Historical Sketches
of
New Mexico

Historical Sketches
of
New Mexico

From the Earliest Records
to the
American Occupation

Facsimile of 1883 Edition

by
L. Bradford Prince

New Foreword
by
Richard Melzer, PhD

SANTA FE

New Material ©2009 by Sunstone Press. All Rights Reserved.

No part of this book may be reproduced in any form or by any electronic or mechanical means including information storage and retrieval systems without permission in writing from the publisher, except by a reviewer who may quote brief passages in a review.

Sunstone books may be purchased for educational, business, or sales promotional use. For information please write: Special Markets Department, Sunstone Press, P.O. Box 2321, Santa Fe, New Mexico 87504-2321.

Library of Congress Cataloging-in-Publication Data

Prince, L. Bradford (Le Baron Bradford), 1840-1922.
Historical sketches of New Mexico : from the earliest records to the American occupation : facsimile of 1883 edition / by L. Bradford Prince ; new foreword by Richard Melzer.
   p. cm.
ISBN 978-0-86534-730-4 (softcover : alk. paper)
1. New Mexico--History--To 1848. 2. Prince, L. Bradford (Le Baron Bradford), 1840-1922. I. Title.
F799.P75 2009
978.9'02--dc22
                              2009029054

WWW.SUNSTONEPRESS.COM
SUNSTONE PRESS / POST OFFICE BOX 2321 / SANTA FE, NM 87504-2321 /USA
(505) 988-4418 / ORDERS ONLY (800) 243-5644 / FAX (505) 988-1025

The Southwest Heritage Series is dedicated to Jody Ellis and Marcia Muth Miller, the founders of Sunstone Press, whose original purpose and vision continues to inspire and motivate our publications.

CONTENTS

I
THE SOUTHWEST HERITAGE SERIES

II
FOREWORD TO THIS EDITION

III
BIOGRAPHICAL SKETCH

IV
IN MEMORY OF
L. BRADFORD PRINCE
Historical Society of New Mexico

V
FACSIMILE OF 1883 EDITION

SOUTHWEST HERITAGE SERIES

I

THE SOUTHWEST HERITAGE SERIES

"The past is not dead. In fact, it's not even past."
—William Faulkner, *Requiem for a Nun*

The history of the United States is written in hundreds of regional histories and literary works. Those letters, essays, memoirs, biographies and even collections of fiction are often first-hand accounts by people who wanted to memorialize an event, a person or simply record for posterity the concerns and issues of the times. Many of these accounts have been lost, destroyed or overlooked. Some are in private or public collections but deemed to be in too fragile condition to permit handling by contemporary readers and researchers.

However, now with the application of twenty-first century technology, nineteenth and twentieth century material can be reprinted and made accessible to the general public. These early writings are the DNA of our history and culture and are essential to understanding the present in terms of the past.

The Southwest Heritage Series is a form of literary preservation. Heritage by definition implies legacy and these early works are our legacy from those who have gone before us. To properly present and preserve that legacy, no changes in style or contents have been made. The material reprinted stands on its own as it first appeared. The point of view is that of the author and the era in which he or she lived. We would not expect photographs of people from the past to be re-imaged with modern clothes, hair styles and backgrounds. We should not, therefore, expect their ideas and personal philosophies to reflect our modern concepts.

Remember, reading their words and sharing their thoughts is a passport back into understanding how the past was shaped and how it influenced today's world.

Our hope is that new access to these older books will provide readers with a challenging and exciting experience.

II

FOREWORD TO THIS EDITION
by
Richard Melzer, PhD

LeBaron Bradford Prince (1840–1922) was a transplanted New Yorker, a tireless judge, a controversial territorial governor, a gentleman scholar, and an early leader of the Historical Society of New Mexico. In all these roles, and others, he was a passionate advocate of New Mexico statehood. In the words of Robert W. Larson, the foremost authority on the struggle for New Mexico statehood, Prince displayed a readiness "to plunge into the statehood fray" whenever and wherever he was needed.

Prince was born, raised, and educated in New York. As a young attorney, his political career in state politics had progressed well until he clashed with leaders of the state Republican Party machine, led by Roscoe Conkling. Salvaging his political fortunes in the West, Prince won appointment as the chief justice of the New Mexico Supreme Court in 1879. By all accounts, no territorial judge worked harder than Prince, often hearing cases from 8:00 in the morning till 11:00 at night. In what time remained in his busy days, Prince compiled a 603-page volume of territorial laws and began to write history with the clear purpose of advocating New Mexico statehood. His first work on New Mexico history, entitled *Historical Sketches of New Mexico: From the Earliest Records to the American Occupation*, appeared in 1883.

After actively lobbying for the coveted position, Prince won appointment as the thirteenth U.S. territorial governor of New Mexico. Unfortunately, his four-year term in office, 1889–93, was marred by property violence (by the *Gorras Blancas*), political violence (by and against the Santa Fe Ring), and almost continuous political controversy. Despite this turmoil, Prince and his wife Mary were known for their generous hospitality at the Palace of the Governors, sparing little to entertain visitors of all social classes.

In relation to his overriding political goal, Prince convened a state constitutional convention shortly after he entered the governor's office. Knowing that the writing of a state constitution was a major step toward statehood, the governor praised the convention's work as "excellent" but blamed his uncompromising Democratic opponents for the draft's decisive defeat at the polls. In 1890 Prince led a delegation of twenty-nine territorial leaders on a trip to Washington, D.C., to lobby for statehood, among other pressing issues. Unfortunately, the sojourn east proved as futile as the drive to pass an acceptable state constitution.

Once out of office, Prince continued to press for New Mexico statehood, especially through the preservation of the region's long history. Realizing that those outside New Mexico thought of the territory's racial diversity as a disadvantage, Prince argued that each racial group (or at least its leaders) had special qualities that had helped to unite, rather than divide the territory during most of its history. Writing to the editor of the *New York Tribune*, Prince asserted that the sum of these special qualities gave New Mexico "special advantages as a self-governing community over most other Territories" that seemed destined to achieve statehood before New Mexico. These "special advantages" became the major theme of Prince's historical work, whether he was collecting artifacts for the Historical Society of New Mexico, serving as that organization's president and most active member from 1884 to World War I, speaking to civic groups, or writing pertinent history, including *New Mexico's Struggle for Statehood*, published in 1910.

L. Bradford Prince was one of seven territorial governors who attended the January 15th inauguration of New Mexico's first state governor, William C. McDonald, in New Mexico's long-awaited statehood year, 1912. Within a year of that auspicious occasion, Prince published *A Concise History of New Mexico*, a condensation and revision of his *Historical Sketches* of 1883. His purpose in 1913 was to be concise by avoiding the "temptation" to provide excessive historical details, a mild criticism of much longer recent histories by Ralph Emerson Twitchell (five volumes, 1911–17) and Benjamin Read (1912). Prince also hoped that his "little volume" might be of use in the now-required teaching of

New Mexico history in the state's public schools. The passage of a public school bill during his term as governor had been considered an important step toward the attainment of statehood. The publication of a state history textbook was meant to be an important contribution to New Mexico public education once statehood had been achieved.

But within a year of its publication, Prince affirmed that the length and price of the already brief *Concise History* was excessive for most public schools and students. While still recommending *A Concise History* for teachers and most adults, Prince offered an even more focused, 174-page work, entitled *The Student's History of New Mexico*.

Now, instead of using history to argue the case for New Mexico statehood, Prince's chief goal was to use history to help create pride in New Mexico for the "clear-eyed, pure hearted, noble minded youth" of the nation's newest state. These future citizens could take pride in both their past, "the most interesting of all American state histories," and in the special qualities of individual groups whose collective story was "unrivaled in ancient or modern times." Proud students would hopefully grow to become good citizens, well prepared to contribute to the making of a strong, modern state. Convinced that *The Student's History* had served its purpose well, Prince later updated his book with an additional ten pages about New Mexico's first few years of statehood. This second edition of *The Student's History* appeared in 1921, a year before Prince's death.

Despite its brevity, *The Student's History* reflects much about Prince and his Anglo generation's thinking about New Mexico and its past, as of the early twentieth century. By our twenty-first century standards, much of this thinking is imperialistic, elitist, and racist. While Prince described most Spanish, Anglo, and Pueblo leaders in appreciative terms and portrayed four of New Mexico's "most noted" Indian fighters with special praise, readers search in vain for references to Navajo or Apache leaders like Geronimo or Cochise, no less for any virtues these Native Americans may have displayed for students to admire and emulate.

The second edition of *The Student's History* is also offered as a brief history of New Mexico of value to the general reader sophisticated enough to recognize its biases, but astute enough to appreciate its many facts. If this unique telling of New Mexico's past adds to our pride in being New Mexicans—or helps others to better understand New Mexico—then L. Bradford Prince will have achieved his purpose long after he departed his beloved New Mexico, once a striving territory and now a productive member of the nation's family of states.

Books by L. Bradford Prince

Prince, L. Bradford. *A Concise History of New Mexico*. Cedar Rapids, Iowa: The Torch Press, 1912.

_____. *Historical Sketches of New Mexico: From the Earliest Records to the American Occupation*. New York: Leggat Brothers, 1883. New Edition, Sunstone Press, 2009

_____. *New Mexico's Struggle for Statehood: Sixty Years of Effort to Obtain Self Government*. Santa Fe: New Mexico Printing Company, 1910. New Edition, Sunstone Press, 2009

_____. *Spanish Mission Churches of New Mexico*. Santa Fe: Museum of New Mexico Press, 1976; originally published in 1915.

_____. *The Student's History of New Mexico*. Denver: The Publishers Press, 1913; second edition, 1921. New Edition, Sunstone Press, 2008

Suggested Readings

Clancey, Frank W. *In Memory of L. Bradford Prince*. Santa Fe: Historical Society of New Mexico, 1923. (See Section IV in this book.)

Donlon, Walter J. "LeBaron Bradford Prince, Chief Justice and Governor of New Mexico Territory, 1879-1893." Unpublished Ph.D. dissertation, University of New Mexico, 1967.

Lamar, Howard R. *The Far Southwest, 1846-1912: A Territorial History.* Albuquerque: University of New Mexico Press, 2000.

Larson, Robert W. *New Mexico's Quest for Statehood, 1846-1912.* Albuquerque: University of New Mexico Press, 1968.

Montoya, María E. "L. Bradford Prince: The Education of a Gilded Age Politician." *New Mexico Historical Review*, vol. 66 (April 1991): 179-201.

Pattison, J. Michael. "Four 'Gentlemen' Historians of New Mexico." Unpublished M.A. thesis, New Mexico Highlands University, 1992.

Poldervaart, Arie W. *Black-Robed Justice: A History of the Administration of Justice in New Mexico from the American Occupation in 1846 Until Statehood in 1912.* Santa Fe: Historical Society of New Mexico, 1948.

Stensvaag, James T. "Cleo On the Frontier: The Intellectual Evolution of the Historical Society of New Mexico, 1859-1925." *New Mexico Historical Review*, vol. 55 (October 1980): 293-308.

Collected Papers

L. Bradford Prince Papers, Center for Southwest Research, Zimmerman Library, University of New Mexico, Albuquerque, New Mexico.

L. Bradford Prince Papers, New Mexico State Records Center and Archives, Santa Fe, New Mexico.

III

BIOGRAPHICAL SKETCH
from
History of New Mexico (1891) by Helen Haines

L. Bradford Prince was born at Flushing (Long Island, New York) on the 3rd of July, 1840. He is a lineal descendant on the maternal side of Governor William Bradford, of Plymouth, one of the "men of the Mayflower," and had for great-grandfather and grandfather respectively Governors Bradford and Collins of Rhode Island. His paternal ancestors are the well-known Prince family of Long Island.

Owing to delicate health much of his early life was passed in the South. As he grew to manhood he engaged in horticultural pursuits at his father's place in Flushing, but after a short experience abandoned this line of employment to study law. Entering Columbia College Law School he passed through the course with special honor, and upon graduating received the $200 prize in political science.

From his youth he was exceedingly active in all matters affecting the welfare and improvement of his native town. In 1858 he originated the Flushing Library Association, obtaining the first subscriptions, drawing its constitution, acting three years as secretary and afterward as president, and from that time until his departure to New Mexico was the leading spirit in all local public affairs.

Very early in life he developed an extraordinary aptitude for political matters, and the activity he displayed in his district during the Frémont campaign won for him a vote of thanks from the town club, of which his age—he was then but a lad of sixteen—prevented his becoming a member. In the canvass of 1860, though still a minor, he was secretary of the local political organization, and worked enthusiastically for the success of the Lincoln ticket. In 1861 he was chosen a member of the Republican county committee of Queens

County, on which he served continuously almost twenty years, during several of which he was its secretary and chairman. He was delegate to all State conventions, during the years from 1866 to 1878, with scarcely an exception; was elected a delegate to the National Republican Convention held at Chicago in 1868, which nominated General Grant, and the following year became a member of the State committee. The political labors of Mr. Prince at this period were all the more honorable from the fact that they were pursued merely as a matter of principle, and without the least expectation of personal advancement, the district in which he resided being strongly Democratic. His qualifications for filling a responsible position were, however, too apparent to be neglected, and in 1870 he was elected to the Assembly, members of all parties joining in his support. In 1871 he was re-elected to the Assembly by a large majority, although his opponent was the strongest Democrat in the district and an experienced legislator, who had already served both in the Assembly and in the Senate. The following year he received the extraordinary compliment of a request for his continuance in office, signed by more than two thousand voters, irrespective of party (being a petition over seventy feet long), and, having been nominated by acclamation, was re-elected without opposition. In 1873, having declined a nomination to the Senate, he was again returned to the Assembly without an opposing candidate. In the fall of 1874 the Democrats made a determined effort to redeem the district, which now for four years had been lost to their party, and placed the Honorable Solomon Townsend—who had served three terms in the Legislature and in the constitutional conventions of 1846 and 1867—in opposition to Mr. Prince. The canvass was an exciting one, but resulted in a victory for Mr. Prince, who secured a majority of 771 votes. There is believed to be no other instance on record of a person being elected five successive times in a district politically opposed to him. In the canvass of 1875 Mr. Prince received the Republican nomination for the Senate, and, although the Democrats were successful in the district on the general ticket by nearly 2700 majority, he won the election by a majority of 904, running 3594 ahead of the ticket. The legislative career of Mr. Prince was an exceedingly useful and highly honorable one. In 1872, 1873 and 1874 he was chairman of the judiciary committee, performing the multifarious and arduous duties in the most creditable manner, and rendering valuable service to the State. While filling this position, over 1100 bills came into his hands for reports—a larger number than were ever submitted to any other committee, either State or national, in a similar length of time. During the winter of 1872 it became his duty to conduct the investigation into the official conduct of Judges Barnard, Cardozo, and McCunn. This investigation extended from the middle of February to about the middle of April, during which time 239 witnesses were examined, and over 2400 pages of evidence taken. The thoroughness and fairness with which the investigation was conducted won the approval of fair-minded persons of all shades of political belief, and its results form one of the brightest pages in the history of the recent "reform movement." The reports of the committee in favor of impeaching two of the judges and removing the other met with general public acquiescence, and were adopted by the House, and Mr. Prince was chosen one of the managers to conduct the impeachment trial, receiving 110 out of 113 votes cast on the ballot in the Assembly. He was also appointed to proceed to the bar of the Senate and formally impeach Judge Barnard of high crimes and misdemeanors. He was active in the matter till the close of the trial, and it has been generally conceded that to no other man is the judiciary of the State so much indebted for being relieved of the disgrace that would have attended the retention of Barnard and Cardozo on the bench. The recent amendments to the constitution of the State received from Mr. Prince special attention. In 1872 he introduced, and succeeded in getting passed, the bill for the constitutional commission. During the sessions of 1873 and 1874 he had charge of the proposed amendments, both in committee and in the Assembly, and the task of explaining and defending them fell almost exclusively to his lot. Just previous to these amendments being submitted to the people for ratification—in the fall of 1874—Mr. Prince, at the request of the Council of Political Reform, wrote a pamphlet on the subject, which was widely circulated as a campaign document, and tended largely to their success at the polls. In the session of 1875 he prepared and introduced nearly all the bills required to carry the new constitutional system into effect, that work being assigned to him by general consent, although the Assembly was Democratic.

While in the Legislature Mr. Prince gave special attention to the canal system of the State and the question of transportation from the West to the seaboard. He made several speeches on this subject in the Assembly, as well as at the organization of the Cheap Transportation Association at Cooper Institute in 1874, and at the Produce Exchange meeting in 1875. The New York Chamber of Commerce twice formally acknowledged these services to the mercantile community by votes of thanks. In 1874 he was chairman of the Assembly committee to conduct the United States Senate Committee on Transportation Routes through the State, and performed that duty in September of that year. At different times during 1874 and 1875 he lectured on this subject of transportation in New York, Albany, Troy, Poughkeepsie, etc.

In May, 1876, Mr. Prince was a member of the National Republican Convention which nominated Hayes and Wheeler. In 1877, though tendered a unanimous renomination to the Senate, he declined to serve again, on the ground that he could not afford longer to neglect his private business.

Mr. Prince's reputation is not, however, confined to the field of politics. As a lawyer he occupies a high position, his clear, incisive reasoning power and rare ability as an advocate rendering him eminently successful. In 1868 he was chosen orator of the Alumni Association of the Columbia College Law School, and for two years was president of the association. In 1876, having again been chosen alumni orator, he delivered an oration in the Academy of Music on "The Duties of Citizenship," enforcing the idea that men of character and education should take the lead in political affairs.

Mr. Prince is well known also as a thoughtful writer and lecturer on various topics, among which those relating to legislative and governmental reform have attracted wide attention.

A work from his pen entitled "*E Pluribus Unum*, or American Nationality," a comparison between the Constitution and the Articles of Confederation, passed through several editions in 1868 and received the warmest commendations from statesmen and political scientists. In 1880 a Chicago firm published a work of Mr. Prince's on a somewhat similar subject, entitled "A Nation or a League."

As a speaker he is well known throughout the State, having been active in the general political canvass every year when not himself a candidate, and in 1876 speaking over forty consecutive nights, from Rochester and Salamanca to Plattsburg and Brooklyn.

He is also a prominent member of the Masonic fraternity, having been district deputy grand master of Queens and Suffolk counties for the years 1868, 1869, and 1870, and again in 1876. In 1877 he was appointed on the grand master's staff as grand standard bearer. He is now grand representative of New Mexico to the grand lodge of New York.

Mr. Prince has always taken a very lively interest in all that pertains to the best interests of the farming community, and has delivered a number of addresses before the various agricultural societies throughout the State—more notably those of Saratoga, St. Lawrence, Tioga, Orleans, Suffolk, and Cattaraugus counties. For ten years he was superintendent or director of the Queens County Agricultural Society, and in 1862 wrote an agricultural history of the county, which was published by that society. He is also a life member of the Long Island Historical Society, and for fifteen years—from 1864 to 1879—was an officer in that learned body.

During 1879, without any application or request, Mr. Prince was offered various appointments, including two in foreign countries, the marshalship of New York, the governorship of Idaho, and the chief justiceship of New Mexico. The latter he declined three times, but finally, at the urgent request of Secretary Evarts and the Department of Justice, consented to accept and left for his new home February 1, 1879.

He reached New Mexico on the first Saturday of February and opened court at Santa Fe on the following Monday. The district then embraced all of the territory north of Bernalillo, and before the advent of railroads was a literal "circuit," as the court traveled from county to county in carriages, crossing the Rocky Mountains from Cimarron to Taos and returning to Santa Fe, after many weeks, by way of Rio Arriba. Owing to the influx of population at the opening of the railroad, the business of the district was much larger during the period of Judge Prince's judicial term than ever before or since, but by administrative ability and an extraordinary capacity for work he cleared the docket of old cases and kept abreast of the new business. Great pains were taken by the judge in the selection of the most competent jurors, and the people of the district recognized an absolute impartiality in the court, which they highly appreciated. The first act of the Legislature of 1882 was the passage by a unanimous vote in each house, of resolutions exceedingly complimentary to the chief justice. In May of that year he resigned in order to become a candidate for Congress, but he continued to act as judge until the following August. To show what was accomplished during the three and one half years that he occupied the bench, we quote the following extract from his letter of resignation: "The Court calendars have been cleared of the accumulated business; no less than 1184 civil and 1483 criminal cases have been finally disposed of during the seven circuits which I have held. The critical period surrounding the coming of the first railroad is ended and good order and prosperity everywhere prevail." At the Republican Convention in September, 1882, Judge Prince's nomination was defeated; he generously accepted his defeat, however, and magnanimously moved the unanimous nomination of his opponent; but the party was so highly incensed at the course pursued at the convention, that for the first time in many years a Democratic candidate was elected. In 1884 he was again proposed for nomination and was heartily sustained by the progressive element of the people; at the Territorial convention of that year he was nominated; owing to an opposition ticket having been put in the field, growing out of a political feud in San Miguel County, an election under these circumstances was impossible. Judge Prince, however, made a campaign of wonderful vigor, speaking in all parts of the Territory and resolutely refusing, as the standard bearer of the party, to take any step which would impair the future of Republicans in New Mexico; he received a vote of 9930 against 12,271 for Joseph, and 5792 for Rynerson.

In 1880 he drew the act for the organization of the Bureau of Immigration, and when that board organized he was elected President and held that position for a number of years. He was one of the organizers of the Territorial Historical Society in 1880, and in 1882 he was elected president of that society, which position he has held up to the present day and has devoted to this institution much time and attention. In 1881 he was elected President of the University of New Mexico, and has continued to hold that position by successive elections to the present day. When the Tertio Millennial Celebration was organized in 1882 he was elected first vice-president, and in that position worked actively for the success of that wonderful exhibition until its close in August, 1883. He was at one time president of the Santa Fe Board of Trade, and in 1887 he was chosen presiding officer of "The United Miners of New Mexico," a territorial mining organization. Through all this period he was the enthusiastic friend and advocate of his adopted home, and by addresses when in the East, and frequent newspaper communications and interviews, he did a great deal toward removing prejudices and adding to the good reputation of New Mexico. On the 2nd of April, 1889, he was appointed governor of the Territory by President Harrison, and was inaugurated in front of the capital on April 17. The demonstration on this occasion was by far the largest ever known in New Mexico, a great procession escorting him from the depot and about 5000 persons being present at the ceremony.

Governor Prince is indeed a man of whom the Territory may well be proud and of whom it may be said, "His aims are noble and his methods just." He has been a leader in public thought, an authority in law and legislation, and there are few instances where a single mind has impressed itself so strongly upon the affairs of the people as his.

He is a man of great and simple nature, of high intellectual powers, of sober and solid judgment, and he has brought to the executive office a well trained mind and a keenness of perception in financial matters that qualify him to make a successful and popular executive.

IV

In Memory of
L. BRADFORD PRINCE
President of the Society
Historical Society of New Mexico, No. 25, 1923

Address by Mr. Clancy

Ladies and Gentlemen:

Although it has been some months since the painful event occurred, this is the first opportunity when announcement could be made to our society of the loss which it has sustained in the death of our president, L. Bradford Prince, who for nearly 40 years was the sustaining influence and the soul of the Historical Society of New Mexico. That this has not been sooner made an occasion of commemoration by us of so great a man, is to be attributed to the fact that our loss has had such an absolutely paralyzing effect upon our activities not only as a society, but as individuals, that it has not been possible at any earlier moment to give expression to our feelings of the loss which our society has sustained, and as well the commonwealth of New Mexico at large, but some record of those feelings must be made by the society to which he so long devoted his great talents, energy and ability, after he cast his lot with the people of New Mexico.

It seems to devolve upon me, as vice-president of our society, and as a close and intimate friend of our late president for many years, to attempt to present to you and to the public, some appropriate recognition of his great character and record as a man, a publicist, a jurist, and especially as the steadfast friend through all his lifetime after he came to New Mexico, of our people with whom he made his home and with whom he identified himself in every possible honorable and unselfish way. I feel that I can not do justice to the subject, but I can not avoid responding to what seems to be a call of duty, from the varying standpoints of public citizenship and personal friendship.

To attempt here to make anything like a record of his career and varied achievements is simply impossible. For me to make a mere enumeration of all that he did, of all that he accomplished in public office, of all that he gave to the public in the way of literary authorship, and of what he gave of himself in many ways to the general welfare, would make a book of hundreds of pages, and would be inappropriate here and would exhaust your patience.

He was born in Flushing, Long Island, in June, 1840 and died at the same place, which had been the home of the Prince family for generations, December 8, 1922, so that he was in his 83rd year at the time of his death, and his public activities which began while he was still a boy, continued until the year of his death. He organized political committees before he was 21 years of age, and while, as before stated, it is useless to attempt even a mere enumeration of all that he accomplished, yet mention must be made of a few things.

He wrote, before he graduated from the law school of Columbia university, a book of 125 pages, which was published by G. P. Putnam & Son in 1867, entitled, "E Pluribus Unum, or American Nationality," and was both historical and political in the proper sense of that word, and reviewed our early attempts at government, beginning with colonial times down to and through the chaotic period of the Articles of Confederation, which led to the formation of our Constitution, expounded that Constitution, and told of our great growth and prosperity thereunder, all in a most wonderful and masterly manner, so that it might well be reproduced in whole or in part, with great benefit at the present time, when attacks are made upon our time-honored Constitution by so many different kinds of honest but misguided minds, from the anarchist and socialist, who sees nothing but evil in all existing forms of government and would destroy them by violence if necessary, and they say it is necessary, to those who call themselves merely progressive and would change and destroy by piecemeal here and there, apparently unconscious of the destructive nature of their efforts. This little book received unstinted praise from many of the men of that day, such as Henry Wilson, Zach Chandler, Millard Fillmore, Reuben E. Fenton, Schuyler Colfax, George William Curtis and even Roscoe Conkling, although later he became personally hostile to Mr. Prince, and was perhaps the principal cause of his leaving New York to come to New Mexico.

His public career in the political arena began in 1871, when he was elected, and later again and again re-elected, as a Republican from a strongly Democratic district to the legislature of the state of New York, where he served with distinction, especially in connection with securing needed amendments to the constitution of the state in 1874, and the impeachment of dishonest judges of the worst period of official corruption in the state.

If he had remained in New York, there is no flight of imagination which can reach the possibilities—the probabilities—of what he might have attained in national politics. Even after he came to New Mexico, again and again he was urged by his former associates to return to New York, with the certainty, as they believed, that he could go to congress as a representative or even as a senator, from the Empire state; but he early became so fascinated and even infatuated with New Mexico and its people, that he turned a deaf ear to all such urgings.

In the '70s of the 19th century, Roscoe Conkling was the dominant political power in New York, and while in some ways he was a great man, of varied talents, he demanded from his party abject and servile obedience, was petulant and childishly vindictive towards all who would not bow the knee to Conkling, and Mr. Prince was not one of that kind, so that when opportunity presented itself for him to get away from New York, it seemed then the part of wisdom to embrace that opportunity. The dominance and downfall of Conkling, due to the qualities above mentioned, are a part of the political history of our country, and need not be considered now.

In 1878 the president offered to appoint Mr. Prince governor of the territory of Idaho, but he conceived a prejudice against Idaho, after calling upon the delegate from that territory, and finding him without shoes and with his wool-clad feet obtrusively elevated to a highly unornamental position, and declined the appointment. This was not perhaps altogether reasonable, as that delegate may not have been a fair representative of the people of his territory. Shortly thereafter the president appointed him chief justice of New Mexico, and he arrived in Santa Fe in the winter of 1878–79. From that time on he was a prominent and active part of New Mexico, giving his time and great abilities to everything which could tend to the development of his adopted land.

As a judge, with six counties over the district courts of which he presided, there had not been, nor has there been since, anyone in such a position in New Mexico who disposed of so much business in the same length of time. My personal acquaintance with him began in 1879. I became clerk of his court in the summer of that year, and so continued until he resigned in 1882, and thereafter until March, 1883.

His only fault as a judge, if it were a fault, was in the excessive amount of work which he performed and imposed upon the members of the bar and court officers. He was never harsh or inconsiderate of litigants or their lawyers. I remember having seen, more than once in the district court in the old town of Las Vegas, when counsel asked for time to get a witness or client from the other side of the Gallinas, that he would grant the request, but in order to expedite business, he would empanel another jury for the trial of a different case and proceed therewith until the absentee arrived, when the trial of the first case would be resumed.

At that term in Las Vegas he opened court at 8 in the morning, adjourned from 12 to 1 to permit the eating of a midday meal, and from 6 to 7 for supper, and never stopped before 11 at night. He was always alert, and apparently untired, but everyone else was worn out.

My personal belief is that no judge should hold court much beyond five hours in a day, as with long hours, the bench, the bar and jury are not fit to do their best work, and therefore I do not wholly approve of Judge Prince's judicial record; but it was characteristic of the man to do so much work in a limited time and do it so well. It is difficult to understand how any man could do so much of a high order of merit as he did. An instance of this is to be found in what he did quite soon after he became chief justice.

There had been a compilation of the statutes of New Mexico in 1865, which, although poorly done and badly arranged, was the book of reference of all statutes in existence in 1865, but after that there had been many sessions of the legislature, at each of which numerous statutes were enacted, and in 1879 and 1880 it was very difficult to procure a copy of the compiled laws of 1865, and almost impossible to secure a complete set of the session laws adopted after 1865. And yet Judge Prince, within a year and a half after he became judge, prepared and had published a compilation of all laws then in force, and that book was the only standard as to our statutes for the guidance of territorial and county officers, of the courts and of all the bar until some time in 1885, when the compilation of 1884 became available. I never heard of any complaint of the completeness or accuracy of Prince's compilation, and no one could understand how he found the time to do such work. A story was circulated that he did it all on the train between Santa Fe and New York, whither he went when the courts were not in session. At that time it took 48 hours—often more—to go from Santa Fe to Kansas City, and nearly as much more from there to New York. When we reflect upon the rapidity and accuracy with which that work was done, we may be able to understand, or if not to understand, to believe that he did so much work that most of men would have required a lifetime of continuous labor to accomplish. Among other things, he found time to write a history of New Mexico which is a standard work and constantly referred to by all writers on New Mexico history, and a little later the Student's

History of New Mexico, which might be well adopted as a part of the curriculum of all schools in the state, and which ought, at least, to be in the library of every educational institution, including all high schools.

He wrote a book of nearly 400 pages on the "Spanish Mission Churches of New Mexico," which is a treasure-house of information on a subject to which no other before him had given more than slight attention. He wrote interesting and erudite monographs on "The Stone Lions of Cochiti," and "Old Fort Marcy," and a historical review of "The Struggle for Statehood 1850 to 1910," and a bewildering number of magazine articles and letters to the press on New Mexican subjects, which required an enormous amount of time, research and labor, difficult of belief when we consider the immense amount of time which he gave to so many other fields of work, such as the Trans-Mississippi congress, of which he was president in 1892, 1893, and 1899, the International Mining congress, of which he was vice-president in 1900–03, and in every thing connected with the Protestant Episcopal church, of which he was an untiring and devoted member, whether in national or local affairs. As I have already said, it seems an unnecessary and difficult task to attempt to enumerate the many things which he did, and all so wonderfully well.

It is much better to turn our attention to his individual characteristics as a man, in contact with his fellow beings, which so greatly endeared him to all who knew him.

First, I invite you to consider that from the very beginning of his life in New Mexico, he never failed when opportunity offered to raise his voice, or use his pen, in defense of our people of Spanish descent, against the unjust and villainous attacks upon them made by English-speaking persons inspired by ignorance and ignoble race prejudice, against a kindly, hospitable, open-hearted people, who have from 1846 received and treated the gringos who came here as their conquerors and oppressors with a degree of forbearance and toleration which is almost incredible. He thoroughly appreciated their good traits and, with that sense of justice which was always a part of his nature, he was ever ready in every possible way to give expression to his feelings in their behalf. This is only one evidence of his just and kindly nature, which was readily aroused by any exhibition of dishonesty and unfairness, whether in the form of the disgraceful neglect by our national government to keep its promises, of which a most glaring instance can be found in the failure to pay what are known as the French Spoliation Claims, as to which he made a violent and memorable attack and protest, or in the form of intolerance, political, religious or racial.

This naturally leads one to the consideration of his toleration of every form of honest opinion, no matter how divergent from his own. He was one of the most devoted and zealous members of the Episcopal church in the United States, taking an active and leading part in all concerns of that church, national or local, from early youth to the end of his life, yet he was never known to say an unkindly word, nor can anyone who knew him believe that he ever harbored even an unkindly thought as to any other form of honest religious belief.

He was a total abstainer from alcoholic or even vinous liquors, but he never said a word or had a thought of criticism of those whose habits of life were different from his own. He never sought to impose upon any fellow being his own standard or conduct as that to which others must conform, whether by moral suasion or by legislative mandate.

He was a Republican in politics from conviction based upon fundamental principles of political thought, but he was never harsh or unfair to his adversaries, and as to this I feel moved to become reminiscent. He believed in party politics and party organization as the safeguard of our institutions and form of government. In 1882, while he was judge, prompted by his years of success in politics in New York, he conceived the idea that he might reasonably hope to get the nomination for delegate to congress in that year, but believing that there would be gross impropriety in seeking other and political office while occupying a judicial position, an idea which has since been embodied to some extent in our state constitution, which declares that no judge shall be nominated or elected to any other than a judicial office, he resigned his office as judge with the avowed purpose of seeking the nomination for delegate to congress.

The convention to make the nomination was held in the new town of Albuquerque, which was then in its beginning, and he was defeated by what his supporters believed to be unfair and dishonest tactics of the opposition. After the nomination was made, there was an assembly of his disappointed and angry supporters in an unfinished storeroom, somewhere north of Railroad avenue, and there were many loud and vociferous appeals to him to run as an independent candidate, but after listening until the angry ones had somewhat talked themselves out, he addressed them something like this, for I cannot recall his exact language, "No, gentlemen, I cannot do that; I am a Republican and believe in party organization, and to preserve that organization is of more importance than the gratification of any man's individual ambition. I cannot be an independent candidate." His calm words quieted the angry excitement and the junta soon dispersed.

Two years later he was the regular nominee of the Republican convention, but a defeated candidate from the southern end of New Mexico, who had not had the political party education or training which New York had given Judge Prince, but looked on a political contest as one of purely personal character, with his friends bolted and made a campaign as an independent candidate without any reasonable hope of success, and thereby defeated Judge Prince, who lost by a plurality of about a thousand only, and thereafter until 1894, New Mexico was steadily represented in congress by a Democrat. In the campaign of 1884 he was doubtful of success, but declared that, having been selected by the convention as its candidate, it was his duty as a Republican to make the best fight possible, even if he were certain to be defeated. He would have been elected if some disaffected members of the party had not been lukewarm in their support.

He was appointed governor of the territory of New Mexico in 1889, and served in that position for four years, until the national administration passed over to the Democratic party. Of his administration as governor, it is sufficient to say that it was creditable to him and of benefit to New Mexico. It will be recalled that during that period, in 1891, the public school system much as it exists today, was created by legislative action, largely due to his influence as our chief executive. Animated by a regard for the historic past, and by what seemed to him to be the natural fitness of things, he made his residence while governor in this Old Palace of the Governors under Spanish, Mexican and American governments, where we now stand, and, with the assistance of his brilliantly gifted wife, made it the scene of social functions of the most varied and ornate character.

This naturally leads me to say a word about his wife, who survives him, Mary Catharine Beardsley, daughter of a distinguished officer in the Union army during the great Civil War, of Oswego, New York, connected with many of the prominent families of that historic region of north central New York, as to her must be given the principal credit of the brilliant social success of her husband's administration as governor.

One of the most important and enduring achievements of Governor Prince was the creation by him in 1909, of the Spanish-American Normal School, which is located at El Rito. I am told that this school has been of great and most beneficial importance to the development of our educational facilities. For several years after this school was established he was president of its governing board, and many of his friends felt grieved and aggrieved that he was not restored to that board by the governor under the last Republican administration, in 1921, and were inclined to consider that the failure so to restore him was a sin of omission of that administration, as that school which he had created was very dear to his heart, and he was then still in perfect mental vigor, as indeed he remained up to the time of his death, and with sufficient physical strength to discharge the duties of the position with benefit to the public interest.

Coming now to the subject of our own society, it may truthfully be said that of all his varied interests and activities in many fields, only a few of which have been touched upon in what I have set forth, there was nothing which became so thoroughly a part of his life, and so engrossed and permeated his mind and almost every thought, as did this society and all matters connected with it.

The Historical Society of New Mexico was created by a special act of the legislative assembly of New Mexico on February 2, 1860, which was not long before the Civil War. What were its activities immediately after its creation, I do not know, but it is certain that during the war, and for years thereafter, it remained in a state of suspended animation until about 1880, when through the efforts of Governor Ritch, a man of high character with imagination and ideals for the future, the society was reorganized with Ritch as president. Right here, if time and your patience would permit, I would like to expatiate at length upon the great value of imagination, which is not, by the generality of people, even yet thoroughly appreciated, but without which nothing great has ever been accomplished in art, science, literature, philosophy, religion or government, but being of a kind and benevolent disposition, I forbear.

Governor Ritch at that time was able to do nothing more than to lay some foundation for the future, but in 1883 Governor Prince became our president, a man who combined imagination with practical executive ability, and he soon infused life into us. He gave his time, varied research, and even his private means to the acquisition of objects of historical interest. Almost everything in our present collections, is due to his personal exertions, whether it be from Indian, Mexican, Spanish or American sources. We may well feel some pride in what has been accomplished, but we should not forget that but little is due to our individual efforts, or to our collective efforts as a society, and that nearly all is due to our late president, L. Bradford Prince, after he took charge of our interests and put some life into us, beginning the arduous work of collecting objects of historic interest from all available sources, the work of arranging these acquisitions in presentable shape being in itself a task of great difficulty. In this part of the work he had the valuable assistance of Mrs. Prince, as much interested as he, who arranged, classified and labeled with her own hands the greatly diversified objects, and arranged them appropriately in cases and shelves, many of which were the creations of her own zealous and skillful hands.

In grateful remembrance of that great man and his exertions, we should strive to preserve, as he always sought, the identity of this society and its collections, and I call upon all of you to join in efforts to accomplish that purpose, first of which should be some intelligent effort toward increasing our membership.

Before closing I feel impelled to recur to what I earlier referred to, and that is the personality of our departed and beloved president. He was of most distinguished ancestry, as far as ancestry can go in our comparatively young country, as may be apparent from the fact that he was a member of such societies as the Sons of the Revolution, the Order of the Cincinnati, the Mayflower Descendants of the Colonial Wars, and of the War of 1812.

He was a direct lineal descendant of William Bradford, who came over in the Mayflower in 1620, and was governor of the Plymouth colony from the spring of 1621 until shortly before his death in 1657, with the exception of five years, 1633, 1634, 1636, 1638, and 1644.

The Encyclopaedia Britannica says of him:

"Bradford's rule was firm and judicious, and to his guidance more than that of any other man the prosperity of the Plymouth colony was due. His tact and kindness in dealing with the Indians helped to relieve the colony from conflicts with which almost every other settlement was afflicted."

To those who believe in the influence of heredity, there must seem to be found in L. Bradford Prince a survival of the traits and temperament of William Bradford. He had the "tact and kindness" in dealing with all kinds of men which William Bradford had "in dealing with the Indians." He was most human and humane in all relations of life, and in Shakespearean language, you may all well join me in saying,

"He was a man, take him for all in all, I shall not look upon his like again."

Resolutions of the Board of Regents of the State Museum

WHEREAS, in due course of nature, and ripe in years and honors the earthly life of Honorable L. Bradford Prince, President of the Historical Society of New Mexico, ended December 8, 1922, thus forever stilling the compelling call of duty, and the urge of helpful service to his fellows. Like autumn fruit, he lingered long and it was even wondered at that he dropped no sooner. Nature seemed to have wound him up for four score years, yet ran he freely on three winters more; until, like a clock worn out with eating Time, the wheels of weary life at last stood still.

Born in Flushing, New York, July 3, 1840, of a long line of illustrious, one hundred per cent American ancestors, he measured up completely to their standards of citizenship, during his many years of active life and service to his fellow-citizens, in his native state of New York, his adopted state of New Mexico, and to the Republic at large. Early in life he developed an aptitude for political matters. By persistent, toilsome effort, he stored his splendid intellect with valuable knowledge. He graduated from the Columbia Law School.

While still a young man, he became interested in politics. He was a delegate to all the state conventions in New York, from 1866 to 1878, and was elected a delegate to the National Republican convention which nominated General Grant for President. The following year he became a member of the New York State Republican Committee. In 1870, '71, '72, '73 and '74, he was a member of the New York Assembly, and in 1875, was elected to the State Senate by an overwhelming majority. His public service there was highly honorable and splendidly useful.

Coming to New Mexico in the later seventies, he immediately took great interest in this, then territory, and soon came to the front as one of the most influential advocates of statehood. In 1878, he was appointed Chief Justice of the Supreme Court of New Mexico, by President Rutherford B. Hayes. He served in that capacity until May, 1882, when he resigned. The efficiency and impartiality of his administration as Chief Justice were approved by the business interests of the territory. He showed a remarkable capacity for expediting business that came before the Court.

"And he judged therein as a just man should; His words were wise and his rule was good."

There was no time after he became a citizen of New Mexico that he was not foremost in the ranks of our citizens, doing his utmost, at home and abroad, for the welfare and prosperity of the people. He framed the act under which the Bureau of Immigration was organized. As early as 1881, he prepared a compilation of the laws of New Mexico. In 1883, he became President of the Historical Society of New Mexico. For years he was identified, either as officer or member, with the Trans-Mississippi and National Irrigation Congresses, where he accomplished much for the best interests of the entire west.

In the spring of 1889, President Benjamin Harrison appointed Honorable L. Bradford Prince governor of New Mexico. His administration of the affairs of the territory, while governor, was characterized by its progressive spirit, always having in view the educational, social and industrial advancement of the territory. Socially, no occupant of the old Palace of the Governors, before or since, so elaborately entertained the people of all classes. His wife, Mrs. Mary C. Prince, nee Beardsley, of Oswego, New York, a descendant of one of the most prominent families of that state, was a charming hostess, and a great favorite with the guests on these occasions.

After retiring from the office of governor, Governor Prince practiced his profession in the courts of New Mexico, devoting considerable time to horticultural pursuits, maintaining his legal residence in Rio Arriba County, near Chamita. From this county he became a member of the legislative council, in the 38th legislative assembly.

But now his work is finished. He has gone to a well earned rest. His reward is to be that of the faithful. We shall miss him. But his good works will live as long as enlightened citizenship stands ready to offer up the supreme sacrifice, on the altar of freedom. The key to his life was service. His philosophy of life was helpfulness. He accepted the fundamental truth that he who serves best is greatest among us, and he who serves well shall indeed be well served in his own soul.

He felt that representative government comes to an end when outside influence of any kind is substituted for the judgment of the representative. He deplored the unsound social and economical theories that deluge our country from time to time, and felt that they are not the progeny of stalwart men and women; that sound bodies do not breed unsound doctrine. That along with a vigorous physical training, should go a mental calisthenics for creating healthful thoughts, and that after all, it must be remembered that "as a man thinketh in his heart, so is he."

He held that government is not-must not be-a cold, impersonal machine, but a real, genuine, human agency, appealing to reason, satisfying the heart, full of mercy, assisting the good, resisting the wrong, delivering the weak from any imposition of the strong. That this is not paternalism, is not servitude imposed from without, but freedom of a righteous, self-direction from within. That laws are not manufactured, are not imposed; but are rules of action, based upon the principles of eternal Truth; and that there is no greater service this Republic can render the oppressed of the earth than to maintain inviolate the freedom of its own citizens.

He had complete faith in the moral power of the United States. He believed that the nation with the greatest moral power will win; that this power gave us independence under Washington and freedom under Lincoln. That here, in the United States, right has never lost, and wrong has never won. However powerful the forces of evil may appear, there are somewhere, more powerful forces of righteousness. That we have a priceless heritage of confidence and courage, and that justice is our might. With our late lamented President Harding, he proclaimed Americanism and acclaimed America, in the Spirit of the Republic.

Like other great Americans, he thanked God that the spirit of a free people can be created, animated and cheered out of the storehouse of its historic recollections. He thanked God that the exemplars of patriotic virtue have abounded in our own country, on our own soil; that strains of the noblest sentiment that ever swelled in the breast of man are breathing to us out of every page of our country's history in the native eloquence of our native tongue; that the Colonial and Provincial Councils of America exhibit to us models of the spirit and character which gave Greece and Rome their name and their praise among nations.

His interpretation of patriotism included more than a willingness and readiness to fight and die for one's country and its institutions. He believed that if a man loves his country and is true to her institutions, and is affectionately concerned for their quality and permanence, there will be something which he will be all the time doing in her behalf. To his way of thinking, going to war is only a small and incidental part of the matter. He felt that what our country needs most is men who will live for her, and during all of her times of peace, work for the consummation of her noble ideals.

He believed that the spirit of nationalism is essential to the perpetuity of this Republic. That such a spirit is as the sun in the heavens, diffusing light and warmth, and by its subtle influence holding the planets in their orbits and preserving the harmony of the universe. So he maintained that the sentiment of nationality in a people diffuses life and protection in every direction, holding the faces of Americans always toward their homes, and preserving the harmony of all. He cherished the idea that while the states have their rights, sacred and inviolable, which we should guard with untiring vigilance, never permitting an encroachment upon them, and ever remembering that such encroachment is as much a violation of the Constitution of the United States as to encroach upon the rights of the general government, still we should ever bear in mind that the states are but subordinate parts of one great nation, that the nation is over all, even as God is over the universe.

Longfellow had Governor Prince's type in mind when he wrote:

> "The heights by great men reached and kept
> Were not attained by sudden flight,
> But they, while their companions slept,
> Were toiling upward in the night."

THEREFORE, Be it Resolved, that in the death of Honorable L. Bradford Prince, New Mexico has sustained an irreparable loss; that Santa Fe has lost one of its most illustrious, useful and patriotic citizens, and that the great republic of the United States is vastly poorer because of his passing.

Resolved, That the Board of Regents of the State Museum extend to his bereaved wife and family its sincere and heartfelt sympathy, in this day of their affliction, and,

Resolved, That these resolutions be spread upon the records of the Board of Regents of the State Museum of New Mexico, and that a copy be presented to the widow of the late Honorable L. Bradford Prince.

        RALPH E. TWITCHELL, Chairman
        FRANK SPRINGER
        JNO. R. McFIE
        N. B. LAUGHLIN
        J. L. SELIGMAN,
              Committee.

V

FACSIMILE OF 1883 EDITION

HISTORICAL SKETCHES

OF

NEW MEXICO

FROM THE

Earliest Records to the American Occupation,

BY

L. BRADFORD PRINCE,

President of the Historical Society of New Mexico,
Late Chief Justice of New Mexico, Etc.

LEGGAT BROTHERS,
CHAMBERS STREET, NEW YORK.
RAMSEY, MILLETT & HUDSON,
KANSAS CITY
1883

Entered, according to Act of Congress, in the year 1883, by

L. BRADFORD PRINCE,

In the Office of the Librarian of Congress, at Washington, D. C

Electrotyped and Printed by Ramsey, Millett & Hudson, Kansas City, Mo.

DEDICATION.

TO THE

PEOPLE OF NEW MEXICO,

Three-fold in origin and language, but now one in nationality, in purpose, and in destiny;

TO THE PUEBLOS,

Still representing in unchanged form the aboriginal civilization which built the cities and established the systems of government and social life which astonished the European discoverers nearly four centuries ago;

TO THE MEXICANS,

Who, in generosity, hospitality, and chivalric feeling, are worthy sons of the *Conquistadores*, who, with undaunted courage and matchless gallantry, carried the cross of Christianity and the flag of Spain to the ends of the earth;

TO THE AMERICANS,

Whose energy and enterprise are bringing all the appliances of modern science and invention to develop the almost limitless resources which nature has bestowed upon us;

TO ALL, AS NEW MEXICANS,

Now unitedly engaged in advancing the prosperity, and working for the magnificent future of the Territory, of which the author is proud to be a citizen,—these sketches of part of its earlier history are respectfully dedicated.

CONTENTS.

	PAGE.
PREFACE	7
CHAPTER I—INTRODUCTORY	11
II—THE PUEBLO ABORIGINES	20
III—THE JOURNEY OF CABEZA DE BACA	40
IV—THE EXPEDITION OF MARCOS DE NIZA	96
V—THE EXPEDITION OF CORONADO	116
VI—THE MISSION OF FRIAR RUIZ	149
VII—THE EXPEDITION OF ESPEJO	153
VIII—THE COLONIZATION BY OÑATE	161
IX—1600 TO 1680	167
X—THE EXPEDITION OF SALDIVAR	176
XI—THE QUIVIRA EXPEDITION OF PEÑALOSA	179
XII—THE REVOLUTION OF 1680	190
XIII—THE PUEBLO GOVERNMENT 1680-1695	197
XIV—THE RECONQEUST BY VARGAS	206
XV—THE 18TH CENTURY	221
XVI—1800 TO 1846	228
XVII—PIKE'S EXPEDITION	246
XVIII—THE SANTA FÉ TRAIL	266
XIX—THE INSURRECTION OF 1837	285
XX—THE AMERICAN OCCUPATION	290
XXI—THE REVOLT OF 1847	313

PREFACE.

The present volume has been prepared in order to meet, to some extent, the felt want of some book containing, as far as practicable, in a connected form, the historical items relative to New Mexico, heretofore scattered, and often unobtainable, or only preserved in the memory of persons fast growing old.

I have called it "Historical Sketches," instead of "A History of New Mexico," because it is not possible at this time to write a satisfactory continuous account of the history of the Territory. The most of the records prior to 1680 were burned in the Pueblo Rebellion; many of those of more recent date were sold for waste-paper, and so lost or destroyed, in the days of Governor Pile; and the remainder are unpublished, and generally unavailable, at present, for the purposes of the historian. It is to be hoped that before many more years pass, a sufficient appropriation will be made by the Government for the classification and arrangement of all the existing archives, and the publication of such documents as may have historic value.

It had been hoped that records of interest relating to New Mexico might be preserved in the archives at Guadalajara, as all the territory north of Zacatecas was subject to the *audiencia* of that city; but the official investigations made by Hon. John W. Foster, the

American Minister, in the year 1873, destroyed any expectations from that quarter; as it appeared that, even if documents of that character had previously been in existence, they were destroyed by the great conflagration of 1859.

In the preparation of this volume the following books (among others) have been consulted: Relation of Cabeza de Vaca, Buckingham Smith; Relation of Friar Marcos de Niza, Hakluyt; Letters of Coronado, Hakluyt; Castañeda's Relation of Coronado's Expedition, Ternaux-Compans; Relation of Juan Jaramillo; Histories of the Conquest of Mexico, by Bernal Diaz, Antonio de Solis, and Prescott; Histories of Mexico, by Clavigero, Mayer, and Frost; W. W. H. Davis' "Spanish Conquest of New Mexico" and "El Gringo;" Gemeli Careri's Travels in New Spain; Humboldt's New Spain; Peñalosa's Quivira Expedition, Shea; Bonnycastle's Spanish America; Pike's Expedition; Gregg's Commerce of the Prairies; Marcy's Prairie Traveller; Kendall's Santa Fé Expedition; Ruxton's Mexico and the Rocky Mountains; Meline's Two Thousand Miles on Horseback; Explorations in Texas, New Mexico, etc., Bartlett; Mexico, New Mexico, and California, Branz Mayer; Reports of Operations in 1846-7, Emory, Abert, Cooke, and Johnston; Abert's Examination of New Mexico; Hughes' Doniphan Expedition; Campaign with Doniphan, Edwards; Conquest of New Mexico, Cooke; Reconnaissances in New Mexico, Johnston, Smith, etc.; Simpson's Navajo Expedition; Sitgreaves' Zuñi Expedition; Heap's Central Route to the Pacific; Hayes' Santa Fé Trail; Inman's

Trail Sketches; Anderson's Silver Country; Peters' Life of Kit Carson; Cozzens' Marvelous Country; Reports of Wheeler, Powell, Jackson, Stevenson, etc.; New Mexican Blue Book, Ritch; Bancroft's Native Races; North Americans of Antiquity, Short; Morgan's Homes of American Aborigines; Putnam's Archæology of Pueblos, etc.

I beg to tender my acknowledgments to Sergeant Francisco de la Peña, who was in the Mexican Military Service as early as 1832; Hon. Levi J. Keithley, member of the First Territorial Legislature (1847); Hon. Gabriel Lucero, Hon. Samuel Ellison, Capt. J. M. Sena y Baca, Henry O'Neill, Esq., Hon. Amado Chavez, and others, for information of value relative to the more recent history of the Territory.

L. B. P.

Santa Fé, June, 1883.

HISTORICAL SKETCHES.

CHAPTER I.

INTRODUCTORY.

THE history of New Mexico may be divided into three epochs—the Aboriginal or Pueblo, the Spanish, and the American.

The aborigines had no written records, and consequently what is known of their history is from tradition or the relation of such Europeans as came in contact with them. Several times before the final conquest and occupation of the country by the Spaniards, travellers or explorers traversed the country; sometimes by accident, as in the case of Cabeza de Vaca; sometimes bent on conquest, as with Coronado; sometimes as missionaries, as with Friar Ruiz; sometimes to spy out the land for others, as with Marcos de Niza. Each of these, in the narrative of what he saw and did, has given us a brief glimpse of the country as it existed just at that time; and this is all we have from which to gain a knowledge of the history, condition, and customs of the people during long periods. These narratives are of great interest, as they afford us life-like views of a unique form of civilization, existing almost isolated, in the midst of encircling deserts and nomadic tribes. But the absence of chronicles from native sources makes it impossible to give a connected and continuous history of that time. We have isolated glimpses, and nothing more. As the Wandering Jew is said in the legend to visit the same locality at intervals of 500 years, and to find on each occasion a new people and altered customs, without having any knowledge of intervening events or the causes of such changes,—so the brief views into the interior of New Mexico presented by the early narratives (separated sometimes by nearly half a century) reveal changes for which, with no knowledge of the occurrences between, we cannot account. Thus, when Coronado marched through New Mexico, Tiguex and Cicuyé were the two most important cities in the valley of the Rio Grande; but forty years later, when Espejo travelled over the same ground, it is impossible to distinguish them either by description or by name. In the days of Coronado, of Oñate, and of Peñalosa, much was heard of Quivira as the great city of transcendent riches and glory across the eastern plains; but during the 200 years which have since passed its name is not mentioned.

All, then, that can be done in the way of a history of the earlier epoch is to bring together what we know from various sources of the origin and life of the Pueblo aborigines, and then to present, one by one, the brief glimpses that we have of the country from the observations of those who from time to time penetrated to its interior. The earliest of these is Cabeza de Vaca, the first European who ever stood on New Mexican soil. While his visit was unpremeditated and involuntary, yet the story of his long journey across the continent, of its strange adventures, its dangers and privations, can never lose its interest; and in New Mexican history his name will always have the leading place. Fortunately, he has left us a full narration, made to the king on his return to Spain. Then comes the expedition of Marcos de Niza, the record of which, written by himself, is so extravagant and exaggerated that it might thereby lose in interest if his had not been the first journey made for purposes of exploration, the first coming across the western desert, and the first which brought any European in sight of one of the great cities of the

Pueblos. This was immediately followed by the celebrated march of Coronado, who with an army not only traversed the whole of New Mexico, but even crossed the Great Plains to the valley of the Mississippi. Of all the expeditions this was the most important, as it occupied a sufficient time for a full examination of the country; and it is matter for congratulation that we have so perfect a narrative of it as that of Castañeda, supplemented by the letters of Coronado himself, and the relation of Captain Jaramillo.

Forty years pass, and then we have the brief account of a journey of another kind, not undertaken for glory or conquest, save the glory of God and the conquest of souls—the missionary effort of Friar Ruiz and his companions, in 1581. That led to the expedition of Espejo, for the rescue of the monks; and the wide extent of country which he traversed—from El Paso to Zuñi— gives us a brief vision of many places rendered familiar in Coronado's day. Passing less-important travellers, we next come to the colonization of the Rio Grande valley by Oñate, and the establishment of a regular Spanish government in the Province; with the building of churches and the rapid spread of Christianity.

Then ensues a long period of which the records were probably nearly all destroyed at the time of the Pueblo Revolution, though some may yet be recovered in Mexico or Spain; and in 1662 we have the romantic and brilliant expedition of Peñalosa across the Great Plains again to the city of Quivira, which might have brought great results had he been permitted to carry out his programme of conquest and colonization. Throughout this period we find the natives being gradually reduced to more and more severe bondage, until in 1680 they at last rose in successful revolt, and drove the Spaniards from the country. From the history of this contest and their subsequent action, we learn that their long servitude had made them cruel and revengeful, and had unfitted them for self-government; as the years of their supremacy mark a period of jealousy and conflict, and that in which they suffered greater diminution in numbers than ever before. Then comes the protracted contest for new supremacy by the Spaniards, ending at last in 1696 by the final subjugation of the natives and pacification of the Province. After this follows a period during which no events of great interest occurred—generation following generation in an existence almost entirely isolated from the world, and the monotony of life varied by little save almost continual warfare with one or another Indian tribe which desolated the borders. Whatever there is of interest in the succeeding century is hidden among the remaining archives at Santa Fé, or lost with those which were so needlessly destroyed. But nothing occurred sufficiently important to cause a ripple on the surface of the general history of the world, or even of Mexico. The people lived happy, peaceful, tranquil lives, except when aroused by Indian troubles; they improved their surroundings and amassed property and wealth, and were less troubled by the fierce conflicts which shook the world during that period than any other civilized people. The revolution in Mexico made a change in government, and aroused the sentiment of independence among the people; but New Mexico was too remote to be a scene of conflict, and quietly passed from being the dependency of a kingdom to its position as part of a republic. Meanwhile the overland trade with the United States had commenced, and the Santa Fé Trail was the route which made the capital of the Territory the great distributing point for merchandise in northern Mexico. The revolutionary spirit which for so long a time prevented stability in government in the Mexican Republic affected New Mexico as well as other sections; and the year 1837 saw an insurrection which resulted in the killing of the Governor and other high officials, and the proclamation of a Pueblo Indian as Provisional Governor, soon followed by a counter-movement which executed Gonzales and brought Armijo into power.

Less than ten years after, the American "Army of the West," under General Kearney, entered Santa Fé, New Mexico was proclaimed American territory, and a provisional government established. The "Taos insurrection," in which Gov. Bent and a number of others were killed, followed; but this was speedily suppressed, and the treaty of Guadalupe Hidalgo finally ceded the Territory to the United States. Of late years, with more perfect protection from Indians, the introduction of railroads, telegraphs, and other modern inventions, a rapid increase in population, and a general development of her unequalled natural resources, New Mexico is making rapid strides in progress and swiftly fitting herself to be a rich and influential State in the American Republic.

This is an epitome of the history of New Mexico. Under the peculiar circumstances it is not possible to arrange a continuous narrative, and all that is attempted in the chapters to follow is to present the various scenes in the historic drama as truthfully as may be. In presenting the substance of the narrations of the early expeditions, the spirit of the old chronicles has been retained as far as possible, although it might be strongly tinged by exaggeration, as in the case of Marcos de Niza; for the reason that only by that means can we properly appreciate the influence which those reports had on the actions of others. One thing has to be specially borne in mind in judging either of the grade of civilization which the Pueblo Indians had attained, or the dangers and difficulties encountered by the early adventurers, and the courage and endurance necessary in surmounting them—and that is, that many of the events narrated occurred nearly three and a half centuries ago; that the whole world has made vast strides in progress since that time, and that systems of various kinds which to-day may seem crude were then fully equal to the average civilization of the world; while a journey, which, with our geographical knowledge and rapid conveyance, appears but a holiday trip, was then a plunge into an unknown wilderness, requiring enterprise and fearlessness of the highest type. It is difficult for persons in our generation to realize the circumstances under which the various expeditions and explorations connected with New Mexico were made during the sixteenth, and indeed the seventeenth century. We have been so accustomed to the general geographical contour of the American continent from our earliest youth, we know so well the distance from ocean to ocean, and from the gulf to the Arctic region, that it seems difficult to remember that the intrepid explorers who penetrated to the north, after the fall of the Montezumas, had no idea at all of the extent of the main-land, and were never sure, as they ascended a mountain, but that its summit would bring to view the South Sea to the west, the North Sea or Atlantic to the east, or the great Arctic Ocean toward the Pole. Yet we know that Columbus thought he had reached the East Indies when he first discovered land in the western hemisphere, and that after all his voyages he died with no idea of the true distance to that goal; that Hudson ascended the river which bears his name, supposing it to be a strait leading to the China Sea, and that the Chesapeake was explored in a similar belief; that California was for long years represented on all maps as an island apart from the American continent, and that the narrowness of the land between the oceans at Darien, and even in Mexico, naturally gave rise to the idea that the *terra firma* was of no great width at any point, and the great seas of the earth nowhere very far apart. The universality of this opinion among all nations is illustrated by the fact that the early charters of the

English colonies extend their limits westward to the South Sea, with no knowledge as to whether it might be a 100 or a 1,000 miles distant, but in a belief that would have been shocked if any one had suggested that it was giving them an area 2,500 miles in length.

The explorer of those days was travelling entirely in the dark. Nothing in more modern times has been similar to, or can again resemble, the uncertainty and romance of those early expeditions. For the recent explorers of Africa, for example, had a perfect knowledge of the shape of the exterior of the continent, and knew exactly what tribes lived on each shore, and what rivers emptied into each ocean. All that was left as a *terra incognita* was a certain area in the center, and that of known length and breadth. But the early explorers of America literally knew nothing of the land they entered. It was absolutely virgin soil. They might find impassable mountains or enormous lakes; they might have to traverse almost interminable deserts, or discover rivers whose width would forbid their crossing; they might chance upon gigantic volcanoes, or find themselves on the shore of the ultimate ocean. And as to inhabitants and products they were equally ignorant.

We are sometimes induced to smile at the marvelous stories related by some of the older explorers, at their still more extravagant expectations, and the credulity with which everything (however exaggerated or unnatural) relating to the new continent was believed. But we must remember that it was a day of real marvels, and that nothing could well be imagined more extraordinary and unexpected than those things which had already been discovered as realities. An entire new world had been opened to the enterprise, the curiosity, the cupidity, and the benevolence of mankind. It is as if to-day a ready mode of access to the moon were discovered, and the first adventurers to the lunar regions had returned laden with diamonds, and bearing tidings of riches and wonders far beyond the wildest imagination of former generations. Just so the early explorers had returned to the Eastward, telling of the marvels of the new Indies; of the luxuriant vegetation, the vast extent, the untold riches, the silver and the gold, of the western continent. As one adventurous explorer followed another, new discoveries were constantly made; each apparently exceeding its predecessor in importance, in riches, and in glory. Americus Vespucius landed on the main-land of the south, and the Cabots and Verrazani skirted the shores of the northern parts of the continent. Then Cortez discovered and conquered the great empire of the Montezumas, and Pizarro subdued the rich dominion of the Incas. The wealth of these two fallen kingdoms was a marvel, as the accumulated treasures of generations fell into the hands of the conquerors as it were in a moment.

After such discoveries, what might not be expected? When the realities already known so far surpassed all former extravagance of imagination, why might not the future bring forth things even more surprising? Why might not kingdoms be found as far transcending Mexico and Peru as those kingdoms exceeded the barbarism and poverty of the savage inhabitants of some of the first-discovered islands? There was nothing impossible in this, nor illogical in the anticipation; and this should be borne in mind in reading of the later expeditions into the interior of the continent, of the readiness with which stories of marvelous riches and stores of gold and precious stones were credited, and of the eagerness with which men braved danger and hardship in the venturesome expeditions of that day.

And another element is not to be overlooked, and that is the religious one. In many hearts this was a strong, impelling principle. Here were unknown heathen nations to be brought to the knowledge of the faith; here were untold thousands of souls to be saved. In this view it was the old spirit of the Crusaders that was aroused. As men left their homes, abandoned their property, deserted their families and friends, and encountered every form of difficulty and danger to rescue the tomb of the Lord from the dominion of the unbelievers; so, a little later, others imbued with the same martyr spirit were ready to venture all and suffer even death to carry a knowledge of Christianity to heathen tribes.

With these facts in our minds, we can better understand how it was that, within twenty years after the fall of Montezuma, Castilian enterprise and prowess had penetrated more than 1,500 miles to the north, over mountain and desert, to the Land of the Seven Cities, and how, later on, they travelled hundreds of miles further into the interior, in search of new lands to conquer, new riches to acquire, and new tribes to christianize.

CHAPTER II.

THE PUEBLO ABORIGINES.

THE origin of the aboriginal inhabitants of New Mexico as found by Cabeza de Vaca, Coronado, and the other early travellers and explorers, and as existing to-day in the persons of the Pueblo Indians, is involved in such obscurity that nothing certain can be positively asserted of it. We have, in the description given by the first Europeans who penetrated the country, the pictures of populous communities, occupying the valley of the Rio Grande and its branches, and extending westward as far as Zuñi and Moqui, entirely different in character from the nomadic tribes of the plains, but so analogous to each other as to show a common origin and early history. Their villages were alike in all important respects, in the material, the height and peculiar terrace form of the houses, in the smallness of the rooms and the presence of estufas, in the methods of ingress and of defense. Their dress was similar, their customs identical, their agricultural products the same, their pottery uniform in general design and ornamentation. In all these respects they were unlike the tribes which surrounded them, and more similar to the civilized people of Mexico than to any who dwelt nearer. This is not the place to trace out all the features of resemblance, although the subject is one so interesting and inviting that it is difficult to forego its discussion; but suffice it to say that everything in analogy, as well as in tradition, points to the truth of the words of Baron von Humboldt, where he says: "Everything in these countries appears to announce traces of the cultivation of the ancient Mexicans. We are informed, even by Indian traditions, that twenty leagues north from the Moqui, near the mouth of the Rio Zaguananæ, the banks of the Nabajoa were the first abode of the Aztecs after their departure from Aztlan. On considering the civilization which exists on several points of the north-west coast of America, in the Moqui, and on the banks of the Gila, we are tempted to believe (and I venture to repeat it here) that at the period of the migration of the Toultecs, the Acolhues, and the Aztecs, several tribes separated from the great mass of the people to establish themselves in these northern regions."

Without going into any details of early Mexican history, which would be out of place here, it is well to remember a few leading facts. The Toltecs started on their southern pilgrimage from the old home at Huehuetlapallan in the far north-west, in the year 1 Tecpatl, which Clavigero considers equivalent to 596 of our era. "In every place to which they came," says that author, "they remained no longer than they liked it, or were easily accommodated with provisions. When they determined to make a longer stay they erected houses, and sowed the land with corn, cotton, and other plants, the seeds of which they had carried along with them to supply their necessities. In this wandering manner did they travel, always southward, for the space of 104 years, till they arrived at a place to which they gave the name of *Tollantzinco*, about fifty miles to the east of that spot where some centuries after was founded the famous city of Mexico." Twenty years later they moved forty miles westward and founded the city of Tollan, or Tula, named after their native country, and which continued as their capital. Gondra makes the date of their arrival in Anahuac 648, and the foundation of Tula 670; but for some reason he states the year of their departure from the north as 544, or just a Mexican century (fifty-two years) earlier than the chronology of

Clavigero. After them came the Chichimecas, likewise from the north, where their country was called Amaquemecan (Mr. Short says "Amaquetepic," probably meaning the "Mountain of the Moquis"), marching under Xolotl, the brother of their king, who had heard of the rich country to the south and was determined to found an independent empire. They were a less civilized and more violent people than the Toltecs, and Torquemada says that before the migration they lived in caves in the mountains, which may have some connection with our cave and cliff dwellings. They were soon succeeded by the three princes of the Acolhuan nation, with a great host of followers, coming from Tenoacolhuacan, which we are told was near Amaquemecan, and who by marriage with the daughters of King Xolotl became dominant in the valley of Mexico. And last came the Aztecs, who left their home in Aztlan, which Clavigero says was "a country situated to the north of the Gulf of California, according to what appears from the route they pursued in their migration." They crossed the Colorado River and proceeded as far as the Gila, where they remained for some time; the Casa Grande, of Arizona, now so well known through the descriptions of Emory, Bartlett, and others, and the sketches of Ross Browne, and at which both Marcos de Niza and Coronado stopped, being part of the remains of their city. From thence they journeyed to the place called the Casas Grandes, in Chihuahua, "where," says Clavigero, "the immense edifice still existing is constructed on the plan of those of New Mexico; that is, consisting of three floors with a terrace above them, and without any entrance to the under floor. The door for entrance to the building is on the second floor, so that a scaling-ladder is necessary; and the inhabitants of New Mexico build in this manner, in order to be less exposed to the attacks of their enemies—putting out the scaling-ladder only for those to whom they give admission to their house." The famous picture which was afterwards shown by Don Carlos de Siguenza to Dr. Gemeli Careri, in 1698, and copied in the history of the travels of the latter, and more recently reproduced in the interesting work on Mexican antiquities by the learned Ysidro R. Gondra, in Mexico, gives a graphic representation of the wanderings of the Aztecs from the time of their leaving Aztlan until their final settlement in Mexico. The date of the commencement of this migration is given by Clavigero at 1170, and Boturnini, Veitia, etc., make it 1168; but there seems to be an error respecting this, for Gama puts it at 1064, and Humboldt, who had the benefit of all the earlier researches, at 1038; the principal discrepancy arising from the omission by the former writers of two Mexican centuries amounting to 104 years.

The historical picture referred to was found on a sheet of maguey paper, thirty-three inches long by twenty-one in width, and hieroglyphically represents each of the places at which the Aztecs remained for any length of time during their journey. After a representation of an ancient flood, in which only one man and one woman were saved, and in the history of which a dove plays an important part, the picture presents the march of the Aztecs from "a place of magpies," (called by Gondra "flamingoes"), through "a place of grottoes," "a place of the death's head," "the woody place of the eagle," "chalco, the place of the precious stone," "the place of passes," "a whirlpool where the river is swallowed," etc., to the final arrival at Chapultepec, "the hill of grasshoppers," to which they came in 1245.

The legend of their seeing the eagle perched on the cactus, and in obedience to that omen determining to found their capital on that spot, gave rise to the emblem on the Mexican coat-of-arms, and is well known; but can be no more than thus briefly alluded to in this place.

Whether the aborigines of New Mexico are of Toltec

or Aztec origin, there can be little doubt that they are a portion of one or the other of these nations that for some reason was left behind in the great migrations. It will be observed that all of the successive waves of population that succeeded each other in Mexico came from the north-west. They all appear to have taken about the same route through Arizona. Their journeys were not continuous, nor with any predetermined plan as to the locality of ultimate settlement. On the contrary, they sometimes occupied centuries, and the moving nation stopped for many years at places which suited its convenience or its fancy. There is nothing unnatural in the supposition that an offshoot from the Toltecs or the Aztecs settled along the rivers of New Mexico, while the main body of their people was in that vicinity, and when the general migration continued still farther to the southward, remained contentedly in the homes they had established. In no other way can we account for the existence of an intelligent people, living in great houses of excellent workmanship and most admirably adapted for defense against all the weapons of that day; with successful agriculture, skillful manufacturers, and an excellent system of government;—existing in the midst of the savage and wandering tribes without home or property, who surrounded them. And their own traditions, though vague and unsatisfactory, all point to the same origin. The name of Montezuma runs through all of these (not generally referring to the king whom we are accustomed to identify with that name, but to the great chief of the golden or heroic age—the demigod of their earliest traditions, watching over them from heaven and waiting to come again to bring to them victory and a period of millenial glory and happiness). They call themselves the People of Montezuma, or the Children of the Sun; for the sun was the real object of their adoration. The use of the estufa for religious and other important purposes is universal, and its origin is attributed to Montezuma. The little idol representing God seen at one of the pueblos, and described by W. W. H. Davis, was called Montezuma. Their ancient dramatic dances generally represent Montezuma and Malinche.

One tradition is that they came from Shipop in the far north-west, beyond the sources of the most distant branches of the Rio Grande. They were wanderers and lived in caves and sheltered cañons. For awhile they sojourned at Acoma, the birthplace of Montezuma, who became their ruler and guide. He taught them to build pueblos with lofty houses, and to construct estufas wherein was to be kept the sacred fire, ever guarded by chosen priests. Pecos was founded by him, and here for a long time he dwelt. He planted a tall tree, saying that when he disappeared a foreign race would tyrannize over his people, and there would also be lack of rain; but they were constantly to watch the sacred fire until that tree should fall, when white men would appear from the East to overthrow their oppressors; then he would himself return to reign, and peace, with plenty and great riches, would prevail. And this they say was in part fulfilled by the coming of the Americans; and that the sacred tree fell as Gen. Kearney entered Santa Fé.

The fire in the estufa at Pecos was carefully guarded for hundreds of years, by vigils which grew in rigor as the number of participants decreased, until less than half a century ago the Indians at that pueblo became so reduced in numbers that they determined to abandon their home, and preserving the sacred fire with jealous and untiring care, they carried it still burning to the pueblo of Jemez, where their own language was spoken and where they and their descendants still live.

Lieut. Simpson relates that Hosta, his guide, and a very intelligent Pueblo Indian, said of the great pueblos in the Chaco valley, that " they were built by

Montezuma and his people when on their way from the north to the region of the Rio Grande and to Old Mexico," and, " that after being there for a while they dispersed, some of them going east and settling on the Rio Grande, and others south into Old Mexico." Mr. Short, in his "North Americans of Antiquity," says: " The many-sided culture-hero of the Pueblos, Montezuma, is the centre of a group of the most poetic myths found in ancient American mythology. The Pueblos believed in a supreme being—a good spirit, so exalted and worthy of reverence that his name was considered too sacred to mention, as with the ancient Hebrews Jehovah's was the 'unmentionable name.' Nevertheless, Montezuma was the equal of this great spirit, and was often considered identical with the Sun. The variety of aspects in which Montezuma is presented to us is due to the fact that each tribe of the Pueblos had its particular legends concerning his birth and achievements. Many places in New Mexico claim the honor of his nativity at a period long before those village-builders were acquainted with the arts of architecture which have since given them their distinguishing name; in fact, this culture-god was none other than the genius who introduced the knowledge of building among them. Some traditions, however, make him the ancestor and even the creator of the race; others its prophet, leader, and lawgiver." Mr. Bancroft says, on the same subject: " Under restrictions, we may fairly regard him as the Melchizedek, the Moses, and the Messiah of these Pueblo desert-wanderers from an Egypt that history is ignorant of, and whose name even tradition whispers not. He taught his people how to build cities with tall houses, to construct *estufas*, or semi-sacred sweat-houses, and to kindle and guard the sacred fire." It has been aptly remarked by Mr. Tyler, that Montezuma was the great "somebody" of the tribe to whom the qualities and achievements of every other were attributed. The legends of Montezuma are almost innumerable, and as various and contradictory as could well be imagined. In some of them an abrupt connection takes place between Montezuma, the demi-god of the golden age, and Montezuma who was conquered by Cortez; but no doubt the latter idea was engrafted after the Spanish occupation.

At some of the pueblos are old documents which are apparently legends of the conquest of Mexico. These are held in great veneration, and are guarded most carefully against the prying eye of the stranger. Meline, in his "Two Thousand Miles on Horseback," quotes one of these which was with great difficulty obtained for a few minutes by the Indian Agent, Major Greiner, in 1862, at the San Juan Pueblo, and of which he made a hasty copy. The following are a few passages to show the style, although the legend is probably not of very ancient origin, and seems to include matter suggested by the early priests in order to lessen the opposition to the introduction of Christianity. It opens with Cortez as speaker: "They will respect and obey me in whatever I will command. I will teach them the law of Jesus Christ, God of Heaven, him unto whom all should render infinite thanks for the benefaction about to be received by the Children of the Sun; that they should always cheerfully receive the waters of baptism." "From this issued much pleasure among all the people, dances taking place in which there was shown no rancor against the Children of the Sun; and seeing this, the King Montezuma said to the great Cortez that as his children had so much joy in being transferred to the control of Cortez, he charged him that he would treat them with great kindness." "Cortez said to the King, 'I wish you to tell me concerning how many provinces has New Mexico, and its mines of gold and silver.' The monarch said, 'I will respond to you forever as you have to me. I command this province, which is the first of New Mexico, the Pueblo of Teguayo, which governs 102 pueblos. There is a great mine near by, in which they cut with stone hatchets the gold of my crown. The great province of Zuñi, where was born the great Malinche. This pueblo is very large, full of Indians of light complexion who are governed well. In this province is a silver mine, and its capital controls eighteen pueblos. The province of Moqui. The province of the Navajoes. The great province of the Gran Quivira, that governs the pueblos of the Queres and the Taños. These provinces have different tongues, which only La Malinche understands. The province of Acoma, in which is a silver mine in a blackish colored hill.' Seeing this, the great monarch sent Malinche to these provinces to new conquests."

As will appear further on, when the Europeans first entered the country the natives were found living in well-built cities of stone and adobe, composed of houses from three to five stories high, usually built around a plaza, the stories decreasing in size at each floor, so that the whole pueblo was of a terrace shape. Their number was then very large. If Espejo's figures are correct, the population must have been nearly or quite 300,000, as he counts 234,000 in the nine provinces of which he states the population; and this does not include Zuñi, nor the first two that he passed through on the river. Probably this is considerably exaggerated, but yet no one can be acquainted with the vast ruins which exist all over the country from the cañons of the Colorado, the San Juan, the Chelly, and the Chaco, at Abiquiu, Ojo Caliente, and all through the valley of the Rio Grande, to the now desert country of the south-east around Gran Quivira—without recognizing that a numerous, intelligent, and industrious people lived there before the Christians ever heard of the Seven Cities of Cibola; and it is not extravagant to put the population at 150,000 at least.

The architecture of the Pueblos was analogous to that of the Aztecs of Mexico; and indeed as nearly similar as the varied circumstances relative to material and the requirements for defense would permit. They were constructed of adobe, of cobble-stones and adobe mortar, of hewn stone and mortar, or of matched stone, carefully put together without mortar, as the case might be. At Quarra the walls yet standing show the buildings to have been of red sandstone, the pieces used being not more than two inches thick, the walls two feet wide, and the outer face dressed off to a plain surface. The walls of Abó, according to Lieut. Abert's description, were "beautifully finished, so that no architect could improve the exact smoothness of their exterior surface." The ruins west of the Rio Grande, near San Yldefonso, are of buildings made of blocks of lava or *malpais*, roughly squared and put together with adobe mortar; the blocks are comparatively small. Some of the great pueblos on the Chaco (first described by Lieut. Simpson in 1849) were built of tabular pieces of sandstone, laid with adobe mortar; the stones being from three to six inches in thickness, and from six to eighteen inches in length. The Pueblo Bonito showed great beauty and precision in its masonry. The material was a firm, hard, gray sandstone, in blocks of a uniform thickness of three inches, and laid without mortar; the joints are always carefully broken, and the crevices between the ends filled with thin pieces of stone, not over one-fourth of an inch thick. In the Pueblo of Peñasco Blanco the manner of building was "a regular alternation of large and small stones, the effect of which is both unique and beautiful. The largest stones, which are about one foot in length and one-half foot in thickness, form but a single bed, and then alternating with these, are three or four beds of very small stones, each about an inch in thickness." These ruins in the Cañons of Chaco and Chelly are of special interest because there is no possibility of Spanish influence on the architecture, as there may have been at Quarra and Abó.

The general design of all the great pueblos was the same. They were communal buildings, or as some late archæologists word it, "joint-tenement houses." They contained from 50 to 500 apartments, and would accommodate from 200 to 1,000 inhabitants. A whole town was contained in one building; or rather, perhaps, we should say, all the houses of a town were built together, forming one continuous structure. In this they resembled the edifices further to the south. "From Zuñi to Cuzco," says Mr. L. H Morgan, "at the time of the Spanish conquest, the mode of domestic life in all these joint-tenant houses must have been substantially the same." Speaking of the Pueblo of Hungo Pavie (which Simpson's Report describes as 300 feet long, with wings each 144 feet in length, three stories high, in terrace form, and built of stone, the first story containing seventy-two apartments, the second forty-eight, and the third twenty-four) Mr. Morgan says: "We may recognize in this edifice a substantial reproduction of the miscalled 'palace' of Montezuma in the Pueblo of Mexico, which, like this, was constructed upon the three sides of a court, in the terraced form, and two stories high. In the light which these New Mexican houses throw upon those of the Mexicans, the house occupied by Montezuma is seen to have been a joint-tenement house of the American model. It is therefore unnecessary to call any of these structures palaces in order to account for their size, or to assume a condition of society in which the palace of the ruler was built by the forced labor of his subjects."

Some of the pueblo edifices were of great size. Among those in the Chaco Cañon that of Wege-gi was 700 feet in circumference, and contained 99 rooms; Chethro-Kettle, 1,300 feet, and 124 rooms; Peñasco Blanco, 1,700 feet, and 112 rooms on ground-floor; and the Pueblo Bonito was 544 feet long, 314 in width, and contained 641 rooms. The ruined Pueblo of Chipillo, west of San Yldefonso, measures 320 feet by 300, surrounding a plaza containing two estufas; and the Cuesta Blanca Pueblo, not far distant, is 450 feet in length. The ruins of most of these buildings, and notably those in the Chaco Cañon and Cañon de Chelly, agree exactly with Castañeda's description of the large pueblos which Coronado visited in the Rio Grande valley; as they were built around courts, with a high, straight wall on the outside, without openings for either doors or windows, and terraced in stories on the inside like an amphitheatre. All were furnished with estufas, some as large as sixty feet in diameter, and frequently considerable in number. Speaking of the analogy between these buildings and those of Mexico and Central America, Mr. Morgan says: "These seem to have been the finest structures north of Yucatan, and the largest ever erected by the Indians of North America. There is no reason for supposing that the Pueblo of Mexico contained any structures superior to them in character."

What gives special interest to the pueblo dwellings of New Mexico is that nowhere else on the continent are buildings still inhabited precisely as they were when Columbus discovered America. In several instances, as at Taos and in the western pueblos, the people are now living in identically the same houses which were then occupied. "These pueblos," says the author last above quoted, "were contemporary with the Pueblo of Mexico, captured by Cortez in 1520." The buildings at Taos are about 250 feet long, 130 feet deep, and five stories high. While they are irregular in form, and rudely built in comparison with some of those described by Castañeda and the stone structures of the Chaco, yet they preserve the general idea and the ancient manner of living in all essential respects. Another point of similarity between the pueblos of New

Mexico and those situated farther south, is the custom of building on the tops of hills, or mesas. This was the usual course with the older pueblos in New Mexico, the great majority of the ruined villages being so situated. Acoma is the best illustration among existing pueblos; but Zuñi, the town on the "Moro," and many ruins in the valley of the Rio Grande and its tributaries, show how usual it was in the days when safety had to be considered more than convenience — a number being so situated as to be practicably impregnable. It is well known that similar situations were selected for many Mexican pueblos.

When the Spaniards first settled in the country, the pueblos were divided into four groups, by reason mainly of difference of language. These were the Piros, Teguas, Queres, and Taños. Such a distinction still exists— five entirely distinct languages (not dialects of one language) being in use. So far as existing pueblos are concerned this division is as follows:—

1. Santa Ana, San Felipe, Cochiti, Santo Domingo, Acoma, Zia, and Laguna.

2. San Juan, Santa Clara, San Yldefonso, Nambe Pojuaque, and Tesuque.

3. Taos, Picuris, Sandia, and Isleta.

4. Jemez.

5. Zuñi.

The first represent the Queres group, the second the Teguas, and the third the Piros. In the early records the Zuñis and Moquis are counted as belonging to the Queres, and they were probably originally of the same stock.

Several curious features are presented by this subject, the first being the fact itself of this very difference in language among a people in other respects almost entirely identical, possessing the same appearance, customs, mode of living, manufactures and agriculture. The language of the Tegua towns is almost entirely monosyllabic; the words in the Queres group are usually of two syllables, and the language of the Piros rejoices in words of extraordinary length, as does also that of Zuñi. Take as an example the word "earth," one of the first employed in any language. In Queres it is *hah-ats ;* in Tegua, *nah ;* in Piros, *pah-han-nah ;* in Jemez, *dock-ah ;* in Zuñi, *ou-lock-nan-nay.* What is very singular is that the distribution of these languages is not geographical; that the groups are not compact divisions, but lap over each other in the situation of their towns. For example, at Taos in the north and Isleta in the south, the same language is spoken; but between them are all the Tegua towns and many of the Queres, covering the most of the central valley of the Rio Grande. Again, the language spoken at Pecos was identical with that used at Jemez, but none of the intervening pueblos were acquainted with it; so that when the former Pueblo of Pecos was abandoned by its inhabitants, they had to pass by the Queres pueblos of Santo Domingo, Santa Ana, Zia, etc., before finding a resting-place where their speech was intelligible. The languages are so entirely different that the people of different pueblos, not of the same nation, usually talk to each other in Spanish, with which all are more or less acquainted.

The Taños pueblos are all extinct, not one remaining to represent this once powerful nation. These were situated along the Galisteo, and south of it, including probably Abó, Quarra, and Gran Quivira, and at one time were numerous, thickly populated, and influential. Espejo estimated the number of Taños Indians at 40,000; though this was probably an exaggeration. Several of these pueblos existed during the earlier Spanish occupation, but they appear to have been destroyed or abandoned in the wars between the Pueblos that were so fatal to the native races and towns during the years of the Indian supremacy, from 1681 to 1693. The one whose locality is best known to modern travellers is the Pueblo of San Marcos, though San Lazaro and San Cristobal are frequently mentioned in the earlier histories.

In the time of Coronado's expedition, there were seventy pueblos, according to Castañeda's list, as follows: Cibola, 7; Tucaya, 7; Acuco, 1; Tiguex, 12; Tutahaco, 8; Quivix, 7; Snowy Mountains, 7; Ximena, 3; Cicuyé, 1; Jemez, 7; Aguas Calientes, 3; Yuqueyunque, 6; Braba, 1; Chia, 1. Forty years afterward, Espejo described the provinces, and so far as can be ascertained the number of pueblos had slightly increased. He enumerated them as follows: On the Rio Grande, near Isleta, 10; Teguas, 14; province on the west adjoining Cibola, 11; Queres, 5; Cunames (Zia, etc.), 5; Amies, 7; Acoma, 1—being fifty-three in all; to which are to be added those of the provinces that he describes, but neglects to state the number of villages in, as Cibola, or Zuñi, which we can call seven, Zaguate and the other Moqui towns, which were five, and the provinces of the Tubians and the Taños, whose population he placed at 25,000 and 40,000, respectively, which, at the usual ratio, would represent twenty-five or thirty pueblos, but which was no doubt largely exaggerated as he gave the figures from hearsay, and probably did not represent more than fifteen. Calling the number in these two nations fifteen would give us eighty pueblos in all, existing in 1582. At the present they are reduced in numbers to twenty-five, being nineteen in the valley of the Rio Grande and its tributaries; one at Zuñi and the five Moqui towns; which latter have been the least disturbed in the course of centuries. How or when did the number become so greatly reduced? Partly, we believe, by the consolidation of small neighboring pueblos into one, during the Spanish occupation, and more largely by the destruction and abandonment of villages in the wars between themselves, which occurred in the period of the Pueblo control, from 1681 to 1696. The decree of the Emperor Charles V., issued from Cigales, March 21, 1551, specially looking to the concentration of the peaceful native population into a moderate number of towns, took effect of course in New Mexico, as soon as it was under Spanish control. The object, which was spiritual as well as temporal, is set forth in the decree as follows,—

"The effort has been made with much care, and particular attention, to make use of such means as are most suitable for the instruction of the Indians in the Holy Catholic faith and spiritual law, to the end that, forgetting their ancient rites and ceremonies, they might live in fellowship under established rule; and in order that this object might be obtained with the greatest certainty, the members of our council of the Indies, and other religious persons, on different occasions met together, and in the year 1546, by order of the Emperor Charles V., of glorious memory, there convened the prelates of New Spain, who, desiring to render service to God and ourselves, resolved that the Indians should be brought to settle—reduced to pueblos—and that they should not live divided and separated by mountains and hills, depriving themselves of all benefit, spiritual or temporal, without aid from our agents, and that assistance which human wants require men mutually to render one another.

"And in order that the propriety of this resolution might be recognized, the kings, judges, presidents, and governors were charged and commanded by different orders of the kings, our predecessors, that with much mildness and moderation they should carry into effect the reduction, settlement, and instruction of the Indians, acting with so much justice and delicacy that without causing any difficulty a motive might be presented to those who could not be brought to settle, in the hope that as soon as they witnessed the good treatment and protection of such as had been reduced to pueblos, they might consent to offer themselves of their own accord; and whereas the above was executed in the larger part of our Indies, therefore we ordain and command that in all the other portions care be taken that it be carried into effect, and the agents should urge it according to, and in the form declared by, the laws of this title."

This decree was intended, at the time, for the provinces of New Spain, to the south, but there can be little doubt, from various circumstances, that it was acted on in New Mexico during the seventeenth century, and resulted in the consolidation of numbers of small, adjacent pueblos, bringing the people to the central village, in which was the church, and the priest, and the local civil authority. The great reduction in the number of the native villages took place, however, during the brief period of Pueblo government, after the expulsion of the Spaniards in 1681. When Vargas made the reconquest, twelve to fifteen years later, he found ruined and abandoned pueblos everywhere. Mutual jealousies, and the struggle for food caused by the successive failures of crops, had caused almost constant wars, in which villages had been destroyed by the enemy, or abandoned by their inhabitants in advance of a siege. The result was, that at the time of the final pacification under Spanish authority, say in 1696, the number of pueblos differed very little from that existing at present. The official list made by Governor Mendoza in May, 1742, is as follows (exclusive of the Moquis),—

"Taos, Picuries, San Juan, San Ildefonso, Santa Clara, Pojuaque, Nambe, and Tesuque, north of Santa Fé; Pecos east, and Galisteo south of Santa Fé; Cochiti, Santo Domingo, San Felipe, Santa Ana, Zia, Jemez, Laguna, Acoma, Zuñi, and Isleta south or west of Santa Fé."

In 1796, and again in 1798, the missionaries in charge made reports of the population of the different pueblos, in which the lists of villages only differ from the above in the dropping of Galisteo and the addition of Sandia and Abiquiu Galisteo had been abandoned in the interval (the remaining inhabitants having removed to Santo Domingo, with whose people they had extensively intermarried), and Sandia had been established under peculiar circumstances, which will be hereafter referred to. At Abiquiu 176 Indians are stated to live, but whether at the pueblo on the hill (now deserted and in ruins), or in connection with the Spanish town, does not appear. 124 Indians are also reported at Belen. The total Pueblo population at the time, according to these statistics, was 9,453 in 1796, and 9,732 in 1798. In 1805 Governor Alencaster prepared a complete census of all the inhabitants of New Mexico (divided by races), according to which the Spanish population was 26,805, and the Pueblos 8,172. The list of pueblos, with their mission names and population, appearing in his report, is as follows:—

San Geronimo de Taos	508
San Lorenzo de Picuries	250
San Juan de los Caballeros	194
Santo Tomas de Abiquiu	134
Santa Clara	186
San Ildefonso	175
San Francisco de Nambe	143
N. S. de Guadalupe de Pojuaque	100
San Diego de Tesuque	131
N. S. de los Angeles de Pecos	104
San Buena Ventura de Cochiti	656
Santo Domingo	333
San Felipe	289
N. S. de los Dolores de Sandia	314
San Diego de Jemez	264
N. S. de la Asumpcion de Zia	254
Santa Ana	450
San Agustin del Isleta	419
N. S. de Belen	107
San Estevan de Acoma	731
San Josef de La Laguna	940
N. S. de Guadalupe de Zuni	1470

Both Albiquiu and Belen are reported with large Spanish populations, so that it does not appear whether the Indians were in separate pueblos there or not. This list, it will be observed, agrees perfectly with that of 1796. The report of Lieut. Whipple (Pacific R. R. Surveys, 35° parallel) contains the same list, with the addition of Cuyamangue and Chilili. But their insertion was a mistake, as both were destroyed in the Pueblo revolt 160 years before. An old deed in the archives at Santa Fé refers to "Cuyamangue, a pueblo abandoned and in ruin, since the insurrection in 1696 by the native Tegua Indians of said pueblo." Since Gov. Alencaster's census, no change has taken place, except in the abandonment of the Pueblo of Pecos by the removal of its surviving inhabitants to Jemez. We are, therefore, safe in saying that the Pueblo towns exist to-day as they did at the final reconquest in 1696, with the exception of abandonment of Galisteo and Pecos, and possibly of the pueblo near Albiquiu, and the establishment of Sandia; the great reduction in numbers as previously stated, having taken place in the 17th century.

The circumstances of the establishment of the Pueblo of Sandia, which is the only modern one, were as follows: In 1748 Friar Juan Miguel Meuchero, Preacher and Delegate, Commissary General, made a petition to the Governor, in which he stated that for six years he had been engaged in missionary work among the Indians, and had "converted and gained over 350 souls from here to the Puerco River, which I have brought from the Moqui Pueblos; bringing with me the cacique of these Moqui Pueblos for the purpose of establishing their pueblo at the place called Sandia," and thereupon asked for possession of the land at that point "so as to prevent any converts from returning to apostasy." Thereupon the Governor made the desired grant, and the new pueblo was established in due form by the name of "Our Lady of Sorrows and Saint Anthony of Sandia."

From the beginning the Spanish authorities sought first to conciliate, and afterwards to protect the pueblos by confirming to them considerable tracts of land around each village. The decree of Philip II., in June, 1587, had special reference to this subject, and the limits were afterwards extended until in most cases the pueblo land constituted a square—measured one league in each direction from the parish church.

In local government the pueblos have always been practically independent; each one elects annually a governor, a war captain, and a fiscal, and in each is a cacique, usually an aged man, who holds his position for life, and is consulted on all matters of special importance. These officials govern the community according to their own rules of justice, and to this time no criminal complaint has ever been made by one Pueblo Indian against another in any Territorial court. Industrious, frugal, honest, and hospitable, they still retain the characteristics which were noticeable in the days of Cabeza de Vaca and Coronado, and remain in the midst of surrounding changes the most interesting existing illustration of the higher aboriginal life of the native American people.

CHAPTER III.

CABEZA DE VACA.

THE first European to set foot on New Mexican soil, to meet with any of its original inhabitants, and see the "fixed habitations" in which they dwelt, was Alvar Nuñez Cabeza de Vaca, who came not as a conqueror, a missionary, or even an explorer, but by an accident, which led him through this portion of the continent while endeavoring to reach some European settlement, after long years of wanderings, sufferings, and virtual imprisonment. He came of noble lineage, and held many high positions, but that which carries his name down on the page of history most securely is his brief connection with New Mexico. Here his name stands at the head of the roll, his narration is the first written word descriptive of the country and its people; he can claim to be its discoverer, and the father of all Europeans who came after. Among the people of New Mexico his name will always be held in veneration, and every circumstance connected with his famous journey be considered of interest. On this account, and because it so thoroughly illustrates the methods of the early Spanish expeditions and conquests, and the condition of the natives in various sections surrounding New Mexico, as well as within its borders, we give it an extended space.

The expedition of Panphilo de Narvaez set sail from San Lucar de Barrameda, on the 17th of June, 1527; its object being the conquest and colonization of the mainland of Florida, Narvaez having been empowered by the Emperor Charles V. to take possession of all the country from the Rio de la Palsmas to the southerly extremity of Florida, and to assume the government thereof. This Rio de las Palmas was on the east coast of Mexico, 100 leagues north of Vera Cruz, so that the country which was to be occupied and governed embraced all of the present States of the Union bordering on the Gulf of Mexico, besides a part of north-eastern Mexico itself; in which was included New Mexico. The principal officers of the fleet, under the Governor, were Cabeza de Vaca, who was Treasurer of the expedition, and had the title of High Sheriff; Alonzo Enriquez, Comptroller; Alonzo de Solis, Royal Distributor and Assessor; and for spiritual duties, five Franciscan Friars, headed by Juan Xuarez, who was also Commissary.

The manner in which the expedition was undertaken appears from the petition of Narvaez to the king of Spain, and the order made thereupon; all of which are still in the "Archivo de Indias" at Seville. The following extracts from the petition quaintly show the objects and ambition of the leader:

"SACRED CÆSAREAN CATHOLIC MAJESTY: In-as-much as I, Panfilo de Narvaez, have ever had and still have the intention of serving God and Your Majesty, I desire to go in person with my means to a certain country on the main of the Ocean Sea. I propose chiefly to traffic with the natives of the coast, and to take thither religious men and ecclesiastics, approved of your Royal Council of the Indies, that they may make known and plant the Christian Faith. I shall observe fully what your Council require and ordain to the ends of serving God and Your Highness, and for the good of your subjects. I propose to undertake this in person, with my experience in those countries, and when the occasion shall present itself, to the extent of my property, which, to God be the praise, I have to employ in that enterprise, and am ready to make manifest when that shall become necessary. I ask that the subjugation of the countries from the Rio de Palmas to Florida might be given me, where I would explore, conquer, populate, and discover all there is to be found of Florida in those parts, at my cost; and to that end I beg Your Highness to bestow on me as follows: Your Majesty be pleased to make me Governor and Chief Justice for my term of life, and Captain General, with adequate salary for each. I entreat Your Majesty to confer on me the High Constabulary of said lands I shall people in your Royal name, for me, my heirs, and successors. I entreat Your Majesty to grant me the tenth of all that you may have of royal rents forever. I ask that Your Majesty will make me Adelantado of those territories, for me, my heirs, and successors, That Indians who shall be rebellious after being well admonished and comprehending, may be made slaves, etc."

The order made by the Council was that the king concedes the conquest requested to Narvaez on condition that he take no less than 200 colonists from Spain, founding at least two towns; and he was made Governor with a salary of 100,000 maravedis, and Captain General, with a salary of 50,000, besides being Adelantado. He was furnished with a proclamation to be made "to the inhabitants of the countries and provinces that there are from Rio de Palmas to the Cape of Florida," which is interesting as showing the grounds to the Spanish claim of sovereignty over America. It reads in part as follows: "In behalf of the Catholic Cæsarean Majesty of Don Carlos, King of the Romans and Emperor ever Augustus, and Doña Juana, his mother, Sovereigns of Leon and Castilla, Defenders of the Church, ever victors, never vanquished, and rulers of barbarous nations, I, Panfilo de Narvaez, his servant, messenger, and captain, notify and cause you to know in the best manner I can, that God our Lord, one and eternal, created the heaven and the earth. All these nations God our Lord gave in charge to one person called Saint

Peter, that he might be master and superior over mankind, to be obeyed and be heard of all the human race where-so-ever they might live and be, of whatever law, sect, or belief, giving him the whole world for his kingdom, lordship, and jurisdiction. This Saint Peter was obeyed and taken for King, Lord, and Superior of the Universe by those who lived at that time, and so likewise have all the rest been held, who to the Pontificate were afterward elected, and thus has it continued until now, and will continue to the end of things. One of the Popes who succeeded him to that seat and dignity, of which I spake as Lord of the world, made a gift of these islands and main of the Ocean Sea to the said Emperor and Queen, and their successors, our Lords in these Kingdoms, with all that is in them, as is contained in certain writings that thereupon took place, which may be seen if you desire."

Having thus demonstrated the rightful power of the sovereign, the proclamation calls on them "to recognize the Church as Mistress and Superior of the Universe, and the High Pontiff, called Papa, in its name; the Queen and King our masters, in their place as Lords Superiors, and Sovereigns of these Islands and the main, by virtue of said gift. If you shall do so, you will do well in what you are held and obliged; and their Majesties, and I, in their Royal name, will receive you with love and charity. If you do not this, and of malice you be dilatory, I protest to you that with the help of Our Lord I will enter with force, making war upon you from all directions and in every manner that I may be able, when I will subject you to obedience to the Church and the yoke of their Majesties; and I will take the persons of yourselves, your wives, and your children, to make slaves, sell and dispose of you as their Majesties shall think fit; and I will take your goods, doing you all the injury that I may be able."

As the peculiar interest which the student of New

Mexican history feels in this expedition arises from the narrative of Cabeza de Vaca of the long journey of himself and the other three survivors of the party across the continent, in the course of which they traversed New Mexico, and were thus the first Europeans who ever visited our territory, we give some particulars of his personal history, before proceeding with the account of the expedition itself. Alvar Nunez Cabeza de Vaca came from one of the oldest and most renowned of Spanish families, whose lineage a chronological history traces back to the 12th century. His grandfather was the Conqueror of the Canary Islands, and from him came his proper patronymic of Vera; but for reasons unknown he preferred the name of his mother's house, "Cabeza de Vaca," or "Cow's Head." Various accounts are given of the origin of this rather undignified appellation, of which we reproduce the one narrated by M. Ternaux, in the preface to his French translation of Cabeza de Vaca's Commentaries: "In the month of July, 1212, the Christian army, commanded by the kings of Castile, Aragon, and Navarre, advanced against the Moors; and arriving at Castro-Ferrel, found all the passes occupied by the enemy. The Christians were about to return on their steps, when a burger named Martin Alhaja presented himself to the King of Navarre, and offered to indicate a route by which the army could pass without obstacles. The king sent him with Don Diego Lopez de Naro and Don Garcia Romen; in order that they might recognize the pass, Alhajo placed at the entrance the skeleton of the head of a cow (Cabeza de Vaca.) The twelfth of the same month the Christians gained the battle of Navas de Tolosa, which assured forever their supremacy over the Moors. The king recompensed Alhaja by ennobling him and his descendants, and to commemorate the event by which he had merited the honor, changed his name to Cabeza de Vaca."

Our cavalier having been appointed Treasurer of

the new colony to be established, received a lengthy document of instruction, signed by the king and dated at Valladolid, February 15, 1527, which commences, " What you, Alvar Nuñez Cabeza de Vaca, will perform in the office you fill as our Treasurer of Rio de las Palmas and the lands which Panfilo de Narvaez goes to people, on whom we have conferred the government thereof, is as follows"— and proceeds with great particularity to charge him with the collection of the various percentages, rents, duties, and fines belonging to the royal treasury; and as to the manner of safely transmitting the " gold, guaniñes (impure gold valued by the nations of the Antillas partly for its odor), pearls, and other things," to the officials at Seville.

Thus furnished with documents sufficient for the government of an Empire, Narvaez and his companions started with five vessels and about six hundred men, and sailed first to Santo Domingo for the purpose of laying in stores and procuring horses, but their forty-five days stay at that island produced rather more loss than gain, as no less than 140 men deserted the expedition to try their fortunes on the luxuriant shores. Here also an additional ship was purchased and added to the fleet. They proceeded thence to Cuba, where a tremendous hurricane destroyed two of the vessels, with all the men and material on board. Cabeza de Vaca had command of one of them, and only escaped through his good fortune in being on shore at the time. He tells us that "nothing so terrible as this storm had ever been seen in these parts before;" and it must have been of tremendous force, as the only small boat that was ever found belonging to the lost vessels, was discovered in the branches of a tree at quite a distance from the shore. So tempestuous was the season that Narvaez determined to proceed no further until spring, and so the four remaining vessels wintered at Xagua, under the charge of Cabeza de Vaca. On the 22d of February, 1528, the fleet again set sail, having been augmented by the addition of a brigantine from Trinidad; but again misfortune followed it, as the vessels became grounded on the shoals called Canarreo and were detained there fifteen days; and were overtaken by a great and dangerous storm at Guaniguanico, and another at Cape Corrientes. They then attempted to reach Havana, but violent winds drove them northerly, and on Tuesday, April 12, they came in sight of land on the west coast of Florida; and the next day, which was Holy Thursday, they anchored near the shore in a bay, at the head of which they saw some Indian habitations.

On Good Friday the Governor landed with a number of men, but found the houses all deserted, the inhabitants having fled in their canoes at night. Their houses were called "buhios," and had double-shedded roofs, which were their distinguishing feature among Indian dwellings. One of these buildings, probably used for tribal purposes, was so large as to accommodate 300 persons. On Saturday the Governor raised the Spanish ensign and formally took possession of the country for his imperial master. He proclaimed his authority to act as Governor, and was acknowledged as such; and then the other officers presented their commissions for his inspection. These formalities being concluded, the whole force was disembarked, as well as their horses; but the latter had been reduced to forty-two in number during the passage, and were in wretched condition.

On Easter day some of the natives appeared, and made signs for the Spaniards to leave the country; but there being no interpreter present, they could only be imperfectly understood. The next day a party of forty men, under the Governor, Enriquez, Solis, and Cabeza de Vaca, commenced to explore the main-land toward the north, where they found a large bay stretching far inland, and soon afterward captured four Indians. (This bay was undoubtedly the Tampa Bay of our geographies.)

As the language was wholly unintelligible, recourse was had to signs; and various things were shown to the natives, to see if they were acquainted with them before. Led by these Indians, the Spaniards went to their town at the head of the bay, where they found corn, linen and woolen cloth. and bunches of feathers, and what was the special object of all their expeditions—gold. On being asked whence these things came, the Indians pointed to the north, where they said was a great country called Apalache, which abounded not only in gold but in the other articles which the Spaniards desired. Ten or twelve leagues further on, the expedition found another town, where a large amount of corn was cultivated; and soon after returned to the place where their ships and comrades were, and communicated the results of the trip.

The next day the Governor held a consultation with the principal officers, and some others in whom he had confidence, as to the best course to be pursued. He desired to march into the interior in order to explore the country, and have the ships sail along the coast until they found a harbor, which the pilot insisted existed not very far to the north-west; but he wanted to hear the opinion of the others. Cabeza de Vaca strenuously opposed any separation from the vessels until the latter should be safely moored in a secure harbor, and he called attention to the fact that the pilots were far from agreeing as to the situation of the wished-for haven. He showed the danger of starting off to explore a country of which they had no knowledge or information, and where they could not communicate at all with the natives for want of an interpreter; especially in their present condition of scarcity of food. In short, he opposed the plan with many arguments, and recommended that they should re-embark in the vessels and explore the coast until they found some satisfactory locality, especially as the country where they now were was the poorest and least valuable of any that had been found in the new world. The Commissioner, Xuarez, gave exactly contrary advice. He favored following along the line of the coast by an expedition on land, while the ships kept within easy distance by sailing along that same shore. He based his argument on two principal grounds: Firstly, that the looked-for bay could more easily be found from the land than from the sea, as it was represented to extend a considerable distance back into the country; and secondly, that it would be tempting Providence again to take to the water after the many misfortunes which had befallen the fleet ever since it first left Spain. The feeling with regard to the course to be pursued evidently ran high, for when the Governor concluded to continue the expedition by land, Cabeza de Vaca made a formal demand that the ships should not be left until they were in a safe harbor, and asked a certificate from the notary that he made such a demand; and the Governor, on his part, asked of the notary a certificate that he moved on with his colony in quest of a better country and port, for the reason that the place in which they were would neither support a population nor afford a haven for their ships. What the notarial official did in this dilemma does not apppear from the chronicle, but the Governor went on with his preparations for advancing, and then, in presence of the officers, offered Cabeza de Vaca—as he was opposed to the land expedition—to give him the command of the fleet. This Vaca refused; and when repeatedly urged by the Governor to accept the position, and finally asked why he so persistently declined, he answered, as he himself relates, that "I rejected the responsibility, as I felt certain that he would never more find the ships, nor the ships him; and I preferred to subject myself to the danger which he and the others were exposed to, and to undergo what they might suffer, rather than take charge of the ships and give occasion for any to say that I remained behind from timidity, and so my courage be called in question. I chose rather to risk my life than to endanger my reputation."

The Governer thereupon appointed a Spanish Alcalde, named Caravallo, as Captain of the fleet, and proceeded to arrange for the march. Provisions were already scanty; on the day of starting the men were given a ration of two pounds of biscuit and one-half pound bacon, but thereafter the bread was reduced to one pound. The whole land expedition consisted of 300 men, of whom the officers, etc., who were mounted, were forty. On Sunday, the 1st of May, they took up their march and proceeded northerly for fifteen days, without seeing any kind of habitation or a single Indian. During this time they found nothing eatable to add to their scanty store, except the palmetto or fan palm, which abounded and from which they ate the heart. At the end of the fifteen days they came to a river so wide that it was passed with much difficulty—rafts having to be made for those inexperienced in swimming, and the crossing occupying an entire day. (This undoubtedly is the river now called Withlacoochee.)

On the north side of this river the expedition for the first time encountered a considerable number of natives. They were about 200 in all, and the Governor attempted to open communication by signs, but the Indians made such insulting gestures that the Spaniards could not bear it; and so, rushing forward, they captured several, and compelled them to show them where their village was. This was found about half a league away; and more important to the invaders than the poor Indian cabins, were large fields of corn, just ready to be gathered. "We gave infinite thanks to our Lord for having succored us in this great extremity," piously exclaimed the chronicler, "for we were yet young in trials, and besides the weariness in which we came, we were exhausted from hunger."

Here the army rested for three days, when the chief officers all besought Narvaez to send to search for the sea, so as if possible to find the safe harbor of which the Indians spoke. He gave them no satisfaction at the time, but afterwards authorized Cabeza de Vaca to take forty men and make the exploration. So he set out on foot on May 18th; but the result of the search was, that if a harbor was to be found at all, it was by following the river down on its south side and not on the north; so the Treasurer returned, and Captain Valenzuela was sent on a second expedition; but this only discovered that the bay was too shallow for vessels of any size, although a number of canoes carrying Indians wearing plumes was seen passing across its waters.

Abandoning, therefore, the hope of finding a suitable place for a permanent port in that vicinity, the expedition recommenced its march toward the land of Apalache, of the riches of which they heard so much; having now for guides the Indians they had captured. For almost a month they travelled without meeting any natives, when on June 17th, just before they reached the banks of a very wide and rapid river (which is easily distinguishable as the Suwanee of modern times), they were approached by a chief, covered with a painted deerskin, and carried in the arms of another Indian Many of his people attended him, and in advance were musicians playing on flutes of reed. This appears to have been the method in which they showed hospitality and good will; as eleven years later, when De Soto arrived at the same place, he was met by Indians "playing upon flutes, a sign among them to others that they come in peace." A conference by signs ensued, the Spaniards endeavoring to convey the idea that they were going on to Apalache; and understanding in reply that the chief was an enemy to the Apalachians, and would accompany and assist the expedition. Presents were then exchanged, the chief giving the Governor the deer-skin which he wore; and the next day the army attempted the difficult passage of the river. A boat was constructed, and on this all were finally taken across safely, except one horseman, Juan Velasquez, who was too impatient to wait for his turn, and plunging into the river, was carried away by the swift current. His horse, found drowned on the bank below, furnished the first fresh meat that the soldiers had enjoyed for many days. The next day the expedition reached the town of the chief, whose name is given by Cabeza de Vaca as Dulchanchellin, but by other writers as Uzachil, Osachile, Ochile, etc., (all evidently mispronunciations of the same name), and received some corn as a present.

But now, for some reason, the demeanor of the Indians changed. Heretofore they had been hospitable, and helpful; indeed, without their assistance the army could not have crossed the Suwanee; but now they assumed a hostile attitude. Some slight conflicts ensued, in which three or four natives were captured; and then Narvaez proceeded on his march, on June 20th, the latest captives being now his guides. The country now traversed was covered with dense forests of enormous trees, of which so many had fallen to the ground that travelling was very difficult and slow. After six days of toilsome march their eyes were at length gladdened by the sight of the city which was the goal of their hopes. "We gave many thanks to God," says the Treasurer, "at seeing ourselves so near, having confidence in what we had heard of the land, and believing that here was the end of our great hardships; and having come to the wished-for place, where we had been told was much food and gold, we felt that we had already recovered in part from our suffering and fatigue."

After viewing the town from a distance, the Governor directed Cabeza de Vaca to take nine horsemen and fifty foot soldiers and enter the place. This was done without difficulty, as all the men were absent from their homes and only women and children remained; but shortly afterwards the men returned, and seeing the strangers in possession, commenced discharging arrows at them. This, however, did no damage beyond killing the horse of the Assessor, and the Indians then took to flight. The Spaniards then proceeded to explore the town, but were entirely disappointed both as to its size and riches. Instead of a large city, they found a village of forty small, low houses, scattered in sheltered places, and built of thatch. No gold was to be found, or anything of value, except corn and deer-skins. The whole country was level and sandy, but pines, cedars, oaks, liquid amber, and palmettos abounded. In openings in the country around were patches of corn, but the whole presented a scene of barrenness and poverty far different from what the adventurers had hoped. Within a short time the Indians who had fled returned in peace, asking for their wives and children, who were restored to them; but for some reason Narvaez detained one chief, which produced much excitement and brought on hostilities anew, which were kept up as long as the Spaniards remained in the town, which was twenty-five days. During this time they endeavored by explorations and inquiries to ascertain regarding the surrounding country and any cities of wealth that it might contain; but their expeditions showed them simply a sparsely populated plain, and the answer to all inquiries was, that no other town was as large or as good as their own, except one called Aute, near the sea, and distant nine days' journey.

Finding nothing worth conquering where they were, the Spaniards determined to march to this city, not only because it was the most important that they could hear of, but also because it would bring them again near to their ships. So they set out on the 20th of July, but were greatly annoyed in their march by the Indians, who assailed them with arrows from behind trees and fallen timber, and from the shallow lakes, in which they stood nearly covered by the water. These Indians appear to have been powerful and expert archers, for they wounded many of the men and horses, and drove their arrows with almost incredible force into the bodies of great oaks and elms. Their bows are described as being as thick as a man's arm, of eleven or twelve palms in length, and their aim at 200 yards was almost infallible.

After nine days of hard travel the army arrived at Auté, but found that the news of their approach had preceded them, for the houses had all been burned and the inhabitants had fled. However, they found corn, beans, and pumpkins in great quantities—a most welcome sight to the hungry and weary Spaniards. Here they rested for two days, and then Cabeza de Vaca, at the request of the Governor, went to discover the sea. After a day's march he arrived at a bay where there were good oysters, but examination showed that the Gulf itself was far distant; and so he returned again to the camp. (This bay was probably Apalachicola Bay.) Everything now was in a most discouraging condition. An unknown malady had appeared and spread with great rapidity among the men. Among the stricken were the Comptroller, the Inspector, and the Governor himself. The Indians had taken advantage of this season of weakness and made an attack which had well nigh been disastrous. The position of the army was very embarrassing, and there was no hope of improvement where they were; so it was determined to set off immediately for the shore. But this journey, though short, was no easy task. The sick increased in number daily, and there were not enough horses to carry them. Scarcely any of the men continued fit for active duty; and while thus compassed by difficulties their danger was increased by a plot entered into by those who were mounted to abandon the Governor and their comrades and press on themselves to a place of safety. This scheme, however, was fortunately frustrated and abandoned.

On arriving at the bay the condition of the army was not much improved—except that they could obtain oysters from the water. Affairs soon became so critical that the Governor asked the advice of all the leading men as to the course which promised best to relieve them in their emergency. A third of the men were sick, and the number was continually increasing. Every day augmented their difficulties. It was dangerous to move, and dangerous to remain still. They were on an arm of the Gulf of Mexico, but the whereabouts of their vessels no one knew. Yet they were unable to march farther, and the sea presented their only means of escape. At last, after all their circumstances were considered, all agreed that they must endeavor, if possible, to build boats which would carry them away from this land of misfortune. But no project could well seem more impossible of execution. They had no tools, no iron, no forge, no rigging—in short, no single thing of those most necessary; and no man who had a knowledge of the manufacture. Besides all this, they were nearly out of provisions. They were about abandoning the idea when one of the men said that he believed he could make a bellows from a wooden pipe and some deer-skins; and in their despondent condition even this suggestion seemed like a ray of hope from heaven. They agreed to use their stirrups, spurs, and everthing which they had of iron, in the manufacture of nails, axes, and other tools. From the outer fibrous covering of the palmetto they prepared a good substitute for tow. A Greek named Teodoro made pitch from the adjacent pine-trees. From the palmetto leaves and the tails and manes of their horses, ropes and rigging were ingeniously manufactured; and sails were made from the shirts of the men. But a single carpenter was in their entire company; but under his direction they worked with such diligence that in the period from August 4th to September 20th they built five boats, each twenty-two cubits in length. Meanwhile a good supply of provisions was obtained by making armed excursions to Aute, from which, in all, about 640 bushels of corn were brought; and on every third day a horse was killed to furnish meat. The skins from the legs of these animals were taken off entire, and by rude tanning made into bottles to hold water for the coming voyage. They also obtained shell-fish from the adjacent coves; but this work proved dangerous, for bands of Indian archers attacked all isolated parties, and so powerful and accurate was their shooting that their arrows even pierced the armor of the men, and in one day ten soldiers were thus killed in sight of the camp. More than forty died from the disease before mentioned, and when the boats were completed, but one horse remained unconsumed. There was, therefore, little time to lose, and on the 20th they embarked in their frail boats, which were found scarcely sufficiently large to convey the whole number. The company, which now consisted of 247 persons, was divided equally, from forty-eight to fifty going in each boat. One was commanded by the Governor, Narvaez; one by the Comptroller and Commissary; one by Captain Alonzo del Castillo and Andres Dorantes; one by Captains Peñalosa and Tellez, and one by Cabeza de Vaca and the Assessor. So heavily were the vessels loaded when all were on board that not more than a span remained above water; and the men were so crowded that they could not move without danger. What greatly added to their difficulties was, that among the whole company there was not one who understood even the first principles of navigation.

Never, perhaps, in all history, has an enterprise been undertaken in the face of more discouragements and difficulties than this embarkation of the army of Narvaez. For a single man cast away, to frame a raft on which to attempt escape, is not rare; but without a nail or tool of any kind, to build boats capable of carrying a quarter of a thousand people, working in the midst of sickness and the attacks of the enemy, is without a parallel. The place where this work was accomplished the Spaniards called "Bahia de Caballos," the "Bay of Horses." A few years later (1539), a party from the army of De Soto, under Juan de Añasco, visited it and heard from the natives an account of the sojourn of the army of Narvaez, being shown the spots where the ten Spaniards had been killed and other memorable events had occurred. He even found the furnace in which the spikes had been made for the boats, still surrounded by charcoal, and some large hollowed logs that had been used for horse-troughs. This bay is easily recognizable, from its situation and description, as Appalachee; and this theory is confirmed by the extract from Charlevoix in 1722, given hereafter. It is possible, however, that it may have been near the mouth of the Apalachicola River.

The army embarked on the 22d of September, and proceeded along the shallow waters of the coast, seeing nothing of unusual interest until toward evening of the 28th, when they approached an inhabited island, from which five canoes full of Indians came toward them. The natives, however, were overcome with fear at the sight of the number of the pale-faced strangers, and hastily abandoning their canoes, swam to the shore for safety. The Spaniards pressed on to the island, where they found a number of houses, and what was most acceptable in their condition, some dried mullet and fish-roes. The abandoned boats they made useful in heightening the sides of their own dangerous vessels, until they were two palms above the water. In these frail crafts for thirty more long days they moved along the coast, their sufferings from lack of food increasing as time passed and stores became exhausted, and their difficulties much enhanced by the scarcity of fresh water, which could only be procured by entering creeks and going beyond the reach of the tide, which of course entailed the loss of much time. Unfortunately, their singular bottles of horses' legs did not meet the hopes of their ingenious inventors, for they soon rotted and became worthless, leaving the boats without any vessels in which to preserve any quantity of the necessary water.

On the 30th day they saw a small island, and went on shore in hopes of finding a spring, but in this were disappointed; and while thus on land so violent a storm arose that they were afraid to tempt the waters again, and were thus detained for six days, during the last five of which they were utterly destitute of drink. So frightful became their sufferings from this deprivation that at length some of the men in desperation drank the salt sea-water, and in a short time several died. In this terrible position, death from thirst threatening them if they remained, and destruction by the storm impending if they took to the sea, they chose the latter horn of the dilemma as that which, at all events, presented some chance of escape, and so pushed out again into the Gulf. The waves were so high, and the weather so tempestuous, that many times they were nearly overwhelmed; but when death seemed almost inevitable, just at sunset, they passed around a projecting point of land and found a calm harbor beyond. What was equally welcome at such a time, they saw an Indian village and a number of natives in canoes. The Spaniards quickly approached the shore, and lost no time in gaining the land, being hastened by the sight of jars of water standing in front of the houses. From them they quenched their almost inexhaustible thirst, and then proceeded to observe the surroundings. The houses of these Indians were made of mats, and appeared to be permanent dwellings. The men were tall, of fine form, and when first seen had no arms of any kind.

The Cacique of the village soon appeared and invited Narvaez to his home, where he supplied him with cooked fish, and in return the Governor presented the chief with various trinkets. The Spaniards gave the Indians a little of their remaining scanty store of corn, and the natives supplied them with fish and whatever they had to offer. The best of feeling appeared to prevail on both sides; but just at midnight, when the Spaniards, exhausted by their long watching, were heavily asleep, the Indians suddenly made an attack on them, and killed three of those who were sick and had been brought on shore. They made an attempt to kill Narvaez, and succeeded in striking him in the face with a stone. Some of the Spaniards seized their chief, but the Indians being greater in number rescued him. The Governor was carried to his boat, and the sick and feeble were also put on board, while fifty of the strongest of the Spaniards remained to meet the attack of the Indians. The latter fought with bravery and determination. Three times during the night they drove the Europeans back, and but for lack of arrows, the historian (who was an active participant) thinks that they would have inflicted great damage. As it was, every Spaniard was more or less wounded; Cabeza de Vaca himself being stricken in the face. The next day, as soon as the weather permitted, the boats set sail again; having, however, unfortunately, no means by which to carry any sufficient supply of water.

One trophy they retained from this adventure of which the chronicler makes special mention. When the Cacique was rescued by his people, they left in the hands of the Spaniards his robe of civet-marten. "These skins," says Vaca, "are the best, I think, that can be found; they have a fragrance which can be equalled by amber and musk alone, and even at a distance is strongly perceptible. We saw other skins there, but none to be compared with these."

Sailing along the shore, the little squadron soon came to the mouth of a river, and again saw Indians in canoes. The Governor made signs that he wanted water, and they replied that they would bring it. Thereupon Don Teodoro, the same Greek who manufactured the pitch for the boats at the *Bahia de Caballos*, insisted on going on shore with them, and in spite of all the protestations of his companions went, taking with him a negro from one of the boats. All that could be done by the captains to secure his safety was to detain two Indians on a boat as hostages. At night the Indians came again, bringing the vessels but no water, and without the Greek or the African. They said something in their own language to the two hostages, whereupon the latter attempted to jump into the sea, but were seized and restrained by the Spaniards. Seeing this, the Indians who had come fled in their canoes. The next morning a large number of Indians in boats surrounded the little squadron and demanded the delivery of their two companions, but were answered that they must first return the two Christians. To this they gave no satisfactory answer, only saying that if the Spaniards would come on shore they would not only deliver Teodoro and the African, but would also supply them with water and other necessaries. The Spaniards, however, feared some treachery, and as the Indians seemed to be attempting to cut off their retreat, by taking possession of the entrance of the bay, Narvaez immediately set sail for the sea. The natives then showed their hostile intentions, for they began to hurl clubs and throw stones from slings at the Spaniards, and threatened to shoot with arrows. The wind, however, favored the latter, and they succeeded in getting into the open sea and beyond the reach of their assailants; but while thus saving themselves, they had to abandon the Greek and negro to their fate. Years afterwards, when De Soto passed through, his soldiers heard of Don Teodoro, and were shown a dirk which had been his; but the accounts of his fate, and that of his companion, were conflicting. At all events, they never lived to return to their homes, or even to see a European face again.

The little fleet sailed westward all that day, but about the middle of the afternoon came in sight of a point of land and the mouth of a broad river. So great was the volume of water brought down by this stream that the sailors took fresh water from the sea which was fit for drinking purposes; and shortly afterwards, attempting to pass the mouth of the river, they found it to be impossible, as the current was so violent that it continually drove them out to sea, while they were straining every nerve to reach the land. Three full days they toiled in this way, trying to gain the shore against the mighty current which was stronger by far than anything which human arms could do, and before which the frail boats were but as bubbles on an ocean; and on the morning of November 3d the little vessels had become so far separated that none of the others could be seen from that of Cabeza de Vaca.

There can be no doubt from the description, as well as from the locality, that this river with the enormous current of fresh water was the Mississippi; and that while De Soto has the honor of being the first to see it in its proper form as a river running through the land, the fleet of Narvaez, several years before, was in sight of its mouth and felt the force of its mighty current, and actually drank of its waters as they made a channel through the salt waves of the Gulf of Mexico.

We can imagine the feelings of the party in the boat of the Treasurer when they found themselves alone in the open sea. They had suffered almost every possible privation before, but always in the companionship of their comrades—but now even that consolation was removed. Keeping on their westerly course, however, just at evening, they were rejoiced again to see two of the boats, one near at hand, and one far out at sea. Approaching the former, they found it to be that of the Governor, and a consultation took place as to the best course of action. Cabeza de Vaca contended that they ought to join the other boat at all hazards, so as to be together, and then proceed on their way; but the Governor answered that the other boat was too far out at sea, and that they ought to reach the shore as soon as possible. He expressed his own determination to take that course, and told Vaca that if he wanted to remain in his company he must keep every man at the oars in order to bring the boat to land. This the Treasurer did, taking an oar himself to aid and encourage the men; but the soldiers were worn out with fatigue and hunger, and could not compete as oarsmen with the stronger men in the Governor's boat—which had been manned by the healthiest and most athletic of the army. Finding that he could not keep up with the Governor's boat, Vaca begged them to give him a rope so that his boat could be towed along; but this the Governor refused, saying that it would be all they could do, with every exertion, to reach the shore that night, alone. Vaca then asked what could be done, as his men were too feeble to follow the Governor's boat without assistance; and Narvaez answered that it was no longer a time for one man to give orders to another; that each should do what seemed the best to save his own life; and that he had determined to act on that principle himself. And with this abdication of control, and cry of *"sauve qui peut,"* he pressed forward with his own boat, and was soon lost in the darkness.

As Vaca could have no more hope from that quarter, he directed his course to the other boat, which awaited his approach and which he found to be that commanded by Peñalosa and Tellez. These two little crafts, companions in misery, and laden with as unhappy a set of men as ever burdened a vessel, kept company with each other four days, while the passengers were reduced to a diurnal allowance of half a handful of raw corn. Then a storm arose and they became separated, never more to see each other. The wretchedness of the situation in his own boat is so vividly described by Cabeza de Vaca himself that it seems best to use his own words. "Because," says he, "of winter and its inclemency, the many days we had suffered hunger, and the heavy beating of the waves, the people began next day to despair in such a manner that when the sun sank all who were in my boat were fallen one on another, so near to death that there were few among them in a state of sensibility. Of the whole number at this time not five men were on their feet; and when night came, only the master and myself were left who could work the boat. Two hours after dark he said to me that I must take charge of her, as he was in such condition he believed he should die that night. So I took the paddle, and going after midnight to see if the master was alive, he said to me he was rather better, and would take the charge until day. I declare in that hour I would more willingly have died than seen so many people before me in such condition. After the master took the direction of the boat, I lay down a little while, but without repose, for nothing at that time was farther from me than sleep." Toward morning the Treasurer heard the roaring sound which told of waves beating on a shore, and on sounding found that they were in seven fathoms of water. The Captain advised that they should keep off shore until it was light enough to land with safety, and so Vaca himself took an oar and pulled the boat out into the Gulf. There a great wave struck the boat, throwing it entirely out of the water and arousing all of the men within it, no matter how exhausted; and as she was forced near the shore again, they got out on the rocks and crawled to the land on their hands and feet to the shelter of some ravines. There they made a fire, parched and ate the scanty remainder of their corn, and relieved their thirst from pools of rain-water.

The morning having come, and the men being somewhat refreshed, Vaca ordered the strongest of the party, one Lope de Oviedo, to climb to the top of some trees near at hand and reconnoitre the country; and he soon returned to say they were on an island which seemed inhabited. This aroused mingled feelings of joy and fear, which were enhanced when the same messenger returned from a second trip to tell of finding some empty huts, and bringing an earthen pot, a little dog, and a few mullets, which he had found in them. Just as he arrived three Indians came in view following him, and half an hour later their number was increased by fully 100 of their companions, all armed with bows. "They were not large," says the chronicler, "but our fears made giants of them. The Spaniards were in no condition to meet any hostile attack, so they attempted to conciliate the natives. The Treasurer and the Overseer went to meet them, and by signs endeavored to open friendly intercourse. They gave them beads and bells, and in return each Indian gave Vaca an arrow in token of friendship, and promised to bring some provisions the next day. True to this promise, at sunrise the Indians brought a quantity of fish and a kind of edible root, about the size of a walnut; and again at evening they returned with more of the same supplies. The Spaniards in return gave such presents as they could to the women and children, who flocked to see them.

Being thus refreshed, they began to think of pursuing their journey, and with much difficulty dug their boat out of the beach-sand, under which it was buried. They were still so weak that all exertion was a great burden, and in endeavoring to launch the craft they stripped off their clothes so as to work the better. The boat was scarcely in the water, and but a little way from shore, when a wave passed over her, making the oars so slippery as to be temporarily useless, and the next minute another wave completely capsized the boat. Three of the crew, including Don Alonzo de Solis, the assessor, seeking to save themselves by clinging to the vessel, were carried under and drowned; the rest of the Spaniards being thrown violently upon the beach, naked and half dead. Here the cold wind, beating upon their wet and unprotected bodies, would have caused them to perish, but that they found a few embers still remaining from their last fire, and soon had a bright blaze to warm and comfort them. When the Indians came as usual at sunset to bring fish and roots, they were so amazed and alarmed at what seemed to them a miraculous transformation of their strange guests, that they immediately fled; but on learning the true state of affairs by signs, and seeing the dead bodies washed onto the shore, they returned and expressed their sympathy and condolence by loud and mournful lamentations for the space of half an hour. "It was strange," says Vaca, "to see these men, wild and untaught, howling like beasts over our misfortunes. It caused in me, as in others, an increase of sorrow and a more vivid sense of our calamity." Nothing could well exceed the kindness experienced at the hands of these Indians. Cabeza de Vaca suggested to his comrades that in their forlorn condition it would be best to ask the natives to take them to their homes. The soldiers generally objected to this, fearing that they would be sacrificed to the native idols; but Vaca persisted, and begged the Indians to take care of them. The proposition was received with great favor, and so careful and considerate were the Indians that they carried the half-starved and exhausted white men in their arms up to their village, and on account of the extreme cold and the nakedness of their guests, built four or five large fires at easy distances along the road with which to warm the Spaniards on the way.

Arrived at the village, the strangers were lodged in a house just constructed for them, and were supplied with fires; and would have been most comfortable but for an unpleasant idea that they were only being well cared for at the present in order to be prepared to be suitable victims in a great sacrifice. Meanwhile the Indians celebrated the event by dancing and rejoicings, which continued all night. The next day the keen eye of Vaca observed with one of the Indians an European article which their own party had not brought, and on inquiry was told that it was a gift from some other men similar to the Spaniards, who were not far off. Amazed and delighted by this intelligence, the Treasurer sent a small party to seek their countrymen, who were soon met, as they had heard of the arrival of Cabeza de Vaca and were hastening to visit him—and who turned out to be the entire company from the boat of Captains Dorantes and Castillo. Their respective stories were quickly told; and it appeared that the day before Cabeza de Vaca and his comrades were cast on that shore the other boat had been capsized a league and a half from there, but all the men were saved, and succeeded in preserving a large proportion of their goods. It was soon agreed that the best plan was to repair their boat so that the strongest of the united company could proceed along the coast in search of assistance, while the others remained to regain their strength, or until succor should arrive. In accordance with this plan they set at work; but their efforts were fruitless and their hopes disappointed, for the boat proved unfit for service, and finally sank to the bottom of the sea. There was then no alternative but to winter on the island; for the weak condition of the men, as well as their lack of covering, prevented further effort at that cold and boisterous season.

Four of the most powerful of the company, however, being all expert swimmers, volunteered to make one more attempt to reach the Spanish settlement at Panuco in Mexico (which they all believed to be not far distant), in order that, if a good Providence crowned their efforts with success, relief might be sent to the wretched party on the island. The men who thus risked their lives were a Portuguese named Alvaro Fernandez, and three Spaniards named Mendez, Figueroa, and Astudillo. They were accompanied by an Indian of the island—which was called by the natives Auia, but which the Spaniards, from their own sad experiences there, appropriately named Malhado, or Bad Luck.

And now these experiences were to become more and more unfortunate. The weather soon became so tempestuous that the natives could no longer find the roots which grew at the water's edge, and the fish-nets caught nothing, so that semi-starvation ensued; besides this, the exposure to the winter blasts without any sufficient protection made many a stout heart but emaciated body succumb. Five Spaniards living by themselves in an isolated place near the shore were reduced to such straits that as each died the survivors lived on his dead body; so that when visited, only the corpse of the last survivor was found unmolested. So great was the suffering and mortality that before spring sixty-five out of the eighty who had come on shore in the two boats had perished. Then the Indians themselves, probably on account of their insufficient food, became afflicted with a disease of the bowels, which proved so fatal that full half of the whole population fell victims to it. Never having been so afflicted before, they attributed their misfortune to the malign influence of the pale-faced strangers, and determined to put the surviving Spaniards to death for their own safety, if not in retaliation for the scourge inflicted on their people; and this purpose would, no doubt, have been put into execution but for the enlightened advice of the Indian who had special charge of Cabeza de Vaca, who reminded his companions that if the Europeans had power over life and death they would certainly have saved their own people from the dire destruction which had carried off nearly all of their number; that those who remained were not only feeble, but showed no ill will to the natives, and that it would be far better to leave them in God's hands. Fortunately, these arguments prevailed, and the remnant of the Spaniards was saved from the impending peril. Thus they remained on the island until April, suffering great privations themselves, but none greater than those undergone by the Indians; some of whose immemorial customs entailed great inconveniences and danger in such a time of pestilence. For example, if a son or a brother died in a family, none of the household could go out in search of food for three months, but had to be supplied by their friends and relatives; and they would sooner perish than violate this observance. While ordinarily this might produce no inconvenience, yet during this winter, when nearly every house had lost one of its inmates, it caused great hardships. The number of those still permitted to obtain food was so greatly reduced that though they toiled from morning till night, the supply was far less than what was required, and yet none had the temerity to break through the custom; and had not a part of the people passed over to the main-land, where there were oysters, nearly the whole population would have perished. In April the Spaniards under Cabeza de Vaca also crossed over, and lived on blackberries all that month; while the Indians carried on their spring ceremonials and dances. This probably gave rise to the report which was brought back to Cuba by a vessel which had been sent along the shores of the Gulf in search of the expedition of Narvaez, and which is referred to in a report made by Lope Hurtado to the Emperor Charles V., dated May 20, 529, in the following words: "A caraval has arrived here from searching after Narvaez, and brings eight Indians from the coast; they state by signs that he is inland with his men, who do little else than eat, drink, and sleep."

Among this people Cabeza de Vaca and his companions first appeared in the character of physicians, in which they were afterwards compelled to act in many places. The native system of medical attendance was by blowing upon the sick, and with that breath and the laying on of hands they performed the cures. They also made cauteries with fire and then blew upon the spot, which gave the patient relief. The Indians insisted that the Spaniards should act as their physicians, and when the latter demurred and said that they had no knowledge of medicine, the Indians insisted that it could not be, but that the whites being extraordinary men, must possess this power; and believing that the refusal came from stubbornness, they withheld all food from them until they had starved them into compliance. While thus constrained to obey, the Spaniards were in great fear, lest their ill success should bring new dangers upon them; but these apprehensions seem not to have been realized. Cabeza de Vaca tells us: "Our method was to bless the sick, breathing upon them, and recite a Pater-noster and Ave-Maria, praying with all earnestness to God our Lord that he would give health, and influence them to make us some good return. In his clemency he willed that all those for whom we supplicated should tell the others that they were sound and in health, directly after we made the sign of the blessed cross over them. For this the Indians treated us kindly; they deprived themselves of food that they might give to us, and presented us with skins and some trifles."

As the spring advanced the other Christians returned to the island, but Vaca remained on the main-land, where he became very sick. Hearing of this, the others, under Alonzo del Castillo and Andres Dorantes, desired to visit him, but had considerable difficulty in getting the tribe with which they were to allow them to cross. Those still alive on the island were fourteen in all, but two, named Alviniz and Lope de Oviedo, were too feeble to travel. The other twelve crossed to the main-land, and there found another of their party, Francisco de Leon; and these thirteen started to travel along the coast, leaving Cabeza de Vaca alone and to his fate, as he was unable to move. Here he remained for more than a year, treated by the natives as a slave, and compelled to perform the most toilsome and painful work. During this time he was continually planning how to escape to some other tribe, and so gradually move on to Mexico, but it was long before an opportunity was presented. At length he proposed to his masters to go trafficking for them to the adjacent tribes, and as he was expert in such matters, they soon let him travel on such business to considerable distances. The goods that he took to trade with, were shells, and a peculiar fruit, like a bean, which the interior tribes used as a medicine; and in return he obtained skins, ochre for painting the face, hard cane to make arrows, sinews, flints, etc., etc. This business gave him not only great liberty, but better fare and treatment; and besides, he was continually gaining information as to the best way to go forward when he should escape and start for Christian settlements.

For nearly six years he remained thus among the natives, with no European for a companion, but living naked and in all respects like an Indian. The reason, he says, that he remained so long was that he wanted, when he went, to take with him Oviedo, who had been left on the island, and whose companion, Alvaniz, had soon after died. With this in view he went over to the island every year and saw Oviedo, and tried to induce him to start on the journey toward the Christian settlements. But Oviedo, who seems to have been satisfied with his lot, or else afraid to venture on new trials, kept putting him off, until in the year 1533 Vaca finally took him away and carried him with him toward the West; although as Oviedo could not swim, he had to support him in the water in crossing rivers and bays. So they proceeded until they arrived at a wide expanse of water, which they believed must be the bay called Espiritu Santo. There they met some Indians from the western side of the bay, who said that there were three white men with their tribe, and inquiry showed that these were the sole survivors of the thirteen who had passed on; five of the others having been killed by the Indians, and the others having died of cold or from privations. They gave such a frightful account of the manner in which the three survivors were being treated that the courage of Oviedo completely gave out, and he insisted on returning to the island; and notwithstanding the entreaties of Cabeza de Vaca, he could not be dissuaded from the purpose, and so departed, leaving Vaca again entirely alone among this new tribe of savages. As soon as he could, he ascertained where the three Spaniards were to be found and visited them; his appearance creating the greatest astonishment, as they had supposed that he was long since dead—and the natives had so reported. In the words of Vaca: "We gave many thanks at seeing ourselves together again, and this day was to us the happiest that we had ever enjoyed in our lives." The three Christians who were there found were Alonzo del Castillo, Andres Dorantes, and Estevanico, the latter being an African. They soon talked of plans of escape, and Dorantes said that for a long time he had been urging the others to unite with him in pressing forward, but that they had refused because they could not swim, and were afraid of the rivers and bays which so abounded in that country. They advised Vaca that he must not arouse any suspicions on the part of the natives that he intended to leave there, or he would certainly be killed; and that for success in any project of escape, it would be necessary to wait for six months, until the time when the Indians regularly went to another island to eat prickly-pears. Cabeza de Vaca was given as a slave to the same Indian who owned Dorantes, and so had a further experience in enforced servitude to a native.

While here he heard of the fate of the other boats of the expedition, and of the death of Narvaez and the Comptroller. The boats in which were the Comptroller and the Friars had been cast away on the coast, and that of Narvaez had been carried out to sea by a north wind, while scarcely any except the Governor were on board, and was never more heard of. All of the men in both those parties had perished in various ways, except one, named Hernando de Esquivel, who was believed to be still alive among the Indians to the west. One other Spaniard still survived, Figueroa, one of the party of four who were dispatched from the island the year before to endeavor to force a passage through to Mexico, and send succor to their enfeebled commander. It might be added here, that some time after, information came through the Indians of the destruction of the party under Peñalosa and Tellez, who were in the fifth and last boat. It appeared that they had reached the shore a little farther west than the others, but in so feeble a condition that they were all destroyed by the Camones tribe, who inhabited that region, the Spaniards not having the strength to offer any resistance even when being slain.

While among the tribe where they now were, the Spaniards suffered greatly, being cruelly treated, compelled to work very hard, and suffer much hunger; but the Indians themselves, except in the prickly-pear season, fared little better as to food, as they were compelled to live on roots, which were scarce and difficult to dig, and frequently were reduced to the use of spiders, worms, lizards, and snakes, and even earth and wood. They had a singular custom as to their children, all the female infants being cast away at their birth. The reason of this was that they were surrounded by tribes that were enemies, and if their daughters grew up, they would have to marry into some of these tribes, and so serve to increase the number of their foes—as it was not allowable to intermarry in the tribe. For their own wives they captured or bought the women of their enemies, in that way strengthening themselves and weakening their opponents.

When the prickly-pear season arrived, to which they had looked forward as the time of their deliverance, by great ill fortune the masters of the Spaniards had a quarrel and separated a considerable distance, so that it was impossible for them to meet and escape; and thus a whole year was lost until the same season came again. During the year Cabeza de Vaca suffered many things—three times narrowly escaping being killed by his masters; but at length the summer arrived once more, and the tribe moved as before. After encountering many difficulties in arranging to escape, the Spaniards finally succeeded in uniting beyond the encampment of the Indians, and pressed on as rapidly as possible to avoid being overtaken. After two days they came to another tribe called Avavares. These people had already heard of the Spaniards, and of the wonderful cures which they had performed among the Indians on the island; so that scarcely had they arrived when some of the Indians came to Castillo saying that they had severe headaches, and asking to be relieved. He made the sign of the cross over them and commended them to God; whereupon they all said that the pains had departed, and soon returned with prickly-pears and a piece of venison—a rare treat for our adventurers. As the news of their cures spread, many others came, each bringing a piece of venison as a fee, until more meat had accumulated than the Spaniards knew how to dispose of; whereupon they gave thanks to God for his goodness. As the season was now well advanced and inquiry showed that there were no provisions at that season in the country beyond, the Spaniards concluded to remain through the winter with these Indians who treated them so well. All through that period the sick and wounded of the surrounding country were brought to them for cure; and they had such success that nothing else was talked of by the adjacent tribes but the astonishing power of these pale-faced strangers. At first only Castillo and Cabeza de Vaca acted as physicians; but as time passed, and the number applying for help increased, Dorantes and the negro also commenced to practice—and all with equal success; "although," says Vaca, "in being venturesome and bold in the performance of cures, I greatly excelled." "No one whom we treated," he adds, "but told us he was left well; and so great was the confidence that they would become healed if we administered to them, that they even believed that whilst we remained none of them could die." The Indians not only treated them well, but showed great appreciation of their character as their benefactors: "Thus," says the narrative, "when the Cuthalchuches (who were in company with our Indians) were about to return to their own country, they left us all the prickly-pears they had—without keeping one; they gave us flints of very high value there, a palm and a half in length, with which they cut. They begged that we would always remember them, and pray to God that they might always be well; and we promised to do so. They left the most satisfied beings in the world—having given us the best of all they had."

For eight months they stayed among these people; and then, as the prickly-pears began to ripen, they stole away (as that was the only means by which they could pursue their journey) to another tribe, called Maliacones; and thence to the Arbadaos, a people very weak and lank—probably for lack of food. "Among them," says Cabeza de Vaca, "we underwent greater hunger than with the others; we ate daily not more than two handfuls of prickly-pears, which were green, and so milky they burned our mouths. In our extreme want we bought two dogs, giving in exchange some nets (with other things), and a skin with which I used to cover myself. I have already stated that throughout all this country we went naked; and as we were unaccustomed to being so, twice a year we cast our skins, like serpents. Sometimes the Indians would set me to scraping and softening skins; and the days of my greatest prosperity there were those in which they gave me skins to dress. I would scrape them a very great deal, and eat the scraps; which would sustain me two or three days. When it happened, among these people (as it had likewise among others whom we left behind), that a piece of meat was given us, we ate it raw; for if we had put it to roast, the first native that should come along would have taken it off and devoured it—and it appeared to us not well to expose it to this risk; besides, we were in such condition it would have given us pain to eat it roasted, and we could not have digested it so well as raw. Such was the life we spent there, and the meagre subsistence we earned by the matters of traffic, which were the work of our own hands."

After eating the dogs the Spaniards felt refreshed, and continued their journey, and at night came to a village of fifty dwellings. The inhabitants probably never had heard of white men, as they were greatly amazed at their appearance, showing at first much fear. In the morning the Indians brought their sick, on whom they prayed for a blessing. Here the Spaniards stayed some days; and when they stated that they must leave, the whole town was in tears at their departure, begging them to remain. They went forward, however, and were received by the next tribe with equal hospitality. Here for the first time they saw the Mesquit, and ate of its fruit, and of flour made from it. Though these people arranged a special festival in honor of the travellers, they did not tarry, but passed on; and after crossing a river as wide as the Guadalquiver, arrived at a large Indian town of a full hundred habitations. Here the fame of the strangers had preceded them, and the people came out to receive them, making a barbarous kind of music with their voices and hands, and carrying gourds with pebbles in them, which were used solely on important occasions; because, as the gourd did not grow in their country, but was only found when brought down the river occasionally in times of floods, they considered it peculiarly sacred, and as coming direct from heaven. Having heard of the wonderful cures effected by the pale-faces, the people pressed upon them in crowds, each trying to be foremost in touching them in order to receive some of the miraculous virtue, so that the Spaniards were in danger of their lives and had to retire into a house. All night long the natives danced and sang in honor of the occasion, and the next morning the whole town came to be touched and blessed, as they had heard had been done in other places, and made presents to the Indians who had guided the Spaniards from the last town. This latter custom was continued from place to place in an increasing degree. Those that accompanied the party from the town just mentioned to the next, took from each person who came to be cured his bow and arrows, and any ornaments which he might wear, apparently as payment for having brought the wonderful physicians; and the sick men were so full of rejoicing over what they considered a certainty of cure that they cheerfully yielded all that they had. The people of that town, when they in their turn conducted them to still another, were even more grasping, entering the houses and carrying off whatever suited their fancy; but when the Spaniards showed sorrow and displeasure at this, the people who were thus despoiled assured them that they need not be grieved, as they were so gratified at their coming that they considered the payment by their property but a small equivalent; and besides (and this was perhaps the real reason of their complacency), that as the Spaniards went on, they in their turn would be well rewarded by those in advance, who were very rich.

About this time the four travellers first came in sight of some mountains, all the country heretofore having been a level plain. These were undoubtedly the San Saba Mountains of modern atlases, though Cabeza de Vaca in describing them gives a good illustration of the indefinite ideas of geography then existing in America, by saying that "they appear to come in succession from the North Sea," or Atlantic. They were guided towards them by Indians, who took them to the villages of their kindred, because they did not wish their enemies to enjoy so great a privilege as the presence of the wonder-working strangers; but who, nevertheless, did not forget to plunder the towns visited as a kind of reward. At length this custom became so well known that at any place that they approached the people would hide a portion of their goods. Sometimes they made voluntary presents to the Spaniards, but the latter always distributed them among the natives who were bearing them company, in order to carry out the national custom. At this point they followed up the course of a river for a considerable distance, being desirous to seek the interior, where they found uniform kindness and hospitality, rather than trust themselves again with the tribes near the coast, who were more violent and had proved cruel task-masters.

Once when the Spaniards had preferred to follow their own ideas of the proper route, rather than the suggestion of the accompanying people, the latter left them and the little company of adventurers journeyed on alone; and on arriving at a village found every one in sorrow, because news had come that wheresoever the Spaniards came the town was pillaged by their escort. When they saw that the party was unaccompanied, they gained courage, and gave them prickly-pears to eat. But their sense of security was short-lived, for at dawn a lot of Indians from the preceding town suddenly broke open their houses and plundered them of almost everything. As consolation the marauders told them that the Spaniards were the children of the Sun, having power to cure or to destroy, to cause to live or die. They advised them to do everything to make the strangers satisfied, and to show them the highest respect; not to mind what they lost in doing this, but to conduct the Spaniards to places where the people were numerous, and then to pillage the town, as that was the custom. The hearers were apt pupils, and when Cabeza de Vaca and his party were ready to move, they accompanied them, repeating what they had been told of the Spaniards, and adding much more; for "these people," says the chronicler, "are all very fond of romance, and are great liars, particularly when it is to their interest." On the journey two native physicians presented them with two gourds, which the Spaniards thereafter carried, thus increasing the estimation in which the people held them. Here they reached the base of the range of hills, and proceeded almost directly inland for fifty leagues, when they came to a village, where, among the articles presented to them, was a hawk-bell of copper, thick and large, and figured with a face, which the natives had greatly prized, and brought as their choicest offering. On inquiry they said that it had come from the north, where there was much of that metal, but they had only received this one piece from a neighboring tribe. The next day the travellers passed over a ridge seven leagues in extent, and in the evening came to a beautiful river, on which was a village, where they stopped. Here the people as usual were profuse with their gifts, presenting, among other things, little bags of Marquesite and pulverized galena, with which they rub the face. Here also the Spaniards first found Piñons, which Cabeza describes by saying that "in that country are small pine trees, the cones like little eggs; but the seed is better than that of Castilla, as its husk is very thin, and while green, is beat and made into balls, to be thus eaten. If the seed be dry, it is pounded in the husk, and consumed in the form of flour." At this time Vaca performed a very notable cure, removing from a man's breast, close to the heart, a large arrow-head, which for many years had been imbedded there. "From there," says the chronicler, "we travelled through so many sorts of people, of such diverse languages, that memory fails to recall them. They ever plundered each other, and those that lost, like those that gained, were fully content. We drew so many followers that we had not use for their services. Whatever they either killed or found, was put before us, without themselves daring to take anything until we had blessed it, though they should be expiring of hunger, they having so established the rule since marching with us. Frequently we were accompanied by three or four thousand people, and as we had to breathe upon and sanctify the food and drink for each, and grant permission to do the many things they would come to ask, it may be seen how great was the annoyance."

The party now arrived at a "great river coming from the north," and after proceeding thirty leagues over a level section, met a number of persons who had come out of their town to receive them, and who welcomed them most hospitably to their homes. These obliging hosts also guided them on their way more than fifty leagues, over rough mountains devoid of water or any kind of food, where the party suffered much with hunger; but having accomplished that distance, their eyes were gladdened by the sight of a very large river, the water of which was breast high. (The "great river coming from the north" was almost without a doubt the Pecos, and the "very large river" the Rio Bravo del Norte, now better known as the Rio Grande.) Proceeding westerly, they stopped at a plain at the base of the mountains, where they found a considerable population, who gave them so many goods that half of them had to be left for lack of means to carry them. Vaca told the Indians to take back the goods which were left, or they would soon be spoiled; but they answered that "that was not possible, as it was not their custom after they had bestowed a thing to take it back." It is evident that the phrase "Indian giver" did not originate with this particular tribe of natives, whose customs were so thoroughly based on an opposite principle. The party remained here some days, first letting the natives know that they wished to reach the land of the setting sun. To this the Indians replied that the inhabitants in that direction were remote, and were hereditary enemies of their own tribe. Cabeza then asked them to conduct the party to the north, but of this journey they gave an even more discouraging account, saying that there were neither people, nor food, nor water in that direction. The Spaniards, however, insisted on that course, and when the inhabitants of the village still objected to going with them, Vaca became offended and went to sleep in the woods away from the houses, which so distressed the natives that they went where he was and remained all night, begging him to forgive them and be no longer angry, and saying that they would go whithersoever he desired, even though they were sure they should die on the way. The terror which this display of displeasure on the part of the Spaniards occasioned was greatly heightened by the strange coincidence that on the next day many of the Indians became ill and some of them died. "Wheresoever this became known," says Cabeza de Vaca, "there was great dread, and it seemed as if the inhabitants would die of fear at sight of us. They besought us not to remain angered, nor require that more of them should die. They believed we caused their death by only willing it, when in truth it gave us so much pain that it could not be greater; for beyond their loss, we feared they might all die, or abandon us from fright, and that other people thenceforward would do the same, seeing what had come to these. We prayed to God our Lord to relieve them, and from that time the sick began to get better."

After remaining here over a fortnight the travellers again proceeded on their long journey, a number of women acting as guides, as that was the only possible course when the tribe to be met was hostile to that just left. After marching three days, Castillo, with Estevanico, the African, set off on an expedition with two women as guides, one being a captive from the country they were approaching. The latter led them to the river that ran between some ridges where there was a town in which her family lived, and there it was, to use the language of the narrator, that "habitations were first seen having the appearance and structure of houses." Castillo in his report described them as "fixed dwellings of civilization;" and in speaking of their next journey, Vaca uses the term "settled habitations." The party was certainly then in New Mexico, though in what exact spot it is impossible now to say, but their description seems to point very distinctly to some of the Pueblo towns. The points that would specially strike a man who had lived so long away from civilization, and where a tent is the most pretentious dwelling, would naturally be those of permanence and stability, and of resemblance to the solid houses of European communities, and these are precisely the ones to which the narrators allude. The inhabitants of these towns, of which the Spaniards visited several, are described as the "finest persons of any we saw, of the greatest activity and strength, who best understood us and most intelligently answered our inquiries." "We called them," says Vaca, "'the cow nation' because most of the cattle killed are slaughtered in their neighborhood, and along that river upwards for fifty leagues they destroy great numbers."

The country was found to be very populous, and the inhabitants lived on beans, pumpkins, and corn, although at that time the latter was scarce on account of drought. The people did not understand the language of the Indians who had accompanied the Spaniards, and seemed to be different in many ways. After stopping a few days the Christians told them that they must go on toward the setting sun, and enquired concerning the best route. The Indians replied that the only feasible path was to follow the great river they were on upward to the north, for if they went more directly to the west, they would have a long journey across a desert, where there was nothing to eat except a fruit called by the natives "chacan," which, even when ground between stones, could scarcely be used as an article of food on account of its dryness and pungency. Along the river, on the contrary, there was a continuous population; and though they had few provisions, yet they would receive the strangers with the best of good-will and hospitality. The Spaniards, however, disliked to add anything unnecessary to the length of the journey required to bring them to some of their own nationality, and determined to brave the dangers and sufferings of the desert route. They found it as represented, and indeed were not able to swallow the chacan fruit at all, but had to subsist on a handful of deer suet each day, this being the most concentrated form of nutriment that Cabeza de Vaca could devise, and he having devoted much time to its collection for the purpose

The route here is obscurely recorded, as it appears they did proceed up the river for seventeen days, and then, after crossing, a further journey of seventeen days brought the travellers to a land of plenty again, where were large supplies of flour, grain, beans, and pumpkins; but before reaching this, they had passed through a section where during four months of the year the people lived on nothing but the powder of straw, and their journey happening to come exactly at that time, they were compelled to accept the same scanty diet. It may be added that on the journey they were presented with "coverings of cowhide," meaning buffalo-hides, in considerable numbers. The land of plenty, when reached, was one where the natives had permanent structures for houses, some of earth, and some of cane mats. Through this good land they travelled by their own computation (which is almost always exaggerated) over 100 leagues, finding everywhere settled habitations, and plenty of corn and beans. The people gave them "cotton shawls, better than those of New Spain, many beads, and certain corals found on the South Sea, and fine turquoises that came from the North." "Indeed they gave us," says the chronicler, "everything they had. To me they gave five emeralds, made into arrow-heads, which they use at their singing and dancing. They appeared to be very precious. I asked whence they got these, and they said the stones were brought from some lofty mountains that stand towards the north, where were populous towns and very large houses, and that they were purchased with plumes and feathers of parrots." The "populous towns and very large houses" undoubtedly referred to the greater pueblos to the north. Here for the first time the Spaniards saw the use of the "Soap-weed" (Yucca filamentosa, called also Spanish Bayonet and Amole) for cleansing purposes, and found a people who habitually used coverings for the feet, like shoes or moccasins. "These

Indians," continues the narrative, "ever accompanied us until they delivered us to others, and all held full faith in our coming from heaven. While travelling we went without food all day until night, and we ate so little as to astonish them. We never felt exhaustion, neither were we in fact at all weary, so inured were we to hardship. We possessed great influence and authority; to preserve both we seldom talked with them. The negro was in constant conversation; he informed himself about the ways we wished to take, of the towns there were, and the matters we desired to know. We passed through many and dissimilar tongues. Our Lord granted us favor with the people who spoke them, for they always understood us, and we them. We questioned them and received their answers by signs, just as if they spoke our language and we theirs; for although we knew six languages, we could not everywhere avail ourselves of them, there being a thousand differences. Throughout all these countries the people who were at war immediately made friends, that they might come to meet us, and bring what they possessed. In this way we left all the land at peace, and we taught all the inhabitants by signs which they understood, that in heaven was a man we called God, who had created the sky and the earth; him we worshiped and had for our Master; that we did what he commanded, and from his hand came all good; and would they do as we did, all would be well with them. They are a people of good condition and substance, capable in any pursuit."

Proceeding onward, always to the west, and through a town which they named the Town of Hearts (Pueblo de los Corazones), they came to a village, where the incessant rain detained them for a fortnight; and during that time at length saw the first signs which gave token of an approach to the European settlements which they had so long been seeking. Hung to the neck of an Indian, Castillo saw the buckle of a sword-belt, and attached to it the nail of a horse shoe. While small things in themselves, to the Spaniard these spoke volumes, for they were sure signs of some communication with a civilized and Christian people. Eagerly he inquired of the owner whence they had come, and was told that they had come from heaven. He asked how, and who had brought them, and then came the answer they were so earnestly waiting for, that a number of men with beards like the Spaniards had come from heaven to the river near by, bringing horses, lances, and swords, and that they had lanced two Indians. "What had become of these men," asked the travellers, endeavoring to suppress any signs of their intense interest. The answer was that "they had gone to sea putting their lances beneath the water, and going themselves under the water; afterwards they were seen on the surface of the water going towards the setting sun." Never were men more rejoiced than the Spaniards, at the news which showed that the colonies of their countrymen were near at hand.

From this point information regarding Europeans, and signs of their recent presence, increased at every step. Unfortunately, too much of this was of an unfavorable and shameful character. Everywhere the new-comers had made themselves feared and hated, and not loved. Wherever they had been they had killed, abused, or enslaved the natives. Cabeza de Vaca in pressing westward told the natives that he was going in search of these people to tell them no more to kill or enslave them, nor despoil their houses and lands, nor do other injustices; and at this the poor natives greatly rejoiced. Passing on, they found whole territories depopulated because the inhabitants had fled to the mountains for fear of the Spaniards. For two years they had planted no corn, because whatever they raised was stolen by the marauding parties of the Europeans. They had abandoned their houses, which were found going into decay; and although the land was of great fertility and well watered, they were wretchedly subsisting on roots and the bark of trees. To Cabeza de Vaca and his companions, whom they never associated in any way with these Spanish oppressors from the west, they cheerfully brought the few things which they had saved by concealment; at the same time telling them of the forays of their bearded enemies, who had carried off half the men and all the women and boys from the valleys into slavery, only those remaining who had escaped to the mountains. Contrasting the generous confidence with which his own party was received, and the high respect and veneration paid to them, though they were impoverished, naked, and half starved, with the fear and hatred which the outrages and oppression of the Spaniards of Sinoloa had inspired, the chronicler well says in his report to the emperor: "Thence it may at once be seen, that to bring all these people to be Christians, and to the obedience of the Imperial Majesty, they must be won by kindness, which is a way certain, and no other is."

Trying to collect the natives, as usual, for a conference, the messengers of Cabeza de Vaca returned, saying that it was impossible, as some of the people had seen the Christians from behind trees the night before, and so all were fleeing to the mountains; especially, as they had seen slaves in chains with the Spanish party. The truth of this was soon evident; as the travellers reached a point where the Christians had encamped at night, the stakes showed that they were horsemen. Vaca calculated that the distance from this point to the town where they first saw the buckle and nail was ninety-two leagues; the river, where the Spaniards had first been seen by the natives, being about twelve leagues west of that village. As the Spanish marauding party had now been passed, and Vaca feared that they were killing and enslaving the kind and hospitable people through whose country he had just come, he turned back, with Estevanico and eleven Indians, to seek them; and followed their trail ten leagues, and finally the next day overtook four of them on horseback. What a strange meeting! Men born in the same land, across the Atlantic, meeting in an Indian territory close to the Pacific; one party, after journeying for seven years across a continent, enduring all kinds of hardships, emaciated, and having almost lost the semblance of European civilization; the others coming from the opposite direction, well armed, and on horseback, seeking conquests and riches. "They were astonished at sight of me," says Cabeza de Vaca; "so confounded that they neither hailed me nor drew near to make an inquiry. I bade them take me to their chief; accordingly, we went together half a league to the place where was Diego de Alcaraz, their captain."

After his surprise at seeing Vaca had subsided, Alcaraz told him that he was completely discouraged; that for a long time he had not been able to capture any Indians; and that his men were worn out and discontented from hunger and fatigue. Vaca then told him that his companions, Castillo and Dorantes, were but ten miles off with a multitude of friendly Indians, and desired that they should be sent for; which was quickly done, three horsemen being swiftly despatched, with Estevanico as a guide. Five days afterwards they returned with Castillo and Dorantes, and more than 600 Indians; many of whom were those who had fled from Alcaraz, but who gladly showed their confidence in Cabeza de Vaca and his companions. Alcaraz begged that they would ask the Indians to bring food; and this they cheerfully did at the request of Vaca—bringing pots full of corn, which they had hidden in the ground, and Vaca distributed it to the Spanish troops. But no sooner had the latter satisfied their hunger than they forgot all sense of obligation, and wished to capture the Indians and make slaves of them. This outrage Cabeza de Vaca and his companions opposed vigorously, and finally succeeded, after many high words, in preventing it; and persuaded the Indians, by promises of future good treatment, to return to their houses and fields.

The confidence which the natives showed in these wanderers, in contrast to the hatred and fear for the Mexican Spaniards, caused a strange feeling of jealousy on the part of the latter; and calling an interpreter, they told the Indians that Cabeza de Vaca and his friends were of the same people as themselves, only they had been lost a long time; that they themselves were the lords of the land who must be obeyed and served, while the wanderers were persons of mean condition and small importance. But the Indians were not to be influenced by any such talk, and conversing among themselves said, as the narrative of Vaca tells us, "that the Spaniards lied, for we came from the land where the sun rises, while the others came from the land where the sun sets; we healed the sick, they killed the sound; that we had come naked and barefooted, while they had arrived in clothing and on horses, with lances; that we were not covetous of anything, but all that was given us we directly turned to give, retaining nothing; that the others had no other purpose than to rob whomsoever they found, bestowing nothing on any one. Even to the last I could not convince the Indians that we were of the Christians, and only with great effort and solicitation we got them to go back to their residences. We ordered them to put away apprehensions, establish their towns and cultivate the soil. The Indians at taking their leave told us they would do what we commanded, and would build their towns, if the Christians would suffer them; and this I say and affirm most positively, that if they have not done so, it is the fault of the Christians." So early could an experienced traveler and military officer, with no natural predilection in favor of the Indians, state in one brief and terse sentence the fact so often repeated since, of the original cause of the great majority of difficulties between the Europeans and the native possessors of the land.

Dismissing now their Indian escort, the four travellers hastened on to the habitations of their own people; and when three leagues from Culiacan, were met by the Alcalde of that town, Don Melchior Diaz, who was also Captain of the Province, and who had heard of their approach. He wept at sight of them, and gave praise to God who had preserved them through such great dangers. On behalf of the Governor, Nuño de Guzman, as well as himself he tendered all the hospitality and service in his power. The travellers wished to lose no time in journeying towards Mexico, but the Alcalde begged them to remain long enough to give confidence to the Indians and induce them again to inhabit the fruitful valleys which were now going to waste. This was no easy task, as Alcaraz immediately after the departure of Cabeza de Vaca had recommenced his outrages upon the natives; but finally through the influence of those to whom they looked up with so much reverence and respect they were brought in. Many of them were baptized, and the Captain of the Province, in the presence of them all, made a covenant with God no more to invade, or consent to invasion, nor to enslave any of the people. Having accomplished this double benefit to both Spaniards and Indians, the four companions proceeded on their way, arriving at the town of San Miguel on April 1, 1536, and on July 25 at the City of Mexico, where they were welcomed with great rejoicing, and entertained most handsomely by the Viceroy of New Spain, and by Cortez, who now bore the title of Marquis of the Valley. From thence, by reason of storms and the dangers of enemies on the sea in the war then raging, they were over a year in reaching Europe, finally landing at Lisbon on the 8th of August, 1537, more than ten years after they had left San

Lucar, in high hopes of conquering an empire in Florida.

Thus ended the expedition begun with intent to find another El Dorado, similar to those of the Montezumas and the Incas, and which, though doomed to disaster from its very inception, and utterly unsuccessful in accomplishing its design, yet lives in history through the sufferings and endurance of the four men who were the first to cross the continent north of the comparatively narrow domains of Mexico. By the people of New Mexico the name of Cabeza de Vaca will ever be held in special remembrance as that of the first European who ever passed through her territory. While some parts of his narrative are obscure, and in the absence of names that can be identified with any of those of more modern days, or even with those preserved by subsequent travellers among the Spaniards, it is difficult always to determine localities with entire certainty, yet we are enabled with a little care to distinguish quite accurately the general course of this most extraordinary journey.

The following seem to be the points of most interest in this regard: The bay in which the Spaniards first landed and where Narvaez set up the Imperial Ensign, was probably Charlotte Harbor, or somewhere in that vicinity, on the west coast of Florida; and the large bay discovered on Easter Monday, and which stretched far inland, was undoubtedly Tampa Bay. It is possible that the first landing place was one of the coves which are found in the southerly part of the same bay, as the distance between the two places was not great. The river reached after fifteen days travel, and which was crossed with difficulty on account of its width, was certainly the Withlacoochee, as there is no other that answers the description; and the "wide and deep river with the rapid current," where they had to stop and build a canoe in order to cross and where Juan Velasquez was drowned, was undoubtedly the Suwanee. As thirty days were occupied in travelling from one of these rivers to the other, either the journey must have been specially slow and difficult or else the expedition crossed the latter pretty high up, probably just below the junction of the Santa Fe, its eastern branch, as the narrative makes no mention of crossing that stream separately.

The next point of interest is the town of Apalache; and this appears to have been situated in the vicinity of Tallahassee, though from the time required to reach Aute, it may have been further north, in south-western Georgia, or near the locality of Chattahoochee. Of the town of Aute, we know that it was but a days' march from the sea and near a very large stream, which the Spaniards called Magdalena. This may have been near St. Marks, or perhaps the great river was the Apalachicola, and Aute may have been near the site of Fort Gadsden. This seems more probable, as the expedition of twenty men sent out to explore the coast gave a report of the bay being large and the seashore still distant. Charlevoix, however, who was at San Marcos de Apalache (St. Marks) in 1722, writes: "This bay is precisely that which Garcilasso de la Vega, in his history of Florida, calls the port of Aute;" and an ancient map, drawn by no less an authority than Sebastian Cabot, shows Apalache Bay, with the note in bad Spanish, "*Aqui deSan Barco panflo de Narnez.*" (*Aqui desembarcó Panfilo de Narvaez*). If this is true, then the Bahia de Caballos of Narvaez is the Apalache Bay of the present. The village where the battle was had with the Indians, and where the robe of civet-marten was obtained, was probably near Pensacola; and the place where Teodoro, the Greek, was abandoned, at the mouth of Mobile Bay. But there is some authority for believing that the latter point was also in Pensacola Bay, instead of being further west. However this may be, there can be no doubt that the great river which emptied such enormous quantities of fresh water into the Gulf, with such a swift current, was the Mississippi.

From this point it is more difficult to trace the exact route of the travellers, as times and distances are wanting, except in a few instances. The Island of Malhado and Espiritu Santo Bay have been located by different historians in widely varying localities. Buckingham Smith, in the first edition of his translation of Cabeza de Vaca's narrative, places them as far east as Mobile Bay, and traces the travellers' route north to the Muscle Shoals in the Tennessee River. This, however, could not well be, in connection with other parts of the route. And in the edition of 1871, he has changed his views so far as to suggest that the locality may have been as far west as San Antonio Bay in Texas. W. W. H. Davis, in his "Spanish Conquest of New Mexico," expresses the opinion that Malhado was one of the low islands on the coast of Louisiana; and the mention of a tribe called Atayos in the narrative, who are probably identical with the Adayes, who lived in 1805 about forty miles from Nachitoches, and the Hadaies, who years before were reported as being between the Nachitoches and Sabine Rivers,—adds plausibility to this view. It is possible that the island may have been at or near Galveston, or as far west as the beaches or islands known as Matagorda Beach and Matagorda Island, which are the outer protections of Matagorda and San Antonio Bays All that we can say certainly is that the Island of Malhado was one of the low islands so numerous on the coast of western Louisiana and Texas; and rest contented with that amount of knowledge. From here the course of Cabeza de Vaca and his three companions was in a generally northwesterly direction until the plains were reached, and afterwards the mountains seen, and from thence generally south-west into Sonora and Sinaloa.

The country with towns of "fixed habitations"

undoubtedly referred to the domain of the Pueblo Indians in New Mexico; and the great river coming from the north, which they crossed, was in all probability the Pecos. From there they were guided through fifty leagues of desert, and over rough mountains to another very great river, the water of which was breast high. This was undoubtedly the Rio Grande; and it was here that they had the long parleying with the natives as to the route to be pursued, the latter telling them of the great deserts to be passed if they went directly westward. Up this river they marched for thirty-four days —seventeen on the east side and seventeen on the west. Part of the distance was over plains lying between chains of great mountains; and they proceeded till they reached permanent habitations, where abundance of corn was raised, and where the natives, besides pumpkins, beans, etc., had "shawls of cotton." Some of their houses were of earth and some of cane mats. Just how far up the valley of the Rio Grande Cabeza de Vaca came we shall probably never know; but evidently not further than central New Mexico, as the turquoises which were presented to him, and which certainly came from the great Chalchiuitl Mountain in the Cerrillos, twenty miles south of Santa Fé, he mentions as coming "from the north." From the highest point reached, the party seem to have turned quite abruptly west, probably as soon as they had passed by the desert regions on the west of the river; and then marched for more than a 100 leagues, continually finding settled domicils, with plenty of maize and beans. It may be well conjectured that this was along the line of the Puerco and San Jose, and among the numerous pueblo towns, of which we have such full descriptions a few years later, in the time of Coronado; although the route may have been further south. From this time the course of the travellers was south-west until they reached the points in Sonora, where they neard of the nearness of other Christians.

Before leaving the subject of Cabeza de Vaca, it seems only proper to add a few words as to the subsequent history of this extraordinary man—everything in relation to whom is of interest in connection with early New Mexican history: For three years after his arrival in Spain, and the presentation of his "Relation" to the king, he appears to have lived in comparative seclusion; recovering slowly from the terrible exhaustion and after-effects of his wanderings, privations, and sufferings. At the end of that time (1540), news came to Spain of the death, by an Indian ambuscade, of the Commander Ayolas, who had been governor of a colony in South America, where the Republic of Paraguay is now situated. The surviving colonists sent urgent entreaties to the mother country for succor, and Cabeza de Vaca was selected to command the new expedition, and appointed as the governor of the colony. He was to furnish 8,000 ducats towards the expenses of the enterprise, but in return was given the titles of Governor, Captain-General, and Adelantado, and entitled to one-twelfth of the produce of the countries he should conquer.

After many difficulties he landed at St. Catharine's, in Brazil, in March, 1541; and from there marched across an utterly unknown country, and amid dangers which exceeded anything, even, that he had known in North America,—to the River Parana. Arrived here, he expected to be met by boats to convey his troops to Asuncion; but the Lieutenant-Governor, one Irala, was an ambitious man, who had brought about the destruction of the preceding Governor, and was in no way desirous to hasten the advent of his successor—and so none were at hand. With his indomitable energy, however, Vaca surmounted all difficulties, and finally arrived at his capital on March 11, 1542. But Irala secretly labored against him, and finally succeeded in raising an insurrection; in the midst of which the Governor was seized, thrown into prison, and so closely confined that his friends, for nearly a year, thought him dead. At length, more dead than alive, he was carried on board a vessel and sent to Spain, with documents from Irala (now Acting-Governor) accusing him of the gravest crimes. During the voyage he was loaded with chains, and treated in the most inhuman manner; and on his arrival in Spain, in September, 1545, his ill fortune followed him, for his friend, the Bishop of Cuenca (President of the Council), was just dead, and had been succeeded by the stern Bishop of Burgos, the advocate of Indian slavery, who was indisposed to look favorably on Cabeza de Vaca.

His enemies prevailed, and he was thrown into prison to await his trial; and while constantly petitioning to be released on security, remained in confinement for more than six years. Finally, in March, 1551, the Councilors of the Indies delivered their judgment, which was—that he be stripped of all the titles and privileges he had enjoyed, and banished for five years to Oran in Africa, there to serve the king, at his own expense, with horse and arms, on penalty of having the term of banishment doubled. It is doubtful if this sentence was in all respects executed—the history of the remainder of his life being clothed in much obscurity. It is to be hoped that the record of Charlevoix is correct, which says: "At last the Emperor granted him a pension of 2,000 crowns, and gave him a place in the Royal Audience of Seville, where he died at an advanced age." Charlevoix adds: "I have, indeed, seen a memorial in which it is said that he was immediately gratified with a seat in the Council of the Indies."

Altogether he was a remarkable man, and though his cotemporaries differed greatly in their estimate of his character, yet none could disparage his courage or his power s of endurance. Some went so far in their regard for his reputation as to credit him with the working of miracles, and a theological controversy arose therefrom, as to the possibility of the performance of a miracle by a layman. We may all, however, concur in the closing remarks on his character by the late Thos. W. Field: "He attempted the abolition of slavery to which the Indians had been illegally subjected, and a reform of the morals of Christians to a standard which would entitle them to the respect of savages; and in both he failed. He is scarcely to be decried for this, as three centuries elapsed before the first object was accomplished, and of the last history has little to record."

CHAPTER IV.

THE EXPEDITION OF FRIAR MARCOS DE NIZA.

THE next European to enter the territory now embraced in New Mexico was Friar Marcos de Niza, a Franciscan. As will shortly be seen, his expedition, which was purely one of exploration, was the direct result of the news which Cabeza de Vaca brought to Mexico of the rich countries to the north; and the negro companion of Cabeza became the guide of Marcos.

But before proceeding with the story of the journey of the Friar, a few words should be devoted to an attempt previously made to enter New Mexico from the south-west, based on information of the great wealth and splendor of its cities, brought by a native Indian. In the year 1530 Nuño de Guzman, who was President of New Spain, possessed an Indian who was a native of the Valley of Oxitipa, which the Spaniards call Tejos. The Indian told him that he was the son of a merchant who had died a long time before, but who, in his lifetime, used to travel through the interior of the country in order to sell ornamental feathers, to be made into plumes, and who obtained in exchange for them great quantities of gold and silver, which metals were very common in that country. The Indian added that he had accompanied his father on one or two of these trips, and had seen cities which were so splendid and large as to compare favorably with the City of Mexico. These cities were seven in number, and in them were whole streets occupied by goldsmiths. To reach this country, it was necessary to march for forty days across a desert, where there was no vegetation but a species of short grass about five inches high, and to go into the interior of the continent in a northerly direction between the two oceans.

Nuño de Guzman, full of confidence in these statements, raised an army of 400 Spaniards and 20,000 Indian allies, in New Spain, and starting from the City of Mexico, marched through the Province of Tarasca, a dependency of Michoacan. According to the report of the Indian, he would find the desired country—to which he had given the name of the "Land of the Seven Cities"—by proceeding toward the north, and the President believed it to be about 200 leagues distant, calculating from the forty days which his informant had said would be required for the journey. All went well until he arrived in the Province of Culiacan, which was beyond his own government and within what afterwards constituted the Kingdom of New Galicia; but there he began to meet many difficulties. The mountain regions which he had to traverse, were so wild and inaccessible that notwithstanding the most strenuous efforts he was unable to find a passage. On account of this lack of roads the army was obliged to remain at Culiacan, and the rich Spaniards who had accompanied him, and who had left in Mexico large numbers of slaves, became disheartened and very desirous of returning to their homes. Perhaps Guzman himself would have agreed to this and marched back to Mexico, but just then information was received that Cortez had arrived from Spain, with increased powers and honors, and bearing the new title of "Marquis of the Valley." As Guzman, while he had been President during the absence of Cortez, had shown himself his bitter enemy, and had seized and wasted his property, and that of his friends, he was afraid that the new Marquis would retaliate by like treatment, or perhaps worse. So, finding it impossible to go on with the expedition and yet fearing to return to Mexico, he determined to colonize the Province of Culiacan, and so remained there with such of his

Spanish friends as he could induce to take part in the new enterprise. They established themselves at Xalisco, afterwards called Compostello, and at Tonala, which is the present Guadalajara; and finding enough to occupy them in this work, they abandoned all idea of continuing their expedition. The Tejo Indian died, and so for several years the "Seven Cities" remained unknown, except in name.

For eight years Guzman remained and governed this Province, when, with the suddenness which characterized political changes in the Spanish Colonies at that time, he found himself not only succeeded by a new Governor sent from Spain, and named De la Torre; but accused of various crimes and thrown into prison. The new Governor lived but a short time to enjoy his colonial dignity; and the naming of his successor devolved upon Don Antonio de Mendoza, Viceroy of all New Spain, who appointed Francisco Vasquez Coronado. This gentleman was a native of Salamanca, but had established himself in Mexico, where he had greatly strengthened his position by a marriage with the daughter of the Treasurer, Don Alonzo d'Estrada, former Governor of Mexico, and who was generally believed to be a natural son of King Ferdinand, the Catholic. Coronado was a man of wealth and high character, and at the time of his appointment was travelling through New Spain, in order to see the country, and at the same time making valuable acquaintances for the future. Just as Coronado had been appointed by the Viceroy, Antonio de Mendoza, as Governor of New Galicia, Cabeza de Vaca, accompanied by Dorantes, Castillo, and the negro Estevanico, arrived in Mexico from that very Province, after their perilous and romantic journey; and their appearance years after they had been supposed dead, and the strange stories they told of their adventure, attracted much attention. To the Viceroy they made a special report, in which they gave a glowing account of parts of the countries they had traversed, and in particular spoke of great and powerful cities, in which the houses were four or five stories in height, and "of other things," adds Castañeda, writing of it long after, "very different from those which existed in reality." These accounts were quickly communicated by the Viceroy to Coronado, and caused the latter to be so much excited at the thought of the possibilities of discoveries and conquests in the vicinity of the Province which he was appointed to govern, that he abandoned a tour in which he was engaged, in order to hasten immediately to Culiacan. He carried with him the negro Estevanico, who had accompanied Cabeza de Vaca, and also three Franciscan monks, Marcos de Niza, who was a priest and theologian, and Daniel and Antonio de Santa Maria, lay brothers; Marcos having already much experience in hazardous expeditions, under Alvarado in Peru.

No sooner had Coronado arrived at the seat of his new Government than he took immediate measures to send the Franciscans, under the guidance of Estevanico, in search of the Land of the Seven Cities. It appears that the monks were not at all pleased with the conduct of the negro, who carried with him everywhere a number of women, and whose only thought was to enrich himself; but as he was able to understand the language of the natives of the country which they wished to penetrate, and as the Indians were acquainted with him, they concluded to send him in advance, so that they might be able to follow peacefully, and gather the information desired without difficulty or danger. Friar Marcos had received special instructions from the Viceroy Mendoza, before leaving Mexico, as to his duties on this expedition, "undertaken for the honor and glory of the Holy Trinity and for the propagation of our Holy Catholic Faith." The very first sentence shows the good effect of the influence of Cabeza de Vaca, as the Franciscan is told, as soon as he arrives at Culiacan, to exhort the

Spaniards to treat the Indians better, promising them rewards if they obey, and threatening punishments if they refuse, and then to visit the Indians and assure them that the Emperor has been greatly pained at their sufferings, that they shall no more be enslaved, and that every one maltreating them shall be punished. "Make them banish all fear and recognize God our Saviour, who is in heaven, and the Emperor whom He has placed on earth, to reign and govern." The instructions went on to say that if a route was found into the interior, then he was to proceed to explore, taking Estevanico as guide. He was to use great care and avoid all occasions of difficulty with the Indians, and to observe carefully the characteristics of the people, the nature of the soil, the temperature, the trees, plants and animals, the minerals and metals; and, wherever possible, to obtain specimens. In case his travels took him to the South Sea, he was to bury at the foot of some conspicuous tree on the shore such documents as would be valuable, and to raise a large cross there to designate the spot. If a large city was found, where it seemed desirable to found a monastery, he was to return to Culiacan to make the necessary arrangements therefor; "for in the proposed conquest the most important matter is the service of our Lord, and the good of the natives of the country." And lastly, "as all the earth belongs to the Emperor, our master, you are authorized to take possession of new countries in the name of his majesty; and you will make the natives understand that there is one God in heaven, or one Emperor on earth, who reign and govern." These instructions the Friar acknowledged having received, and promised to obey, on the 25th of November, 1538; and very soon after set off with Coronado and the two lay brothers for Culiacan.

We are fortunate in having a full account of the expedition of Friar Marcos written by his own hand. It is full of inaccuracies and extraordinary exaggerations; but we give the substance of it here, as a knowledge of those very exaggerations is necessary, not only to give us a correct view of the spirit of the times, but also to show on what kind of statements the expedition of Coronado, in the succeeding year, was based. The "Relation of Friar Marcos de Niza" is in the form of a report to the king; and was most formally certified by the writer to be absolutely true, in the presence of the Viceroy, the Auditor, Francisco de Ceiños, and Governor Coronado, and attested by various notaries, at Temixtitan, on September 2, 1539. It is published in Ramusio, Vol. III., page 297; Hakluyt, Vol. III., page 438; as an appendix to H. Ternaux's Castañeda, page 256; etc., etc. "By aid of the favor of the Holy Virgin Mary, our lady, and of our seraphic father St. Francis, I, Friar Marcos de Niza, left the city of San Miguel, in the province of Culiacan, on Friday the 7th of March, 1539," commences the "Relation." The Friar was accompanied by Friar Onorato, and by Estevanico, or Stephen, the Barbary negro; and also by a number of Indians whom the Viceroy had freed from slavery for the purpose, and a large body of other Indians belonging to Petatlan, and a town called Cuchillo, some fifty leagues beyond. They first travelled to the town of Petatlan, following the general line of the coast of the Gulf of California, and a short distance from it. Everywhere along the route the people received them with joy, and did everything in their power to show their appreciation of the action of the Viceroy and Governor in saving them from slavery and stopping the outrages to which they had before been subjected. They brought provisions and flowers as presents; and wherever there were no houses, constructed temporary bowers of the branches of trees for shelter for the travellers. At Petatlan, Friar Onorato fell sick, and after waiting a few days Marcos felt compelled to proceed without him,—"continuing my journey as the Holy Ghost did lead me, although I was unworthy of such guidance," as he piously writes Wherever he came, the Indians gave him a warm welcome; raising triumphal arches, and furnishing from their scanty stores the best provisions that they could. So he went on, still following the line of the Gulf, for about seventy-five miles, when he was met by some Indians from the island which Cortez had visited on his voyage not long before; and also by Indians from another island, larger and more distant, who wore shells of mother-of-pearl suspended from their necks, and who told him that pearls abounded on their shores.

Here he reached the border of a desert so wide that it required four days to cross it, and which evidently formed a complete barrier to intercourse between the natives, for when he arrived on the other side and met the people there, they were greatly astonished to see him, because they had never before heard of Europeans, or seen any persons who resembled the strangers. They called the Friar "Hayota," meaning "a man from heaven," and pressed him simply to touch his garments, and in every way showed their respect and veneration. In return, by means of interpreters, he endeavored to teach them of God and the Emperor, the heavenly and earthly authorities whom they ought to obey. As these people were poor, the travellers eagerly inquired for news of any large cities or wealthy tribes; and were told that in the interior of the country, four or five days' journey from the base of the mountains, there was a very extensive plain, which contained a considerable number of great towns inhabited by a people who were dressed in cotton, and whose vessels were made of gold. On further inquiry, they said that these people wore "certain round green stones hanging at their nostrils and at their ears, and that they have certain thin plates of gold wherewith they scrape off their sweat," and that the precious metal was so plentiful that the walls of their temples were covered with it.

This description was certainly sufficiently enticing, but as he wished not to be drawn so far into the interior, the Friar concluded to defer the exploration of this rich country until his return; and meantime proceeded for three days through the domain of the same tribe that he first met beyond the desert, when he arrived at a city of medium size ("reasonable bigness" the old translation in Hakluyt expresses it), where the people received him with great hospitality, and a bountiful supply of provisions, of which they had abundance, as the land was very fertile. The Spaniards arrived here on the Friday before Palm Sunday, and Marcos determined to remain until after Easter, and meanwhile to obtain all possible information of the surrounding country. Understanding that the Pacific coast (South Sea) was but forty leagues distant, he sent Indian messengers by three different routes to bring to him some of the inhabitants of the main-land and the adjacent islands, in order that he might learn from them direct the facts regarding their country. The negro, Stephen, he dispatched towards the north, with instructions to proceed fifty or sixty leagues, to see if anything of importance was to be discovered in that direction. His instructions were, if he gained any information of interest, either to return or to send an Indian messenger; and in the latter case a novel series of signs was agreed on. If the discovery "was but a mean thing, he should send me a white cross of one handful long; if it were any great matter, one of two handfuls long; and if it were a country greater and better than New Spain, he should send me a great cross." Stephen started on his journey on Palm Sunday in the afternoon, and so prompt was he to meet the highest expectation that only four days had elapsed when Friar Marcos was greatly elated by the sight of messengers returning, bringing a great cross as high as a man, and news that Stephen had met people who told him of a country which was the greatest in the world. With the messengers, the African sent one of the people who had visited this wonderful land, in order that the Friar might have accurate information. This Indian told him that it was a thirty days' march from the point where Stephen was to the nearest of the cities of the great nation beyond, whose country he called Cibola. In that land there were seven very great cities, all of which were ruled by one sovereign; the houses were large and built of stone and lime, the smallest being of one story surmounted by a terrace, and others of two and three stories. The palace of the ruler was four stories high and very finely built. The doors of the principal houses were ornamented with many turquoises curiously wrought, that stone being common in that country; and the inhabitants were all well appareled. As if this was not enough, he added that beyond the Seven Cities were other provinces exceeding them in greatness and riches.

Marcos held long conversations with this man, in order to obtain all the information possible, and was more and more convinced of the truth of his statements, as he found him reasonable and intelligent. Naturally, he was eager to push on to the discovery of these wonderful regions, but he felt that he ought to await the return of the other messengers sent to the coast, and so remained several days longer at Vacupa. Meanwhile there arrived three Indians of the race called "Pintados" —on account of their being elaborately painted on the face, breast, and arms—who lived far to the east; and they corroborated all that the natives sent by Stephen had told of the glories of Cibola. Having received the report from the Pacific coast, in which we have no special interest, Marcos lost no time in setting out to overtake Stephen, taking with him the three Pintados and some other Indians, and starting on the Tuesday after Easter. He soon met other envoys from the negro, carrying a cross as large as the first, and a message begging him to hasten on, as more recent information showed the country before them to be even greater and more marvelous than the first accounts had stated. Two days afterwards he arrived at the village at which Stephen had first heard of Cibola, and from which he had sent the first message. The negro had gone on without waiting for the Friar, but the latter found so many persons here to tell him of the country beyond that his time was well occupied. They all bore testimony to the same facts previously stated by the messengers, and added that besides the Seven Cities there were three other great kingdoms, named Marata, Acus, and Totonteac. The Indians said that they were familiar with Cibola, because they went there each year to work in the fields, and received their payment in hides and turquoises; the latter being very common there, so that all the people wore fine and beautiful ones suspended from their ears and noses, and all the principal doors being ornamented with them. They described the dress of the men of Cibola as consisting of long gowns of cotton descending to the feet, fastened at the neck with a button and a long string, which hung down; that the sleeves were of the same size from the shoulder to the wrist, and that they wore belts of turquoise around the waist. From the description the Friar thought that these dresses must be quite similar to those of Bohemia. The women were similarly costumed, wearing gowns which reached their feet.

The people of this town showed great hospitality to Marcos, not only attending to all his wants after his arrival, but sending out supplies to meet him on the road. They brought their sick to him to be healed, and clustered around to touch his garments. They also brought him several "cow skins," (buffalo-hides), so admirably tanned and dressed that they appeared as if prepared by a most civilized people; and all these they told him came from Cibola. From Vacupa the Friar continued his journey, accompanied only by the Pintados, who refused to leave him, and arrived toward evening at another village where he was equally well received, and where he found another large cross, left by Stephen as a token that the news was increasingly good. This, Marcos thought, was a proper place to carry out his instructions as to taking possession of the country for the Spanish Crown, and he consequently set up two crosses, and formally made the appropriate proclamations. Thus he travelled on for five days, finding a succession of villages, in each of which the people vied with each other to do him honor, and finally, just before reaching a desert of which he had been told, arrived at a large town, beautifully situated near several small rivers, and where he was received by a great concourse of men and women wearing cotton clothing, although some were covered with well dressed buffalo-skins, which they preferred to any other material. All the people of this town were "in caconados"—that is to say, wore turquoise ornaments suspended from their noses and ears, which were called "cacona." At their head were the chief of the community and two of his brothers, all exceedingly well dressed in cotton fabrics, and ornamented with caconas, and collars or necklaces of turquoise. They brought to the Friar great quantities of game of various kinds, as well as many buffalo-skins and turquoises, but he declined them all according to the custom which he followed in all places.

Marcos himself was dressed in a kind of gray woolen cloth, then called saragosa, which Governor Coronado had sent to him. The chief, and some others of the principal men, quickly observed this, and examined the material with interest; then said to the Friar that at Totonteac there was abundance of similar stuff, of which the people of that country made their clothes. Marcos, wishing to ascertain if they really distinguished the difference between cotton and wool, laughingly said that the material of their own clothing and his was the same. At this they seemed indignant, and said: "Thinkest thou that we are ignorant that this fabric is different from that which we wear? Thou wilt see in Cibola all the houses full of material such as ours; but at Totonteac there are little animals which furnish the wool from which your kind of cloth is made." This surprised and interested the Franciscan greatly, as it was the first information that had been received of the existence of any kind of sheep in the country. On leaving this town he had to enter the desert, which would occupy four days in crossing; but even here the kindness of the natives had provided for him, for during the whole period he found at each stopping-place, whether at noon or night, bowers made for his accommodation, and provisions prepared to meet his wants.

After passing this desert he came to a most charming valley, through which he travelled for five days, and which was everywhere cultivated like a garden. Villages were scattered all through its extent, being only a league, and sometimes half a league, apart. In one of these he found some very intelligent men, from whom he learned still more of Cibola and Totonteac,—of the great houses of the former, and the sheep and woolen cloth of the latter. In particular, they spoke of the buildings, the streets, and public places of Cibola. Wishing to test their accuracy, the Friar said that it was not possible that houses could be built of the height that they had stated. Whereupon they took some earth and some ashes and wet them, and then showed how the stones were laid one on top of another, and how the building was thus constructed of alternate layers of stone and mortar, until it had arrived at its full elevation. Still feigning ignorance, the Friar asked whether these men had wings so as to be able to fly to the upper stories of the edifice?—at which they laughed heartily, and drew a picture of a ladder as well as he himself could have done it, explaining that by this means the upper portions were reached. Totonteac they said was built of similar houses, but better constructed, and more numerous; it was so great a city that it might be called limitless.

Soon after passing this town Marcos met with an actual resident of Cibola, the first whom he had seen, and from him received a great deal of interesting information. The traveller describes this man as "a white man of a good complexion, of far greater capacity than the inhabitants of this valley or those which I had left behind me." He was quite aged, and had fled from the city on account of some difficulty, but said he would return with the Friar if the latter would procure his pardon. He said that the Lord of the Seven Cities lived at one of them called Ahacus, having lieutenants in charge of the others. Cibola is a very large and populous city having many fine streets and market-places; that in several places there are immense houses five stories in height, (the French version of Ternaux-Compans says "ten stories"), in which the rulers meet at certain times of the year. The houses are of stone and lime, the gates and smaller pillars of the principal residences are of turquoise, while all the household vessels and ornaments are of gold. Satisfied with modestly saying this much as to his own city, the Indian then informed Friar Marcos that all of the others of the Seven Cities were similarly built, but several were larger than Cibola, the most extensive being Ahacus the capital. Toward the southeast was situated another kingdom called Marata, with a large population, and many-storied houses, which was continually at war with the ruler of the Seven Cities. To the west was the kingdom of Totonteac, which was the greatest and most important in the world, thickly populated and very rich. Here the people were dressed in woolen cloth like that of the Friar, only more beautiful. They were highly civilized and very different from those already seen. There was also another very large kingdom called Acus, which he begged Marcos not to confound with Ahacus, the city, although the names were somewhat similar. Among other things the Cibolan said that the people of his city slept on "beds raised a good height from the ground, with quilts and canopies over them, which cover the said beds." In this valley the Friar counted over a thousand buffalo hides, extremely well prepared, and a constantly increasing amount of turquoise, all of which, however, was said to come from Cibola. Here also he was shown an enormous hide, half as large again as that of the largest ox, which he was told was that of a great beast having one horn growing from the middle of his forehead, which bent down towards his breast, but has a point going straight forward, so strong that it would "break anything how strong soever it be, if he run against it;" and the natives told him that these animals were very abundant in that country.

While here, and just before reaching the borders of another desert, Marcos was met by other messengers from Stephen, with most encouraging tidings. The negro sent word that he was "very joyful," because the further he advanced the more he heard of the richness of the country, and the surer he was of the correctness of the reports. Before leaving this fertile valley and entering upon the long march across the desert which separated it from Cibola, the Friar was induced by the people to stop for three days for rest and refreshment, and to allow a number of them to prepare to accompany him on his journey. Three hundred had thus acted as an escort to Stephen, but from the multitude who presented themselves for that purpose at the appointed time, Marcos selected only thirty of the wealthiest and most influential men—those who were best dressed and adorned with the greatest number of turquoise necklaces—as companions, with a number of others as servants to carry provisions; the passage across this last desert being a long and dangerous one, usually occupying fifteen days. They started on this journey on the 9th of May, 1539; finding a broad and well beaten road, which was used for the travel to Cibola, each noon and night stopping at places where an advance party had built a temporary house for the Friar, once or twice recognizing the houses which had been similarly prepared for Stephen a short time before, and seeing the remains of many old ones used by former travellers.

Thus they journeyed for twelve days, full of enthusiasm and high hopes, when they were suddenly met by an Indian who was one of those who accompanied Stephen, and was the son of one of the principal natives then with the Friar. He was covered with perspiration, nearly exhausted with fatigue, and his face was full of sadness and terror; and after the first salutation, he told the following story: "One day, shortly before arriving at Cibola, Stephen sent the calabash, or gourd, which he carried as a mace and which had a peculiar significance, by messengers, according to his custom, in order to announce his arrival. To this gourd was attached a string of bells and two feathers, one white and the other red. When the messengers had arrived in presence of the chief who rules that city for the Sovereign, they handed him the calabash. The chief took it, but when he saw the bells, became suddenly enraged and dashed it on the ground, ordering the messengers to leave immediately; for he knew these strangers, and that they had better not enter the city, or they would all be put to death. The messengers hastened back to Stephen and reported to him what had occurred; but the negro replied that that was of no importance, for those who seemed displeased at his coming always received him the best, and he continued his journey until he arrived at Cibola. At the moment when he was about to enter, he was met by a party of Indians, who took him into a large house just outside of the city, and forthwith despoiled him of all that he had with him, including the articles he had brought for trading purposes, some turquoises, and many other presents that he had received during the journey. He passed the night in this place, without anything either to eat or drink being given to himself or his companions, who were lodged with him. The next morning the narrator, who was one of them, being very thirsty, started out of the house in order to get some water from a river which flowed near by. Soon after, he saw Stephen running away, pursued by the Cibolans, who were killing the Indians who were with the negro. As soon as the narrator saw this, he hid himself by the river, and at the first opportunity started back through the desert."

This news threw the party of the Friar into consternation; they began to lament and murmur against their leader, so that he tells us he began to fear for his life; but he quaintly adds: "I did not fear so much the loss of my own life as that I should not be able to return to give information of the greatness of that country where our Lord God might be glorified." With a keen insight into human nature, he forthwith opened some of the packages of goods which he had brought for traffic, and distributed the contents among the principal men, telling them not to fear but to go forward. This they consented to do; but when within a days' journey of Cibola they met two other Indians who had accompanied Stephen, bloody and covered with wounds. These told the same story as the first comer, as to the capture and attempted escape of Stephen. They had been among those who were with him at the time, when a great multitude of natives had pursued them, killed some and wounded all; but they had fortunately escaped and lain concealed all day thereafter, hearing much noise, and seeing crowds on the walls of the city, but neither seeing nor hearing more of Stephen, so that in their own language, " We think they have shot him to death, as they have done all the rest who went with him, so that none are escaped but we only." The news of the death of so many relatives and friends roused the indignation of the Indians almost to frenzy, and soon the Friar was informed by a trusty servant, named Marcos, whom he had brought from Mexico, that they were conspiring to kill him, as they felt that through him and Stephen their fathers and brothers had been slain, and that they were liable through the same means to meet similar destruction. Friar Marcos tried the same method as before to pacify them, distributing many of the most beautiful and fascinating articles, and succeeded to some extent, and then endeavored to prevail on some of them to go on towards the city so as at least to get further news of the fate of Stephen; but this they absolutely refused to do. Then he told them that God would surely punish the men of Cibola, and that the Spanish Viceroy would speedily send an army to chastise the city when he should learn the news of the death of Stephen; but they only replied that that was not possible, for no people could withstand the power of Cibola.

By this time Marcos was convinced of the impossibility of forcing an entrance into the city or visiting it peaceably, and so concluded to make as thorough an examination of it as he could from without. So he told his followers that he proposed to see it at all events, but not one would accompany him. Finally, when they saw him actually start alone, two of the chiefs consented to join him; and with them and his own Indians from the south he proceeded until he was within sight of the long-looked-for city. He found that it was situated "on a plain at the foot of a round hill, and maketh show to be a fair city, and better seated than any that I have seen in these parts. The houses are builded in order, according as the Indians told me, all made of stone, with divers stories, and flat roofs, as far as I could discern from the mountain, whither I ascended to view the city. The people are somewhat white; they wear apparel and lie in beds; their weapons are bows; they have emeralds and other jewels, although they esteem none so much as turquoise, wherewith they adorn the walls of the porches of their houses and their apparel and vessels, and they use them instead of money through all the country. They use vessels of gold and silver, for they have no other metal, whereof there is greater use and more abundance than in Peru." Having viewed the city, which his comrades told him was the least of the "Seven Cities," the Friar named the country "El Nuevo Reyno de San Francisco;" "and thereupon," he says, "I made a great heap of stones by the aid of the Indians, and on the top thereof I set up a small, slender cross, because I lacked means to make a greater, and said that I set up that cross and heap in the name of the most honorable Lord Don Antonio de Mendoza, Viceroy and Captain-General of New Spain, for the Emperor, our lord, in token of possession." Not satisfied with thus formally annexing the City of Cibola itself to the Spanish dominion, De Niza further solemnly declared that the possession which he then took was "also of the 'Seven Cities,' and of the Kingdoms of Totonteac, of Acus, and of Marata."

Having thus at any rate formally accomplished great political things, and having really penetrated to a region theretofore unseen by European eyes, he turned his back on Cibola and hastened to overtake the little army which had accompanied him on his march across the desert, and which was now moving, as he expressed it, "with more fear than victuals." Here he had an opportunity of learning very soon the old lesson, that the consideration in which a man is held is largely proportioned to his success, for as he briefly puts it, "I was not made so much of as before." Indeed, when he arrived at the town of the valley, whence his companions and those of Stephen had come, he was afraid of his life on account of the great lamentation made by both men and women over the loss of the slain and missing; and so "with fear," he says, "I hastened from the people of this valley and travelled ten leagues the first day, and so daily eight or ten leagues, until I had crossed the second desert." Thence he went back to San Miguel and finally to Compostella, where he found the Governor, and made a report of the wonderful things which he had seen and heard of. This report reduced to writing, was sent to the Viceroy, and he in turn transmitted it to the Emperor, accompanied with an account of the ill success of several more ambitious attempts to discover golden regions, and adding, "It seemeth unto all men that it was God's will to shut up the gate to all those who by strength of human force have gone about to attempt this enterprise, and to reveal it to a poor and barefooted Friar."

Before closing the account of this expedition, it seems proper to notice another version of the death of Stephen, which appears in the "Relation" of Castañeda, and which contains particulars not known, probably, to the frightened Indians who escaped to carry the first tidings to Friar Marcos. Castañeda says: "Stephen arrived at Cibola with a great quantity of turquoise, and some fine women who had been presented to him along the route. With him were a large number of Indians who had been furnished as guides at different places, and who believed that under his protection they could traverse the whole world without having anything to fear. But as the people of Cibola were more brave and spirited than those who accompanied Stephen, they shut up his whole company in a house outside of their city, and there the caciques and aged men of the place questioned him as to the object of his coming into their country. After having continued this inquiry for three days, they held a council to decide as to his fate. As the negro had told them that he was the forerunner of two white men, sent by a powerful prince, who were very learned in the heavenly affairs, which they would come to teach them, they considered that he must be the guide or the spy of some nation which desired to subjugate them. It seemed to them, also, unreasonable to believe that this man who was black came from the country of men who were white. Besides, Stephen had demanded of them their riches and their women; and this seemed to them hard to consent to. So they concluded to kill him, without doing any harm to those who accompanied him. And this they did—taking merely a few young boys, and sending back all the rest, who numbered about sixty."

The route taken by Marcos de Niza on this celebrated expedition is, so far as its main features are concerned, easy to distinguish. He first travelled nearly parallel with the coast of the Gulf of California, until he reached its head, and then turned to the north-east, and continued travelling in that general direction for the rest of the distance. The fertile and populated valleys were along the Gila and its tributaries. There is no doubt at all that Cibola was Zuñi, being what is now called the "Old Pueblo," or "Old Zuñi." The kingdom to the south-east may have referred to the Pueblo country in the vicinity of Acoma and Laguna, or possibly to one still more distant and across the Rio Grande, towards Abó and the ruins now called "Gran Quivira." Totonteac, if situated as stated, to the west, would be identical with the Moqui towns; and Acus might have been the country now represented by the ruins in the Chaco Valley, the Pueblo Bonito, etc. But the experience of Coronado, shortly afterwards, shows these reports of kingdoms to have been very shadowy, and at all events greatly exaggerated.

CHAPTER V.

THE EXPEDITION OF CORONADO.

THE highly colored account with which Friar Marcos regaled Governor Coronado, and afterwards the Viceroy himself, was enough to excite the ambition as well as the cupidity of even less adventurous men. In addition to his written narration, or report, which was sufficiently enticing, the Friar made most exaggerated statements of what he had been told by Indians of the countries beyond Cibola; and his position in the Franciscan order lent weight to his words. The Viceroy became intensely interested, believing that here was an opportunity to obtain both fame and gold, and determined to lose no time in organizing an expedition for the exploration and conquest of the rich kingdoms beyond the desert.

No sooner was it known that an expedition for the conquest of Cibola and the wonderful Land of the Seven Cities had been decided on, than the most adventurous cavaliers of New Spain hastened to take part in the enterprise. The best families of Castile were represented among them, and the troop of 400 which finally started was the most brilliant which, at that time, had ever been raised in the new world. Francisco Vasquez de Coronado, the Governor of New Galicia, was very properly appointed as Captain-General, by the Viceroy, both because the discovery of Cibola had been made through his instrumentality, and because his province was the natural starting-place of the expedition. He was a man experienced both in arms and in government, wise, prudent, and able, and a great favorite with Mendoza. The Viceroy also appointed the other officers of the expedition; and here the only difficulty which arose was from an "embaras de richesses." "Seeing the great number of gentlemen taking part in this expedition," says Castañeda, "the Viceroy would have been glad to give each one the command of an army; but as the soldiers were so few, it was necessary to make a choice. He concluded to name the captains himself, because he was so greatly loved and respected that he knew no one would refuse to obey those whom he designated." "He chose for standard-bearer Don Pedro de Tobar, a young cavalier, son of Don Fernando de Tobar, mayor-domo of the late Queen Joanna, our legitimate sovereign, whose soul may God preserve. He appointed as Maestro de Campo, Lope de Samaniego, governor of the arsenal of Mexico, and a chevalier well worthy of this position. The captains were Don Tristan de Arellano, Don Pedro de Quevara, Don Garcia Lopez de Cardenas, Don Rodrigo Maldonado, brother-in-law of the Duke of Infantado, Diego Lopez, member of the city council of Seville, and Diego Gutierrez, captain of cavalry. All the other gentlemen were placed directly under the orders of the General, because they were men of distinction, and a number of them were afterwards appointed captains." The commander of the infantry was Pablo de Melgosa, and the chief of artillery Hernando de Alvarado. The historian of the expedition, Pedro de Castañeda de Nagera, who accompanied it through all its journeyings, and afterwards in Culiacan wrote a full account of all that occurred, mentions a number of other illustrious names, in order to impress upon the reader the chivalrous and aristocratic character of those who were engaged in it, and to prove that it contained "more men of quality than any which has been undertaken for the making of discoveries," adding that it must surely have been successful but for the great riches, and the young bride, noble and charming, left behind by the commander, to which attractions he attributes his intense desire to return at a later day.

With the 400 Spaniards were 800 Indian soldiers, so that the entire expedition was composed of 1,200 men; and these were directed to rendezvous at Compostella, the capital of New Galicia, in the spring of 1540. At the same time Don Pedro Alarcon was ordered to start from Natividad, on the Pacific, with two ships, and proceed to Xalisco with such munitions as the soldiers could not well carry, and thence sail along the coast as near as possible to the army, so as to keep up communication with it, the supposition being that the route of the expedition was near to the coast of the Pacific. In reality the line of march of the land forces so soon diverged to the east that these vessels were of no service; but they made many very interesting discoveries, as are quaintly recounted in the report made by the commander, Alarcon, after his return, and subsequently published in the collections of Ramusio.

Meanwhile the troops were concentrating at Compostella, and thither the Viceroy went in person in order to give to the expedition the distinction and benefit of his official presence. He was splendidly entertained by Cristoval de Oñate, who had been appointed to act as Governor of New Galicia while Coronado was absent; and he held a grand review of the whole army, which is described as a most brilliant spectacle. The Viceroy was exceedingly popular, and was received with great enthusiasm. He addressed the soldiers on the vast importance of the expedition in a threefold aspect; to their country by conquering this great province; to the Indians by bringing them to a knowledge of Christianity; and to themselves by bettering their fortunes. He then caused each man to swear on a missal containing the gospels never to abandon their General, but to obey all that he might command; and in order to encourage them to the fullest extent, he accompanied them for two days on their march. The army set out early in January, 1541, from Compostella, as brilliant an array and as full of enthusiasm and high expectations as was ever seen in the new world. As soon as the Viceroy had departed, the regular march commenced, and the days of holiday parade were over. Many difficulties were at once experienced. The baggage was found to be a great annoyance; it had to be transported on horses, and the animals proved to be too fat, and ill accustomed to fatigue. Besides, many soldiers did not know how to pack them properly, so that very soon a large part of the baggage was abandoned, or given to any one who would take it. Necessity caused many a cavalier to perform work to which he was unaccustomed, so that it was not rare, we are told, to see men of gentle birth acting as mule-drivers.

After much fatigue, the army reached the town of Chiametla; and here it was discovered that the supply of provisons was already failing, and a halt of some days was required in order to replenish the stock. From this place, Samaniego, the Maestro de Campo, imprudently went with only a few men to an adjacent Indian village, and while there was shot in the head with an arrow and killed. A grand military funeral was had, and all the natives who even "seemed to be" inhabitants of the place where the murder took place, were hung; but the affair naturally cast a gloom over the expedition. Another discouraging event occurred at this town. Some time previously Coronado had dispatched two officers named Melchior Diaz and Juan de Saldibar, with a party of a dozen men, to explore the route toward Cibola, which had been traversed by Friar Marcos de Niza. The party had gone as far as Chichilticale, which was the town so glowingly described by Marcos at the edge of the great desert, but found nothing very inviting nor in any way equaling the report of the Friar; and so had returned and met the army at this point. While they only communicated with Coronado, yet it soon became known in the camp that the news was unfavorable, and many began to be discouraged. Friar Marcos, however, assured them that the countries to be visited were of great richness, and that every man would reap a splendid reward, and in this way somewhat revived their spirits; and they resumed the march to Culiacan. Here they were received on the day after Easter with great demonstrations. The inhabitants arranged a grand sham fight, in which they pretended to defend their town against the approach of the army, and then falling back, allowed the latter to enter the city in triumph. The officers were entertained with marked hospitality by the citizens, who insisted that they should occupy their houses instead of the quarters prepared; but Castañeda throws a doubt on the disinterested character of these professions by saying, "This hospitality was not to their disadvantage, for the officers were very well equipped, and as they could not carry all their baggage on their animals, they preferred giving many articles to their hosts rather than expose them to the chances of the future."

The army remained here for a month, but Coronado himself only stayed half of that time, as he was impatient to press on to the exploration, if not the immediate conquest, of the famed lands before him. So he took a few of his most intimate friends, and with fifty horsemen and a few soldiers on foot, started in advance, leaving the main body of the army under the command of Don Tristan de Arellano, with orders to follow him in a fortnight. The General took with him all of the priests, as for some reason none of them would remain with the army; but after proceeding on the march three days, one of their number, named Antonio Victoria, happened to break his thigh and had to be sent back to Culiacan for treatment; "which," says Castañeda, "was no small consolation for all the people." Meanwhile Coronado and his party were proceeding successfully on their journey, full of enthusiasm, and meeting with no trouble from the natives, as many of the latter were acquainted with Friar Marcos, or had acted as an escort on the recent expedition of Diaz and Saldivar; and so they arrived at Chichilticale. But here a great disappointment awaited them. Instead of the flourishing town they had been led to expect, they found in reality but one single building, and that in ruins and even without a roof. It is true that its proportions and style of architecture proclaimed it to be the work of some superior and civilized nation, differing widely from the inhabitants of the country around, but that was small consolation under the circumstances. They had come seeking the riches of the present, and not the relics of the past. This building, Chichilticale, is almost beyond a doubt identical with the structure now called the "Casa Grande" of Arizona, which has been so frequently described by travellers in recent days; both the situation and the description making the identification almost positively certain.

At this point the great desert began; but Coronado would not wait for his army, but pressed on rapidly with his little escort in hopes of making discoveries of such importance that the present disappointment would be forgotten. For fifteen days they marched through a continuous desert, barren, sandy, and devoid of water; but at length their eyes were gladdened by the sight of a narrow stream, whose waters had such a reddish tinge that they named it Vermejo. What added to their joy was the fact that they were but eight leagues from the special object of their journey—the City of Cibola. Here they saw a few Indians, but could open no communication, as they fled as soon as they were approached. Marching on, on the evening of the next day, when they were but two leagues from the city, they discovered some Indians on an elevation, who raised such a frightful cry that it startled and alarmed the Spaniards, who were unaccustomed to such extraordinary sounds; the fright of some of the soldiers being so intense, Castañeda says, that they "saddled their horses wrong end foremost." "But," he adds "these were men of the new levy." The veterans started in pursuit of the Indians, but the latter succeeded in escaping to the city. The next day the whole army arrived in sight of Cibola; but here their disappointment was even greater than at Chichilticale, and the air was filled with maledictions against Friar Marcos and his enormous exaggerations. Instead of the large city described in his " Relation," they saw a small town located upon a rock, containing not over 200 warriors, but protected from capture by the steepness and difficulties of its approach. It was true that the houses were of three or four stories in height, but they were small and inconvenient, and one courtyard had to serve for an entire quarter. The whole province contained seven cities, some of which were much larger and better fortified than Cibola.

The Spaniards had hoped that their overtures of peace and friendship would be accepted without question or delay, but the Indians seemed to understand that peace meant subjugation, and so only replied to the demand of the interpreter by menacing gestures, and drew up their warriors in good order to resist an attack. This speedily followed, for Coronado led his followers to an immediate charge, with loud cries of "Santiago." The Indians could not withstand this attack, but fled to the shelter of the town. The Spaniards followed, but found that the task before them was not an easy one. The single approach was steep and dangerous, the commanding position of the town on the summit of a rocky mesa giving its defenders an immense advantage. The assailants, as they attempted to carry it by storm, were received with showers of stones, one of which struck Coronado himself to the ground, where he would have been killed had not Hernando de Alvarado and Lopez de Cardenas thrown themselves before him, and protected him from the showers of missiles with their own bodies.

Nevertheless his followers pressed on, and "as it is impossible to resist the furious attacks of Spaniards," says Castañeda, in less than an hour the city was captured, and the Europeans marched in triumph through the streets of the first Pueblo town that had ever felt their tread. The conquerors were rejoiced to find a plentiful supply of provisions, of which they were sorely feeling the need; and after a short period for rest, Coronado succeeded in reducing the entire province to subjection.

Meanwhile the army which had been left at Culiacan under the command of Arellano had slowly proceeded on its march, travelling on foot and with considerable difficulty. They passed through the town which Cabeza de Vaca had called "Corazones," where the commander was so much pleased that he concluded to colonize the country. From here they tried to obtain news of the ships which were to have accompanied them to the head of the Gulf, but could learn nothing, and so they stopped at the new town, which was called Sonora, awaiting news and orders from Coronado. These came in the middle of October, by the hands of Melchior Diaz and Juan Gallegos, and the main army immediately set out for Cibola. Gallegos proceeded to Mexico to carry an account of the expedition as far as it had progressed; and he took with him Friar Marcos, who had been obliged to fly from the army at Cibola on account of the indignation of the troops at the exaggerations and falsities of which it had now been proved he had been guilty, in the relation of his former journey. Arellano and a considerable number of soldiers who were sick, or had not the strength requisite for the hardships of the coming journey, remained at Sonora. The main body marched over the same route taken by Coronado, and were hospitably received by the Indians along the road, who had been well treated by the General. They reached the desert at Chichilticale without notable adventure, except that many were seized with a violent disease from eating preserved Indian figs, given to them by the natives. When almost across the desert, and within a day's march of Cibola, they encountered a violent storm, followed by a very severe and deep snow. The Spaniards resisted the cold without difficulty, but the Indians who accompanied them suffered very severely, as they came from the warm country to the south, and had never experienced such intensely frigid weather before. Some succumbed to the exposure and perished, while many others were only saved by being carried on the horses while the Spaniards walked. On arriving at Cibola, however, the army found not only a warm welcome from the General and their comrades, but that Coronado, with an unusual degree of care, had prepared for them excellent and comfortable quarters in advance.

While the whole army, thus reunited, was resting after its desert march, Coronado endeavored to obtain information of the surrounding country. He was soon told of a province called Tusayan, twenty-five leagues distant, where there were seven cities similar to those of Cibola. The inhabitants were said to be very brave, but the Cibolans could give no very exact information concerning them, because there was no intercourse between the two provinces. Coronado was unwilling to continue his march until this province had been visited, and consequently sent a small detachment under Don Pedro de Tobar, in whose bravery and address he had special confidence, to reconnoitre, and if practicable, take possession of the country. With them was sent as an adviser, half spiritual and half military, Friar Juan de Padrila, a Franciscan monk who had been a soldier in his younger days. The expedition marched so rapidly and secretly that it arrived in the province and up to the very walls of the houses of the first village without being discovered, and encamped after dark in the midst of the unsuspecting population. At dawn the Indians were astonished to see the strangers at their doors, and especially amazed at the sight of the horses, the like of which they had never seen before. An alarm was sounded, and the warriors quickly assembled with bows and clubs to drive away the invaders. The Spanish interpreter endeavored to explain that they came as friends, but the Indians, while hearing them politely, insisted that the strangers should withdraw; and drawing a line on the ground, forbade any of the Spaniards to pass beyond it. One soldier rashly ventured to cross, when he was immediately attacked and driven back. At this the Friar, who seemed to have been more aggressive even than the Captain, urged a charge, exclaiming in vexation at the delay, "In truth, I do not understand why we have come here!" at which the Spaniards rushed forward and killed a great number of Indians, while the remainder fled to the houses for protection. These soon returned in the attitude of suppliants, bringing presents, and offering their own submission and that of the whole province. During the day deputations came from the other towns to confirm their surrender and, to invite the Spaniards to visit them and trade. In this province, which was then called Tesayan, but which is identical with the modern Moqui, were seven villages, which were governed as were those of Cibola, by a council of aged men; having also governors and captains. They raised large quantities of corn, and had well tanned leather; and among the presents which they brought to Tobar were poultry and turquoise.

Having accomplished its object, the expedition returned to Cibola, where Don Pedro gave an account of his adventures to Coronado, and also told him of a great river further to the west, of which he had received information from the people of Tusayan. On this river it was said that a race of giants lived; and so much was told of its extraordinary size and character that Coronado determined to send another expedition to explore it. Accordingly, Don Garcia Lopez de Cardenas with twelve horsemen set forth, proceeding first to Tusayan, where they procured guides and laid in provisions for the desert journey. After traversing an uninhabited country for twenty days, they at length arrived on the banks of the river, which was in so deep a cañon that the sides seemed "three or four leagues in the air." It was impossible to descend the rugged and almost perpendicular banks to the water, so the party marched along the side for three days hoping to find a safe place at which to make a descent. The river was so far below that it appeared but an arm's length in width, but the Indians assured the Spaniards that it was fully one-half a league across. At length they arrived at a point that seemed more favorable for an attempt to descend, and Captain Melgosa, Juan Galeres, and one other soldier, who were the lightest and most active of the company, volunteered to make the experiment; but toward night-fall they returned, torn and exhausted, reporting that they had only been able to accomplish a third of the distance They said that even from there the river assumed large proportions, and that some of the rocks, which from the surface appeared scarcely as high as a man, were in reality taller than the tower of the Cathedral of Seville. The expedition proceeded somewhat further along the river, until it reached some great falls, but was finally compelled to return for want of water. This river the discoverers called the Tison, correctly recognizing it as the same of which the mouth had been seen at the head of the Californian Gulf. It is now known as the Colorado of the West; and its Grand Cañon, along which Cardenas thus marched nearly three and a half centuries ago, is one of the most wonderful natural curiosities of the world.

While these expeditions were being made to the west, a deputation of natives came from a province far to the east, called Cicuyé. This was headed by their chief, a young man, tall and fine-looking, who, from the unusual circumstance of his having long mustaches, the Spaniards called "Bigotes." He said that they had heard in their country, seventy leagues away, of the arrival of the white men, and had come to offer their friendship and services, with the hope that the Spaniards, as they advanced, would consider them as allies. Coronado received them graciously, and an exchange of presents took place, the Indians being specially pleased with some little bells. Bigotes gave a general description of the intervening country, its productions and animals, particularly dwelling on the number of native cows (buffaloes) which were to be found to the eastward. This presented too good an opportunity for exploration to be lost; so Coronado directed Hernando de Alvarado, with twenty men, to accompany the deputation on their journey back to their country, and to return within eighty days with an account of his discoveries.

Proceeding easterly, after a five days' march, they arrived at Acuco—the present Pueblo of Acoma—a town built on the summit of a great rock, with sides so perpendicular that ascent was impossible except at one place, and there only by the use of artificial steps. The situation was practically impregnable; for after ascending 200 steps, it was necessary to climb 100 more that were far more difficult, and then a perpendicular ascent of twelve feet remained to be accomplished, which could only be done by the use of holes made in the face of the rock. On the summit was heaped a quantity of great stones, to be rolled down on the heads of any enemies attempting to scale the height, while those above were entirely protected from danger. The flat crown of the rock contained enough good soil for the cultivation of large quantities of corn, and wells sunk in the solid stone supplied the town with water. Acuco boasted of about 200 warriors, and from their fearlessness, and the security of its position, was the terror of the surrounding country.

On the approach of the little band of Spaniards, the Indians came down boldly into the plain, and haughtily forbade them to proceed further; but finding that Alvarado displayed no fear, but was preparing his company to make an attack, they suddenly changed their tone and sued for peace and amity, which were readily accorded. They soon afterwards presented the Spaniards with a great quantity of poultry, together with bread, corn, piñons, etc., which were very acceptable. Alvarado, however, did not delay, but pressed on his journey, arriving in three days at a province called Tiguex, the inhabitants of which, on seeing Bigotes, who was highly esteemed in all that country, received the Spaniards with great hospitality. The precise location of Tiguex cannot be determined at this time; but from the distance to various surrounding points, such as Jemez, Cicuyé, etc., it is evident that the province lay along the valley of the Puerco River, embracing probably the territory on both sides, and especially to the east. It included twelve villages in all, and its principal towns were probably about west from Bernalillo. Alvarado was so much charmed with the appearance of the country and the kindness of his reception, that he sent an envoy to Coronado at Cibola, recommending that he should bring the whole army to winter there.

Without waiting for a response, the little expedition continued its march, and at the end of five days arrived at Cicuyé, the city of "Bigotes," and which was found to be built of houses four stories in height and strongly fortified. Here they were received with special demonstrations of joy and welcome, escorted into town to the music of drums and fifes, and presented with many cotton goods and turquoises. Cicuyé was situated on the Jemez River, and probably at or near the present pueblo of Santa Ana, as it was about four leagues distant from Cia. Alvarado concluded to remain here some little time to give his troops the much-needed rest; and while so waiting, he met an Indian who was destined to have a great influence on the history of the whole expedition. This was a stranger, held as a servant at Cicuyé, but who had come from the far East, being a native, says Castañeda, "of the country on the border of Florida, of which De Soto has lately explored the interior." He bore such a strange resemblance to the Mohammedans of the Orient that the Spaniards called him "the Turk," and by no other name is he mentioned in the chronicles. This man, from his first meeting with Alvarado, began to tell, in most extravagant terms, of wonderful cities to be found in his own country to the east and of their vast riches in gold and silver. So thoroughly did he impress Alvarado with these stories that the Captain felt it but a loss of time to explore a country containing little else but buffaloes; and so, after proceeding just to the edge of the plains, where he could see those animals, he hastened back to meet Coronado and tell him of the great news he had received.

Meanwhile the latter had concluded to act on the advice of Alvarado as to wintering at Tiguex, and had sent Cardenas in advance to prepare quarters for the soldiers. This was done with much harshness and cruelty, the inhabitants being driven out of their houses, and not even allowed to take their goods, with the exception of the clothes they wore—a poor return for the hospitality extended by them to Alvarado. Coronado himself waited at Cibola until the arrival of Tristan de Arellano with re-inforcements, and then set out for Tiguex with thirty men, leaving directions for the main body to follow in three weeks. Wishing to visit a province of eight villages of which he had heard, called Tutahaco, he took a different route from that by Acuco, and after great suffering from thirst in a desert region—(which must have been west of the present Fort Wingate),—he arrived by an eight days' march at the towns which he determined to see. This province of Tutahaco was evidently in the valley of the river now called San Jose, the only one of its towns still existing being the Pueblo of Laguna. The General found the people friendly and well-disposed, and their towns, clothing, and customs similar to those in the vicinity of Cibola. He followed the San José down to its junction with the Puerco, and then ascended the valley of the latter until he arrived at Tiguex, where he met Alvárado and "the Turk." The latter repeated to Coronado what he had before narrated, with perhaps greater embellishments. He said that in his native country, to the east, was a great river two leagues in width, containing fish of the size of a horse, and navigated by boats carrying twenty oarsmen on a side, as well as using sails; that the nobles sat in the stern of these vessels under canopies, surrounded by all kinds of magnificence. He stated that the lord of the land took a daily siesta in the shade of a great tree, from whose branches hung golden bells that the moving air caused to ring, and added, with a thorough knowledge of the hopes and wishes of the Spaniards, that the commonest vessels for water were of finely worked silver, and the plates and other table utensils of gold.

These stories, however extravagant, the Spaniards believed implicitly, and, as we shall soon see, put such confidence in the Turk as to make them distrust all others. For instance, the former told them, by way of corroboration, that he had brought several golden bracelets from his own country when he came to Cicuyé; and when the Spaniards sent to find them, and were informed by the people that such things had never been seen there, and that the Turk was a notorious liar who could never be trusted, they actually disbelieved the latter; and seizing the Cacique and Bigotes, from whom they had received so much aid as well as kindness, carried them in chains to Tiguex in order to extort a confession as to the missing ornaments, and kept them in confinement more than six months. This conduct naturally caused great indignation among the natives, which was increased by the injustice and rapacity which characterized the actions of the officers appointed by Coronado to collect cotton goods for clothing for the soldiers, and by other outrages not easy to be forgiven. At length they met in their estufa and held an important council, in which, after long deliberation and the consideration of all their wrongs, they concluded that the only course before them was to make war on their oppressors and drive them from the land.

The next morning news came to the Spaniards that the Indians had risen and killed one of their native allies, and were driving off the horses. Pursuit was immediately made, and a few of the animals recovered, but the greater number were lost. Soldiers were sent to several of the neighboring villages, but they everywhere found the houses closed and barricaded, and failed to draw the Indians out from these strongholds. It was evidently an arranged policy to act on the defensive, as by this means they had a large advantage. The General then sent Cardenas with the greater part of the army to lay siege to one of the towns, and bring it to terms. He succeeded in taking the Indians unawares, and gained the tops of the houses before they knew of his approach, but the men then suffered severely from arrows fired from loop-holes in the opposite buildings. The Spaniards maintained themselves in this position all that day and night, and the greater part of the succeeding day, fighting continually; when they were relieved by the strategy of their Indian allies, who dug under-ground passages to some of the houses, and by the aid of certain inflammable materials so filled them with smoke that the inmates were compelled to come out and sue for peace. Pablo Lopez Melgosa and Diego Lopez made the recognized sign of peace in reply, by crossing their hands; whereupon the Indians threw down their arms and surrendered. They were then conducted to the tent of Cardenas, who, it is said, did not know the circumstances of their surrender, but supposed they had been captured without any condition, and thereupon ordered that they should all be burned alive as a warning to the inhabitants of the other towns. Those present who knew that they had surrendered under the promise implied by the sign of peace said nothing, but allowed the horrible preparations to go on in silence. When the Indians saw this, and understood what their fate was to be, they seized pieces of the wood which had been brought for the burning, and attempted to defend themselves; but the soldiers attacked them with their swords, so that of about 100 who had thus surrendered, very few escaped. While this cruel massacre struck terror to the hearts of all who heard of it, yet in other ways it had far from the desired effect. The historian of the expedition evidently appreciated this, as he says, "They made it known throughout all the country that the Spaniards did not regard the compacts to which they had sworn, which did us much harm in the end."

Just at this time the part of the army which had been left at Cibola under Arellano arrived, and never could re-inforcements have been more timely. Simultaneously there commenced a very severe snow-storm, which continued with such violence for the space of two months that it was not possible to undertake any new enterprise. Coronado was specially anxious for peace, in order to pursue his journey, and therefore sent envoys to all the villages, promising pardon and good treatment; but the Indians replied that they could put no trust in people who did not keep their word, and reminded them that they still kept Bigotes as a prisoner, and had broken faith with those who had surrendered. As soon as the weather permitted, hostilities were renewed, and finally the General determined to capture the city of Tiguex itself, as an example to the other towns. He therefore had scaling-ladders prepared, and made all the arrangements possible to insure success, and then with his whole army made a most vigorous assault. But the inhabitants were equally well prepared, and met the assailants with showers of arrows, and with great stones of such weight that they unhorsed many of the Spaniards. The advantage of position was altogether with the Indians, and in a short time Coronado found himself forced to retire with considerable loss. The siege continued for no less than fifty days, the Spaniards showing great gallantry and daring, and the besieged no less courage and endurance. Many assaults were made, but always without success. The Indians lost more than 200 warriors in resisting the various attacks, and several of the most prominent Spaniards perished during the siege. The loss most felt by the latter was that of Captain Francisco de Obando, a distinguished soldier of great popularity among the troops, who was captured and carried alive within the walls. The Indians suffered greatly for want of water, their supply having been cut off, and though they sent their women and children away during a day of truce, yet in the end they found themselves compelled to abandon the place. This they attempted to do secretly at night, but were discovered by a sentinel, and the alarm being given, they were defeated with great slaughter. Those who escaped attempted to cross the river, but the water was so extremely cold that many were drowned; and the few who succeeded in gaining the opposite bank were so benumbed and exhausted that they were easily captured. While this siege was progressing, two of the Spanish captains, Quevara and Saldibar, had been sent to capture another village, and with very similar success; for the inhabitants after a considerable time attempted to leave the place by stealth, but were overtaken and with scarcely an exception killed or taken prisoner; the town being given up to pillage. These two captures occurred just at the end of the year 1541.

While the siege of Tiguex was in progress, Coronado made a trip to Cicuyé in order to regain the friendship of the people of that city. He took with him their cacique, who had been imprisoned for some time—at sight of whom the people greatly rejoiced. The General re-established this old official in his position, and promised that within a short time Bigotes should also be restored to them; and then returned to Tiguex, leaving the people in a most friendly mood. As soon as the siege was terminated, he sent an officer also to Chia (the modern Pueblo of Cia or Zia), a large and populous town four leagues distant, whose people had before sent messengers to present their submission. As a compliment to this town, and a proof of confidence, he left in the custody of its people four bronze cannon, which were not in condition to do service. A small detachment of soldiers was also sent on an expedition to the north, to the province of Quirix, the inhabitants of which at first fled from fear; but being re-assured, returned to their homes.

Meanwhile Coronado was impatiently awaiting the opening of the spring, so that he could proceed on his expedition and reach the wonderful land to the east, of which the Turk gave such glowing descriptions—and especially the great city of Quivira, which that veracious informant said abounded in gold and silver. The season, however, was an unusually severe one, the river (Puerco) remaining frozen for no less than four months, and the ice being thick enough to bear the weight of a horse; but the General did not dare attempt a passage until it had thawed. At length, on the 5th of May (1542), the army broke camp and started on its march trom Tiguex to Cicuyé. Coronado took with him the chief

"Bigotes," and restored him to liberty at the latter town, amid the great rejoicings of the people. Indeed, so pleased were they at the restoration of their favorite that they furnished the whole Spanish army with a bountiful supply of provisions; and the two released prisoners, the cacique and the chief, presented to the General a young man named Xabe, who was a native of Quivira, to act as guide on the expedition. This young man confirmed the statements of the Turk as to the existence of gold and silver in that noted city, but said that the amount was far less than had been stated. But while Coronado seems to have felt implicit confidence in all the stories told by the Turk, many of the Spaniards had begun to distrust him very greatly; and Cervantes, who had the care of him, even asserted that he knew him to have dealings with the devil. He himself, however, never varied in his statements, nor allowed any expressions of incredulity to abate one iota from the extravagant estimates which he gave of the wealth of Quivira and the East.

After a brief stay at Cicuyé the army recommenced its march, and after crossing some mountains, came to a great river, which they called the River of Cicuyé, and which was unquestionably the Rio Grande, or Rio del Norte, of modern times. As this stream was too deep to be forded, the Spaniards were compelled to construct a bridge, which occupied four days; after which the army crossed to the easterly side. The exact locality of this crossing cannot be determined now, but was probably in the vicinity of Santo Domingo, Peña Blanca, or Cochití; that is, a little south of west of Santa Fé. They now marched on over a rugged country, but without special adventures, for ten days; when they came to the camp of some Indians, of a nomadic tribe called Querechos, "who lived like Arabs," and whose tents were made of buffalo-skins. These showed no surprise or timidity at sight of the Spaniards, but cooly came out of their tents to ascertain who they were, and then going directly to the advance guard, asked to see the chief. When brought to Coronado, they showed great intelligence, and expressed themselves so clearly by signs that all that they wished to say could be understood as distinctly as if they had spoken, and there was no need of an interpreter. They reported that far to the east, the expedition would find a very large river, whose length was so great that one could follow its banks for ninety days without leaving an inhabited country. They added that the first village arrived at was named Haxa, and that the river was more than a league wide. They confirmed all that the Turk had told and promised; but as this was not until after they had had a conversation with that worthy, the incredulous among the Spaniards were not much affected thereby. The next morning these Indians broke up their camp and disappeared, carrying all that they possessed on the backs of dogs, of which they had a multitude; but two days afterwards they were again met further out on the prairie.

The army had now reached the great plain east of the mountains, which was covered with such enormous droves of buffaloes that Castañeda says "the number was incredible." When attacked by the soldiers, they would fly in such crowds and confusion that one would fall over another, and thus very many were killed. At one place, while thus running from an attack by horsemen, they came to a great ravine, and not being able to stop in their course, with the multitude in the rear pushing them on, so many fell into the chasm that it was completely filled up, and formed a bridge for the remainder of the frightened herd to cross. The Spanish horsemen who were pursuing came upon this without observing it, and in a moment were entangled in the frenzied and struggling mass. A number of horses were disabled or lost, and the men with difficulty extricated themselves from this novel and unexpected danger.

The plains were perfectly flat and covered with grass, and of such a character that no permanent trail was left even by the passage of the whole army. Monuments of stone had to be raised at frequent intervals in order to guide stragglers, and even with these precautions several soldiers were lost and never returned. The army kept on its march "in the same direction," says Castañeda, "as pursued since leaving Cicuyé—that is to say, towards the north-north-east," daily hoping to see some signs of the town of Haxa, which the Turk assured them was not far distant. Faith in the latter was now greatly diminished in the minds even of the most sanguine, especially as another Indian, named Sopete, who was also a native of the east, gave a very different and far less glowing account of the regions to be found in that direction. In order if possible to get some further information regarding the famous city of Quivira, which was now the special goal of the expedition, Don Rodrigo Maldonado was sent in advance to explore the country. While absent on this excursion, Maldonado came to a great ravine, in which he found a large encampment of Indians, who told him that they had been visited by Cabeza de Vaca and Dorantes on their journey some years before. They brought to Maldonado a great quantity of skins, and presented him with a tent "as large as a house," and many other things. Don Rodrigo sent a messenger to Coronado telling him of the circumstances and urging him to come that way. When the General had arrived and saw the vast quantity of skins, he determined to divide them equally among all the soldiers; but a few having been taken in advance, the men feared that a fair division would not be made, and so made a rush to secure all that they could. A general scramble ensued, and in less than fifteen minutes not a skin remained of the whole store. At this the Indians were amazed, as they had supposed that these white men would simply bless the skins and then restore them, as Cabeza de Vaca had done, and the women and children cried over the loss bitterly.

The part of the plains where the army now was, was well populated; in one place, which they called Cona, they passed an almost continuous succession of cabins or tents for three days. Various fruit-trees and vines were found, including grapes and plums. They passed a number of great ravines or cañons, one of which was a league in width, a little stream running through a fertile valley between the walls. The natives here, with whom the Turk was prevented from communicating, gave a very different account from his of the country beyond, so that Sopete gained in credit while the Turk lost. The Indians were very intelligent and treated their wives with special consideration. The women were well dressed, and wore a mantle or cloak of leather, with neatly ornamented sleeves, over their other clothing.

The army had now marched for thirty-seven days, making six or seven leagues a day; the distance being measured by counting the steps. They calculated that from Tiguex to the last village in the valley of the cañon was 250 leagues. It is to be remembered, however, that all the statements of distance made by the early explorers are greatly overestimated; and also that travelling as Coronado did, over mountains and across plains without any road to guide, the route was often circuitous and far longer than was necessary. As nearly as can be ascertained, the Spaniards were now marching near some of the branches of the Canadian, the large cañons seen corresponding with some of those in North-eastern New Mexico; and this agrees with the general direction of their march, and the ultimate arrival at Quivira. Provisions were beginning to be exhausted, with no prospect of any immediate opportunity to procure new supplies, and altogether the situation was so serious that the General called a council of war to determine the future course of the expedition. After considerable discussion it was determined that Coronado, with thirty horsemen and six soldiers on foot, should proceed with the search for Quivira, and that the rest of the army should return to Tiguex under Tristan de Arellano. This arrangement, however, was far from satisfactory to the soldiers, by whom the General was much beloved, and they besought him not to abandon them, declaring that they were ready to follow him to the ends of the earth, and die with him if necessary. He could not be moved however; but promised to let them know in a week's time whether they could rejoin him.

No delay was now made in setting out. The best mounted and most robust men were selected for the escort, and several Indian guides taken, besides Sopete and the Turk; the latter in chains, as punishment for his willful misrepresentation. They travelled as rapidly as was practicable, but no less than forty-eight days were occupied in crossing the plains to Quivira. "They never lacked for drink," Jaramillo tells us, "marching continually in the midst of cows (buffaloes), whose number constantly increased." Just before arriving at their journey's end they reached and crossed a great river, and Quivira itself seems to have consisted of a succession of towns and villages situated on small streams which ran into this main river. But after all this long journey a great disappointment awaited them; for the inhabitants possessed neither gold nor silver, and indeed had scarcely any knowledge of metals. The Ruler wore on his breast a plate of copper, which he prized very highly; but this was the extent of the existence even of the more common metals. Naturally incensed at the utter falsehood of all the statements of the Turk, the Spaniards asked him as to his motive in thus deceiving them; and he, seeing that there was nothing to be gained by further deception, acknowledged that he had done so at the request of the people of Cicuyé, who wished the strangers to be led astray on the great plains so that their horses would perish, and the soldiers be exhausted by long marches and fatigue, and that thus on their return they could easily be overcome and destroyed. On hearing this, and fearing that if at liberty the Turk might cause new trouble with the people of Quivira, the Spaniards strangled that imposter; to the great satisfaction, we are told, of Sopete.

Coronado seems not to have remained a very long time at Quivira, the object of his present expedition having been simply to find the location of the city and its surroundings with a view of returning with his entire army. He says in his letter or report to the Emperor Charles V. "The inhabitants recognized your majesty, and submitted themselves to the power of their rightful master." At the furthest point that was reached in exploring the city, the General erected a great cross with this inscription: "Francisco Vasquez de Coronado, commander of an expedition, arrived at this place." Castañeda tells us scarcely anything of the city itself, except that the houses were round and without solid walls, that the roofs were made of straw, and that under these the people slept and kept their valuables. Their villages, he says, resembled those of New Spain, and their names and customs were similar to those of the Teyas Indians, who were met on the plains, and at the camp in the wide cañon. The whole surrounding country was well populated, and produced plants and fruits similar to those of Spain; among these were plums, grapes, mulberries, and various grains, together with wild flax. Quivira was surrounded by other populous provinces, but these were not visited. It would be impossible from what is told us by Castañeda alone to fix its location with any certainty. He says it was situated "in the midst of the countries which adjoined the mountains that skirt the sea;" and another illustration of the indefinite geographical ideas entertained at that time is found in the following sentence: "It is in this country that the great river of Espiritu Santo, which Fernando de Soto discovered in Florida, takes its rise; it afterwards passes through a province called Arache. Its sources were not seen; they are very distant and on the slope of the mountain range which borders the plains. It traverses them entirely, as well as the Atlantic range (cordillera de la mer du nord); and its mouth is 300 leagues from the place where De Soto and his comrades embarked." One thing appears distinctly, however, that Quivira was on the edge of the great plain or prairie, that from it the mountains first became visible, and that it was situated on small streams, just east of a great river. Jaramillo, a captain in Coronado's army, describes the houses as follows: "The houses are of straw, very many being circular in shape. The straw reaches almost to the ground, like walls; on the outside on top is a kind of chapel or cupola, having an entrance, where the Indians sit or lie down." This description, together with the direction taken, and the distance travelled, make it almost beyond question that it was the same city of Quivira which Peñalosa crossed the plains to visit 120 years later, and the route followed cannot have been far different. Forty-eight days, march from the cañons of the Canadian would carry Coronado to the Missouri without difficulty, and all things considered, we can well believe that he traversed parts of the Indian Territory and Kansas, and finally stopped on the borders of Missouri, somewhere between Kansas City and Council Bluffs. Of the great country of which this was the key, in the language of Castañeda, "God reserved its discovery for others. He only permitted us to boast of being the first who had any knowledge of it. In the same way Hercules first discovered the place where Cesar was afterwards to found Seville. May the Lord's will be done!"

Meanwhile the main body of the army, which had been left by Coronado in the valley encampment, under Arellano, had returned to Tiguex. They remained for fifteen days at the camp after the General left them, killing vast numbers of buffaloes and losing several of their men, who wandered so far from camp as not to be able to retrace their path; and then having received orders by a messenger from Coronado, commenced their march toward the west. They were fortunate in having better guides than before, and so accomplished in twenty-five days the journey which had occupied thirty-seven in the other direction. The route was more southerly than that by which they went, and passed by a number of salt lakes, which are probably those in the eastern part of Valencia County, bringing them to the Rio Grande River at a point considerably below that at which they had crossed on the bridge, and no doubt somewhere between Albuquerque and Los Lunas. From here they followed the river up to Cicuyé; but finding the natives there indisposed to furnish any provisions, they crossed over to Tiguex, arriving about the middle of July. During their absence the people had begun to return to their homes, but on the re-appearance of the Spaniards, they all abandoned them again; every attempt to inspire new confidence having failed. While waiting here for news from Coronado, Arellano sent exploring parties into different parts of the country for the double purpose of seeking new discoveries and obtaining supplies for the winter. Capt. Francisco de Barrio-Nuevo was sent up the Jemez River as far as the towns of Jemez and Yuqueyunque; and hearing of a large village still higher up, they went on to that and found a very considerable town built on both sides of the river, which was crossed on bridges made of well-squared timber. In this pueblo they found the largest estufas which they had seen, the roofs being supported by large wooden pillars, as much as twelve feet in height. This town was called by the natives Braba, but the Spaniards renamed it Valladolid. Another officer went down the Puerco, and examined that river and the San José, discovering four more towns, and following the Puerco until it sank under-ground, as the Guadiana does in Estramadura.

At length, in August, the General arrived at Cicuyé, having travelled from Quivira by a shorter and better route in forty days; and continued his march to Tiguex, where he expected to recuperate his army during the winter, and then undertake a new expedition to the regions of Quivira and even beyond, in the spring. Soon after his arrival, Don Pedro de Tobar came into camp with the expected re-inforcements from San Geronimo. They came with high expectations of joining in the conquest of a land rich in gold and silver, and were much disappointed at the news which awaited them. However, they became reconciled when told of the great expedition planned for the next spring. Through the fall and winter Coronado busied himself in endeavoring to re-establish friendly relations with the people of Tiguex, Cicuyé, and the surrounding country, and in re-organizing his army for the spring campaign. The soldiers were in wretched condition from their long and arduous marches, and their clothes were literally in tatters; and the General used every exertion to procure cotton stuffs from the natives with which to furnish new suits to his men. His attention to their comfort made him the idol of the soldiers. "Never was a general more beloved and better obeyed," says Castañeda. This very attention to the wants of the privates caused dissensions between himself and his officers, who were too apt to show favoritism and to place additional burdens on those whom they did not like; and once or twice these difficulties became so annoying that the general threatened to abandon the expedition.

But when the spring came, all thoughts were turned towards the new discoveries and conquests that were projected. Orders were issued for the army to be in immediate readiness to march. But just at this moment occurred an accident which changed somewhat the course of history. On a festival day, when various athletic and martial sports were indulged in, Coronado was showing his expertness in the favorite game of running at a ring, and was accompanied by Don Pedro Maldonado. While his horse was running at full speed, the saddle-girth broke, and the General was precipitated to the ground in front of the horse of Don Pedro; and the latter, in trying to spring over him, gave him a violent kick on the head, which came near proving fatal, and confined him to his bed for a long time. This, of course, put a stop to all preparations for the advance, and caused a feeling of despondency among the soldiers. Coronado's own anxiety was added to by bad news from a part of his army left near the Sonora frontier; and he began to wish that he was at home, to suffer, and if need be to die, in the midst of his own family. Many of the officers for various reasons were anxious to return to Mexico, and they obtained a petition from the soldiers asking an abandonment of the expedition. On receiving this, the General called a council of his officers, which decided that, as they had failed to find any treasures, or even a country fertile enough to be divided among the soldiers, it would be best to return; and new orders were immediately issued to prepare for the march. But no sooner was this determined than the soldiers repented of their action, and begged to have the order revoked. But Coronado would not accede to this, and to avoid importunity, shut himself up in a house, with sentinels at the door. A number of the officers also regretted the action, on second thought, and proposed to the General, either to leave them sixty soldiers, with which small number they engaged to hold the country until re-inforcement came; or for him to take sixty men himself as an escort, leaving the remainder of the army under a new commander, who could prosecute the explorations and conquest. But the soldiers objected to this separation, and so nothing was done.

At last the day of departure arrived, and the army set out on its return march, in the beginning of April, 1543. Two of the missionaries, however, expressed their desire to remain, Juan de Padilla, a Franciscan, who desired to travel to Quivira, and Luis, a lay brother, who wished to stay at Cicuyé. They were both pious men, and full of zeal in the work of propagating the faith, and could not bear to leave this great country devoid of any Christian teaching. They were sent under an escort to Cicuyé, and from there Friar Juan, accompanied by a Portuguese, a negro, and some Mexican Indians, proceeded to Quivira, where he was martyred before even entering the town. Friar Luis was last seen by some soldiers who were sent to him with sheep by Coronado, on his way to visit a settlement some dozen miles from Cicuyé. Let us hope that the good wishes of the early historian were verified in his case. "He was a man of good and holy life," says Castañeda; "I hope that our Lord graciously permitted him to convert some of those nations, and that he ended his days in feeding his spiritual flock."

On the homeward march scarcely anything occurred worthy of special mention. The troops rested for a few days at Cibola, and several of the Mexican Indians concluded to remain there and make it their home. At Chichilticale they met Juan Gallegos with re-inforcements and munitions, and again the plan of returning to Quivira was agitated; but nothing could be accomplished. As the army neared the settlements of New Spain, discipline became relaxed, and the authority of the General much impaired. After passing Culiacan it was difficult to keep the soldiers together at all; desertions were constant, and when Coronado arrived at the City of Mexico, he could barely muster 100 men. He was coldly received by the Viceroy, who was bitterly disappointed at the result of the expedition; but yet was given a regular discharge. He had lost his high reputation as a soldier, however, and soon after was deprived of his Governorship. Thus ended this expedition, which, though barren of results at the time, will never fail to be of interest as giving to us the first accurate account of the towns and the people of New Mexico.

It seems proper, before leaving the history of this expedition, to give a description of one of the Pueblo towns of that day, as stated by Castañeda. He describes a number of them in his narrative—particularly Cibola, Tiguex, and Cicuyé; but the account given of the second seems to contain the most of interest. These descriptions are specially valuable in order to compare the manners and customs of these people nearly three centuries and a half ago with those of their descendants that exist to-day. Speaking of the towns in the Province of Tiguex, he says: "The houses are built in common. The women mix the mortar and build the walls. The men bring the wood and construct the frames. They have no lime, but they make a mixture of ashes, earth, and charcoal, which takes its place very well; for although they build their houses four stories high, the walls are not more than three feet thick. The young men who are not yet married serve the public in general. They go after fire-wood, and pile it up in the court or plaza, where the women go to get it for the use of their houses. They live in the estufas, which are under-ground in the plazas of the villages; and of which some are square and some are round. The roofs are supported by pillars made of the trunks of pine-trees. I have seen some with twelve pillars, each of twelve feet in circumference; but usually they have only four pillars. They are paved with large polished stones, like the baths of Europe. In the center is a fire-place, with a fire burning therein, on which they throw from time to time a handful of sage, which suffices to keep up the heat, so that one is kept as if in a bath. The roof is on a level with the ground. Some of these estufas are as large as a tennis-court. When a young man marries, it is by order of the aged men who govern. He has to spin and weave a mantle; they then bring the young girl to him, he covers her shoulders with it, and she becomes his wife. The houses belong to the women, and the estufas to the men. The women are forbidden to sleep in them, or even to enter, except to bring food to their husbands or sons. The men spin and weave; the women take care of the children and cook the food. The soil is so fertile that it does not need to be worked when they sow; the snow, falling, covers the seed, and the corn starts underneath. The harvest of one year is sufficient for seven. When they begin to sow, the fields are still covered with corn that has not yet been gathered. Their villages are very neat; the houses are well distributed, and kept in good order; one room is devoted to cooking, and another to grinding grain. The latter is apart, and contains a fire-place, and three stones set in masonry; three women sit down before the stones; the first breaks the grain, the second crushes it, and the third grinds it entirely to powder. In all the province glazed pottery abounded; and the vases were of really curious form and workmanship." The buildings at Cicuyé were described as follows: "The town is built in a square, around a plaza in the center, in which were the estufas. The houses are four stories high; the roofs arranged in terraces, all of the same height, so that the people could make a tour of the whole town without having to cross a single street. To the first two stories there is a corridor in the form of a balcony, which also passes completely around the town, and under which was a pleasant place to sit in the shade. The houses have no doors below, but were entered by movable ladders which reached to the balconies on the inside of the square."

CHAPTER VI.

THE EXPEDITION OF FRIAR RUIZ.

AFTER the unsuccessful expedition of Coronado, no further attempts were made to penetrate into New Mexico for many years. So many discoveries were being made in Central and South America, of new lands which promised rich returns to the explorer or conqueror, that the adventurous spirits of the time found ample field for the exercise of their enterprise and prowess without returning to any region which had already been the scene of failure. When we consider how remote the Land of the Seven Cities was from the City of Mexico, we may well be surprised, not at the lapse of time between expeditions for its exploration, conversion, or conquest, but that within so few years after the fall of Montezuma it should have been reached at all. Compared with the slow advance of the English colonists on the Atlantic coast towards the Mississippi Valley and the interior of the continent, the swiftness with which the adventurous cavaliers of Spain penetrated to the upper Rio Grande is a marvel. There are traditions and some vague written accounts of missionary journeys made by zealous monks who passed the boundaries of New Mexico in the interval, but nothing of certainty or importance until the coming of Friar Ruiz, forty years after the departure of Coronado.

In the year 1581 Agustin Ruiz, a Franciscan Friar, living at San Bartolomé, in north-eastern Mexico, heard from certain Indians who came from the country around the Concho River, that far to the north there were several large and rich provinces which the Spaniards had never visited. So much was said as to the importance and population of this unknown country that Ruiz was much interested, and finally determined, if possible, to penetrate that region and carry a knowledge of Christianity to the thousands who were then living in heathenism. With this view he made application for permission to undertake the enterprise to both the civil and ecclesiastical authorities, and this having been granted, he lost no time in arranging to start on his benevolent mission. Two other Franciscans, named Francisco Lopez and Juan de Santa Maria, accompanied him, and they had as an escort a squad of twelve soldiers under command of a captain, these last being also directed to make diligent inquiries for any mines that might be near their line of march. All things being prepared, they started toward the north, and after a march of about 500 miles, arrived among the Pueblo villages on the Rio Grande, and continued up the valley of that river until they reached the town of Puara, long since destroyed, but which then stood about eight miles north of the site of Albuquerque. Here the soldiers became alarmed at their position in the midst of such a large native population, and at so great a distance from support or succor, and refused to go any further;—indeed, they insisted on an immediate return to Mexico. The Franciscans endeavored to persuade them to go on, but without effect; and the soldiers in turn tried to induce the Friars to go back with them, but they were equally determined. So they separated; the soldiers of the king returned to the ease and security of their garrison life, and the soldiers of the ɔss went forward, braving hardships, and danger, and death, to carry the words of salvation to the heathen nations around.

The Friars went as far as the Galisteo River, where there was an important pueblo, being everywhere received with welcome and hospitality; and then concluded, as the country was so inviting and the people so ready to receive instruction, to send one of their number back to Mexico in order to bring more of the brethren, and thus enable the work to go on with greater efficiency. Brother Juan de Santa Maria volunteered to undertake the journey, and the other two brethren returned to Puara, as the best point at which to learn the Indian languages. Friar Juan crossed the Sandia Mountains with the intention of proceeding directly south to El Paso from the Salt Lakes, that being a preferable route to the one by the river; but on the third day, when near the pueblo of San Pablo, and while resting under a tree, he was killed by some Indians, who afterwards burned his remains. The two other Friars pursued their studies and missionary labors at Puara, until Lopez likewise fell a victim to the hatred of some of the natives, being killed by a blow on the head while engaged in prayer, in a secluded spot a short distance from the village. No doubt it had been determined by some of those in authority that the missionaries should be destroyed, for their lives were blameless and they had no enemies; and the fate of these Franciscans brings to mind the last words which Brother Luis was heard to utter not quite forty years before, and but a few miles distant up the Jemez River; that "all the Indians treated him kindly, with the exception of the old men, who disliked him and would probably cause him to be put to death."

Friar Ruiz was now all alone. He succeeded in recovering the body of his murdered companion, and gave it Christian burial at the pueblo; but the loss was a severe blow to him, and he felt keenly his isolation and the danger in which he lived. Still he resolutely determined to remain at his post as long as life lasted. The Friar had a faithful friend in the war-captain of the pueblo; and he, knowing that the death of all three of the missionaries had been decreed, endeavored to save Ruiz by removing him to the Pueblo of Santiago, about four miles further up the Rio Grande. But the effort was vain, for within a few days he likewise met a martyr's fate, and his body was thrown into the river as food for fishes. Thus ended the lives of these three devoted men, who came to christianize a great province, and were destroyed before they had really begun the work. But their labor was not in vain, for as will soon appear, as a consequence of their expedition, followed an almost immediate permanent colonization of the country; and the proverb that "the blood of the martyrs is the seed of the church" was illustrated in the baptism, within fifty years, of over 34,000 Indians, and the erection, by the Brethren of the Franciscan Order, of no less than forty-three churches in New Mexico.

The soldiers who returned to Mexico from Puara, arrived in safety at San Bartolomé, and reported the situation in which the three Friars had been left by them. This caused much anxiety among the Franciscans generally, and they endeavored to have relief sent to their brethren. Their appeals at length touched the heart of Don Antonio de Espejo, a wealthy Spanish cavalier, then engaged in the mines at Santa Barbara; who offered his services and fortune for the work, if proper authority could be obtained for the expedition. This was soon arranged, Governor Ontrueros, of New Biscay, granting the permission, which included the right to enlist as many soldiers as were thought necessary for the success of the project.

CHAPTER VII.

THE EXPEDITION OF ESPEJO.

DON ANTONIO DE ESPEJO having received the proper authorization from the Governor of New Biscay, lost no time in making arrangements for the proposed expedition to carry relief to the Franciscan missionaries in New Mexico. He was a man of great energy and large resources, and possessed the confidence of the people so fully that soldiers hastened to enlist under his banner; so that in a very short time all the men required had been enrolled, and the necessary stores and munitions were in readiness. Besides the little company which he was to command, he took with him a considerable number of Indians to perform the more laborious duties of the march, and over 100 extra horses and mules to be used in case of necessity. The expedition set out from the valley of San Bartolomé, on the 10th of December, 1582, marching directly northward toward New Mexico. The first tribe that they encountered was the Conchos, living in the valley of the Concho River, in what is now the State of Chihuahua. These people extended a friendly welcome, and their chiefs sent a messenger ahead from town to town so that the inhabitants should be ready to receive the Spaniards. Two other tribes, known as the Passaguates and the Tobosos, were passed through before the expedition reached the banks of the Rio Grande. All of these Indians lived in rude villages of houses covered with straw. They raised corn and melons, and obtained a good deal of game, especially bears, and also excellent fish from the Concho and other streams. In war and in the chase they used bows and arrows; and their government was of a simple kind, under chiefs or caciques.

It was not until the valley of the Rio Grande was reached that a higher grade of civilization was encountered. Here Espejo found an extensive and populous province, called by the natives Humanos, containing a number of large towns of superior construction. The houses were built of stone, cemented with lime-mortar, and covered by flat roofs. The inhabitants were of large stature and war-like disposition, and the first night that the Spaniards came among them, they attacked the camp and killed several horses. This was probably on account of injuries inflicted by previous expeditions of Europeans; for on being assured that Espejo meant them no harm, and was only passing through their country, they expressed entire satisfaction, and afforded him considerable assistance. This nation was so extensive that the Spaniards were twelve days in traversing their country; but after the first difficulty, they were everywhere well received, and treated with great hospitality — the Indians not only supplying them with all the provisions necessary, but bringing presents of hides and chamois-skins, as well dressed as those of Flanders. Many of the people brought their wives and children to the priests that they might bless them, and in other ways showed that they had a vague knowledge of Christianity; and on being asked how this had been obtained, it appeared that this was one of the tribes visited by Cabeza de Vaca nearly fifty years before; for they answered that they had been taught by three white men and a negro, who had passed that way, and had remained a number of days among them

Several days' journey further up the river, Espejo came to another large and populous province; the inhabitants of which were dressed in well-tanned chamois-skins, and had many beautifully-made feather ornaments, and striped cotton stuffs, which they offered in trade for the trinkets of the Spaniards. Beyond this, was another province still more important, where Espejo stopped for three days, while the Indians held a continual festival—performing dances and other ceremonials in manifestation of their joy. The Spaniards then came to a long stretch of uninhabited country, covered with piñon-trees, and which occupied fifteen days of their journey; at the end of which they found a few small houses roofed with straw. About thirty miles above this they began to see some more important towns; and found the river bordered with cottonwoods and walnuts, the timber being in some places as much as ten miles wide. After being for two days in these groves, the expedition arrived at a province containing ten towns, situated in the valley of the Rio Grande, and on both sides of the river. The houses here were four stories high, and well constructed; and the people much more civilized than those below. They wore clothing of cotton and deer-skins—and what was the cause of much surprise, boots and shoes, with soles made of the strongest and best leather. They were idolaters—having images which they worshiped, although the chief objects of their adoration were the sun and heavenly bodies; and besides public chapels, which were handsomely painted and ornamented, each residence had an oratory for the private worship of its own household. The people were industrious and thrifty. One chief gave Espejo no less than 4,000 bolls of cotton. Apparently they had not been visited by any expedition before, as they had never seen horses; and at first sight were inclined to treat them as superior beings. This province was situated a short distance below Albuquerque, in the vicinity of the Pueblo of Isleta, which may be identical with one of the towns.

After remaining here for four days the Spaniards resumed their march, and in a short time came to the first of the towns of the Tegua nation, which was within a few miles of Puara, the scene of the labors and martyrdom of the Franciscan missionaries. Here for the first time they received news of the death of the Friars, and were greatly disheartened to find that they had arrived too late to be of service in protecting them. About the same time the people of Puara heard that an army of Spaniards was approaching, and supposing that they had come to avenge the death of the priests, they deserted their homes and fled into the mountains. With the news of the martyrdom of the Franciscans, the avowed object of the expedition was at an end. A consultation was therefore held to determine on the course to be adopted, and after some discussion it was decided that the surrounding country should be visited, as many flattering accounts were heard of its richness and the wealth of its cities. The first expedition was made by Espejo himself, with only two men, who travelled west for two days and visited a province containing eleven towns and estimated to have 40,000 inhabitants, which lay in the direction of Cibola. The people lived comfortably, having great herds of cattle, and raising cotton and many articles of food. The Spaniards also found that the wealthier classes had considerable silver and gold in their houses. They were well received by the natives, who welcomed them both in words and more substantially with supplies of provisions.

This encouraged Espejo to undertake a far more important expedition. He proceeded up the river to the province of the Queres, where he found five towns, and estimated the people at 14,000. Continuing to march north, the next province reached was one called Cunames, which also contained five towns—Zia being the most important. This town at that time contained eight market-places or plazas, and the houses were the best that the Spaniards had seen, being plastered and painted many colors. In all respects the people were well advanced in civilization, and among other manufactures had beautiful and curious mantles, some of which they presented to the Spaniards. Turning westerly, Espejo next visited a neighboring people called Amies, who numbered about 30,000 and lived in seven towns, which were similar to those of Cunames. Continuing on fifteen leagues further, he came to Acoma, the situation of which on the summit of its high rock particularly impressed the Spaniards. All along their route the people had received them most hospitably; but Acoma exceeded all others in this respect, the officials bringing various presents, and the inhabitants in general endeavoring to entertain them with characteristic games and dances, which occupied three days.

From here Espejo marched directly west to Zuñi, where he found, still living, three of the Mexican Indians who had accompanied Coronado, and who on the return march had concluded to remain at Cibola. Their names were Andrew, of Culiacan, Gaspar, of Mexico, and Antonio, of Guadalajara. They had been so long (forty years) among the Cibolans that they had nearly entirely forgotten their original language; but their meeting with the new expedition of Spaniards was a most interesting one. Among other things they gave Espejo information of a rich and populous country to the westward, which bordered on a great lake, and in which the precious metals abounded. They said that Coronado had endeavored to reach it, but had been forced to turn back for want of water. Espejo was not to be deterred by the ill success of his predecessor, and so, taking but nine soldiers with him, and leaving the remainder of the army at Cibola, he started on the march. At a distance of twenty-eight leagues he came to the most populous province which he had yet visited, as he estimated its inhabitants at 50,000, and which was no doubt the modern Moqui. Here the chiefs, pursuing somewhat the same course which they adopted in the time of Coronado, warned the Spaniards not to approach their towns under penalty of death; but after being assured that the visit was altogether friendly and pacific, this policy was entirely changed, and they were not only allowed to enter, but received with special honor. No less than 2,000 natives came out from the first town to welcome the strangers, and exchanges of presents of all kinds took place, the festivities continuing a number of days.

But Espejo was anxious to visit the mining district near the great lake of which he had been told, and so taking fresh guides he set out again to the westward, and penetrated the country for forty-five leagues, until he came to a mine containing a vein of silver of great width, from which he took a number of rich specimens with his own hands. This was situated in a mountainous region, beyond which the Indians said was a mighty river, whose width—in their usual style of exaggeration—they stated to be eight leagues! This was no doubt the Colorado; but the constant allusions to the "Great Lake" it is difficult to explain, as there is now no large body of water in that region. Whether it existed only in the imagination of the natives, or whether at that time there really was an inland sea in some of the depressed portions of Arizona, we shall probably never know. It is to be observed, however, that Espejo did not see the lake, and none of the other early travellers allude to it.

Satisfied now of the mineral wealth of the country, the commander returned to Zuñi, where he found his army in good health and spirits, the natives having treated them with great kindness and generosity. The conduct of the troops had also been without reproach, so that when they set out on their homeward march, the Indians not only expressed great regret, but urged them to return and bring other Spaniards with them. Returning once more to the valley of the Rio Grande, the main body of the army marched south to Mexico, leaving Espejo with a small number of chosen companions to prosecute his explorations. This time he went to the northeast, and found a province containing a population of about 25,000 people, living in a mountainous country covered with pines, or piñons, and in which mines abounded. It is impossible now to fix with precision the location of this province, as we do not know the point from which the explorer started on this last expedition; but it is not unlikely that it included the Placer mountains, with possibly the Cerrillos to the north, and part of the Sandias to the south. Unfortunately the narrative does not even state what kind of mines they were that were thus abundant. From this point Espejo continued his march to another province of which he heard, which was said to contain about 40,000 people, called Taños, But here, contrary to the pleasant experience he had heretofore enjoyed, the Indians refused to allow him to enter a town, or to supply him with any provisions.

This cold reception seems to have discouraged him, or at all events led him to realize how powerless he would be with his handful of followers in the midst of populous Indian nations, should they for any reason become hostile. So he determined to return to Mexico, well satisfied however that the country was far too rich and inviting to be neglected in the future. He started early in July, 1584, and by the advice of guides took the homeward route by the Pecos, instead of the Rio Grande, finding in its valley the same great herds of buffaloes which had before given to it the name of the "Rio de las Vacas." He followed the Pecos Valley down into what is now north-western Texas, and crossed the Rio Grande to the Conchos, and so on to New Biscay; whence he sent a full account of his discoveries and adventures to the Spanish court. The reports brought back by the members of the expedition spread throughout the country, and aroused a new and strong interest in the settlement of the regions to the north, which soon developed itself in more important enterprises and the permanent colonization of the country.

CHAPTER VIII.

COLONIZATION UNDER OÑATE.

THE first result of the reports of the mineral riches of New Mexico, brought by the members of Espejo's expedition, was the departure of a small party, under a leader named Humaña, to search for gold in the New El Dorado. Nothing of permanent interest, however, was accomplished by them, for after exploring part of the country east of the Rio Grande, their captain and all but three of the men engaged in the expedition were killed by the Indians. Oñate, when he marched through the country a short time afterwards, saw two of the survivors, a Mexican Indian, called José, and a mulatto girl; and the third remained with the New Mexican Indians, adopting their habits and manners, and being at length elevated to the dignity of a chief. The time was about to arrive, however, when a settlement on a larger scale and of greater permanence than any which had preceded it was to take place; and this, also, was the direct result of the favorable accounts which were brought back to Mexico by Espejo and his companions.

Don Juan de Oñate was a wealthy and influential citizen of Zacatecas, in which city he was born; and his ambition was strongly excited by the opportunities of great riches and aggrandizement which were presented by the reports brought from the almost unknown country to the north. He made a formal application to the Viceroy of New Spain, Don Luis de Velasco, for authority to colonize New Mexico, offering to undertake the work with at least 200 soldiers, and with all the animals, tools, goods, and appliances necessary to make it a success. In return of course he asked for the usual rewards of discoverers and colonizers—authority, nobility, and wealth in lands and money. The Viceroy, after due consideration, granted the authority applied for, so far as the colonization was concerned, and also most of the attendant requests of Oñate, on the condition, however, that the country should be conquered, pacified, and colonized within five years; and this grant was afterwards confirmed by the king of Spain, in very ample form, in a decree dated July 8, 1602. Oñate did not wait, however, for this confirmation, but with characteristic energy made preparations for the work the moment he had secured this permission of the Viceroy. Like almost all enterprises of importance, this encountered opposition from various sources, which it required considerable time to overcome; and the delay added greatly to the expense, as a large number of those who originally enlisted became discouraged and returned to their homes before the preparations were fairly concluded. The expedition, as finally constituted, consisted of over 700 soldiers and 130 families for colonization, the latter carrying everything with them requisite for permanent settlement. Ten Friars of the Franciscan order accompanied the party, which consisted at its start of about 1,250 persons; but after the march commenced and they began to appreciate the real hardships to be endured, while the glamour of romance gradually disappeared, desertions became numerous, so that when New Mexico was actually reached, scarcely more than half the original company remained; the desertions, however, being mainly among the troops, and not materially affecting the families.

The expedition set out in 1591, and proceeded northerly through the present States of Durango and Chihuahua until it reached the Rio Grande, and then marched up the valley of that river much as Espejo had done, encountering the same native nations and being uniformly well treated, until it arrived at a point further north than any to which its predecessors had penetrated, and finally selected as the center of the future colony the sheltered valley on the north side of the Chama, just above its junction with the Rio Grande, thus affording protection to the settlement of all of the fertile valleys which extend north, west, and south. The new town they called the City of New Mexico; and while it never grew to any great importance, and was outstripped in its growth by many places afterwards established, yet its site will never cease to be of interest to New Mexicans. Near by, at San Yldefonso, was founded the first permanent "convento" of the Franciscan fathers, which for a considerable time was the center of their missionary activity and enterprise. The Indians in the vicinity of the new town were kind and disposed to welcome the new-comers, whom they assisted very materially in the building of their houses. They lived as did those previously described, in villages or community houses several stories in height, built around squares and containing many rooms; their food consisted principally of the beans, corn, and pumpkins which they raised, together with the products of the chase, and the fish of the Rio Grande and its branches; and they were comfortably and indeed becomingly dressed in the tanned skins of buffaloes and smaller annimals, and in fabrics of cotton of their own raising and manufacture, ornamented with feathers of the wild turkey and other birds.

As in all other colonies, the first season was one of difficulty and privation. Houses had to be built, the virgin soil broken up for future planting, and many kinds of arduous labor encountered; but the land was fertile, the climate unsurpassed, and in much of the heaviest work they had the assistance of the natives, so that before very long contentment and prosperity prevailed. In the meantime, however, some had become discouraged; those who had come expecting to find a land where riches were to be obtained without labor were dissatisfied, and so a considerable number, especially of the soldiers, took such opportunities as were presented for returning to Mexico, where they spread reports of the barrenness and poverty of the country and the failure of the attempts at settlement.

As soon as the necessary means of livelihood were assured, by the building of houses and planting of fields, the Spaniards commenced extensive explorations for the precious metals, which had been a leading object of their coming. Mines were soon found in very many parts of the country, and in nearly every locality where they are now known, so wide-spread was the rude "prospecting" of those days. Gold or silver was discovered—the former sometimes in veins and sometimes in gravel—from Socorro on the south to the Picuris Mountains on the north, including the Sandias, the Placers, the Cerrillos, etc., and also to the west in the mountains of Jemez. A little later they extended the area of mineral discovery and development even further north, as the shafts of their ancient mines are found as far up as the Rio Hondo and Colorado in New Mexico, and even between the Culebra and Trinchera in southern Colorado.

Settlements were rapidly made in various parts of the country, fresh immigrants following those who composed the first expedition, and no opposition to their settlement being manifested by the resident natives. As soon as Oñate could leave the central town on the Chama, with safety, he undertook a series of peaceful expeditions to the various Indian nations, with the view of obtaining accurate information as to their character and numbers, and also to insure amicable relations with them, and as far as possible to introduce Christian missionaries into their chief towns. After visiting most of the tribes of the Rio Grande Valley and its vicinity, he attempted a more ambitious journey, evidently wishing to emulate the example of Coronado, and resolved to cross the plains to the great city of Quivira, which, perhaps on account of its very distance and inaccessibility, seems to have filled the minds of all the early Spanish adventurers, for over a century, with the most romantic ideas. This expedition set out in the year 1599, and consisted of eighty soldiers, accompanied by two Friars named Francisco de Velasco and Pedro de Vergara, for spiritual duties, and as a guide by José, the Mexican Indian, previously mentioned as escaping from the ill-starred party of Humaña, and who was found by the later Spaniards at the Pueblo of Picuris They marched as Coronado had done more than half a century before, and as Peñalosa was to do more than an equal period afterward, over the great buffalo-plains towards the east; finding the same bright, clear atmosphere, the same unvarying prairie, the same grapes and plums, the same enormous herds of buffaloes, and the same wandering tribes of Indians, which had no doubt been there from time immemorial. After travelling over 200 leagues, and just before reaching the settlement of Quivira, they met, as did Peañlosa, a tribe called Escansaques, on their way to make their annual foray into the cultivated country of the Quivirans, with whom they were in a state of perpetual war. Some difficulty arose between the Spaniards and this marauding tribe, which resulted in a serious battle, in which we are told a thousand of the Indians were slain; "a thousand" probably being a figure of speech, considered allowable when treating of expeditions to such far distant dominions; the old chronicler also giving as a reason for this destruction, a pious desire on the part of the Franciscan Commissary to teach the Escansaques a lesson of peace and honesty, which would lead them to abandon their attacks upon Quivira. However this may be, Oñate very soon approached the wonderful City of the East, which was situated on the further bank of a river; and after some negociations, a treaty of perpetual peace and friendship was concluded between the Spaniards and Quivirans. The country was found to be thickly settled, great numbers of villages being seen; and the people said that to the north it was even more densely populated. As in the days of Coronado, no silver nor gold was seen; but reports were heard that the precious metals were plentiful in the interior. Satisfied with the result of his journey, Oñate returned to New Mexico; and a few years after, in 1606, a party of no less than 800 Quivira Indians came to Santa Fé to ask aid in their war with the Axtaos, which was then being fiercely waged. They gave glowing accounts of the wealth of their ememies, as an incentive to action on the part of the Spaniards; but nothing resulted from it, except that they left with Oñate an Axtao prisoner, who was in their hands, who was subsequently baptized by the name of Miguel, taken to Spain by Don Vicente De Saldivar, and presented to the king, attracting great attention wherever he went.

For several years the Governor continued with a rare combination of energy and prudence to establish new settlements and strengthen those already existing; at the same time conciliating the natives, and preventing, during the period of his authority, any hostilities on the part of either race. He explored all parts of the country, and in 1611 made another trip to the eastward, discovering the Cannibal Lakes, which cannot well be identified at this day, and the deep cañon of the Canadian River, which was appropriately called the "Palisade."

CHAPTER IX.

THE PERIOD FROM 1600 TO 1680.

THE period between the permanent settlement of New Mexico by Europeans, under Oñate, at the end of the sixteenth century, and the revolution of 1680, presents a few salient features which are illustrated by a multitude of lesser occurrences. The principal events of a general character were the increase and extension of the Spanish settlements, the introduction and propagation of Christianity among the natives, the establishment and development of mining as an important industry, and the constantly growing feeling of alienation and hatred on the part of the Pueblo Indians. Each of these had relation more or less to the others, so that they cannot well be treated separately; and in any event, our knowledge of the history of those times is imperfect and fragmentary, as all of the regular records were destroyed during the years of Pueblo supremacy which succeeded. After the successful establishment of the first colonies on the Upper Rio Grande, Spanish communities quickly grew up in all the more accessible parts of the Territory, sometimes in connection with the native Pueblos, and sometimes as independent settlements. Santa Fé, from its central position, between the upper and lower valleys, and on account in part, no doubt, of the charm of its situation and climate, early became the most important of the Spanish towns and the seat of highest authority. It is very likely that Oñate himself transferred his residence there from the banks of the Chama; and, at all events, it is certain that his immediate successors made it the Capital, and that the palace was built at a very early day. It was the long established seat of power when Peñalosa confined the Chief Inquisitor within its walls, in 1663, and when the Pueblo authorities took possession of it as the citadel of their central authority, in 1681.

The Spanish settlers naturally found homes in the fertile and beautiful valley of the Rio Grande, and did not attempt to establish many towns far beyond the mountains which marked its boundaries on either hand; but the zealous missionaries of the Christian faith were not confined within any such narrow limits. As we have seen, ten Friars accompanied Oñate on his first expedition into the country, and their number was frequently increased from time to time by the arrival of new brothers from Mexico and Spain—all being of the order of St. Francis. Their first missionary station after San Yldefonso, was established at a place in the territory of the Tegua nation, and probably at one of their principal pueblos, hence called in the early records "El Teguayo," and which has by many been considered identical with Santa Fé. A strong probability is lent to this from the propriety with which the name of the "La Ciudad de la Santa Fé de San Francisco," "the city of the holy faith of St. Francis," would have been given to the point selected for the earliest settled missionary effort of the Franciscan Fathers. The missionaries traversed the country in all directions, priests were stationed at all the principal villages, and churches erected as rapidly as possible at the important points. As early as 1608 it was reported that at least 8,000 Indians had been baptized. Twenty-one years later the number had increased to 34,650; and not less than forty churches had been built for the performance of the ceremonies of the Roman Church. The most celebrated of the monks who devoted himself to the missionary work during the intervening period was Geronimo de Zarate Salmaron, who established himself at Jemez; and from the facility that he acquired in the use of the languages of the people, preached with such success that he alone baptized no less than 6,566 Indians at that pueblo, besides extending his ministrations to the neighboring pueblos of Zia and Santa Ana, and accomplishing the pacification of Acoma, which until that time had refused to hold any friendly intercourse with the Spaniards.

But as time passed and the colonists became stronger, the priests resorted to other means than by pious example and persuasion to bring converts to the Christian faith. Men whose zeal far outran their discretion took part in the work, and the spirit of persecution then dominant in Europe began to exert its baneful influence among the peaceful and kind-hearted natives of New Mexico. Many of these were naturally attached to the religion of their fathers, in which generation after generation of the people had been educated, and which had become almost a part of their nature. They were evidently a religious people, as Espejo found images and altars in almos every house The estufas were the scenes of their more public ceremonies, and they had priests whom they revered as having special intercourse with the Higher Power. Religious rites were of frequent observance among them, and the "cachina," their favorite dance, had a connection with supernatural things. The great object of their worship undoubtedly was the sun, and around it, according to their crude and superstitious creed, were various lesser powers, which ruled over special subjects, and were the objects of a kind of adoration, and certainly of fear. But while thus far from the truth, their religion was intended to make them better and nobler, and did not call for human sacrifices or the perpetration of any kind of outrage or cruelty. When Christianity was introduced as a religion of benevolence and of blessing, as by Cabeza de Vaca, who taught a few of the essentials of the faith, ministered to the sick, and blessed the skins brought by the people among whom he sojourned; or by the first Friars, who sought by good counsel and holy lives to conciliate and win the hearts of the natives—it gained their affection as well as their respect; but afterwards the "zeal without knowledge" of the ecclesiastical rulers led to unfortunate results   They endeavored to convert by force, instead of by love and persuasion. The ancient rites were prohibited under severe penalties, the old images were torn down, sacred places destroyed, estufas closed, and the "cachinas" and all similar semi-religious ceremonies and festivities forbidden. They were compelled to an outward compliance with the rules and participation in the rites of the Roman Church. They had to attend its services, to submit to baptism, to support its priests, and subject themselves to its authority, whether they really understood and believed its teaching or not. The Inquisition was introduced, and soon became the dominant power in the territory, forcing even the highest civil officers to do its bidding, or subjecting them to removal, disgrace, and punishment, if they dared to exercise independence in their action, or attempted to interfere with the arbitrary and often cruel edicts of its imperious representatives. A conspicuous instance of this is found in the removal of two successive Governors (Mendizaval and Peñalosa) by its influence in 1660 and 1664.

The Spaniards who came at first as friends and were eager to have the good-will and assistance of the intelligent natives, soon began to claim superiority and to insist on the performance of services which originally were mere evidences of hospitality and kindness. Little by little they assumed greater power and control over the Indians, until in the course of years they had subjected a large portion of them to servitude little differing from actual slavery. The Spanish courts assumed jurisdiction over the whole territory, and imposed severe punishment on the Indians for the violation of any of their laws — civil or ecclesiastical; introducing an entirely new criminal system, unknown and certainly undesired by the natives. For slight infractions of edicts of which they were often ignorant, men and women were whipped or condemned to be sold into slavery; the latter punishment being encouraged, because it provided the labor of which the Spaniards stood in need. The introduction of mining, and its rapid extension all over the territory, aggravated their hardships; for the labor, which was exceedingly dangerous, as well as toilsome, was performed almost entirely by Indians forced to work under the direction of unfeeling task-masters. Under all these circumstances the kind-hearted and peace-loving Pueblos, who had lived for generations an easy life of independence and happiness, until the coming of these strangers from the south, naturally changed in their feelings from welcome and hospitality to an intense hatred and a determination to repel the intruders whenever an opportunity should present itself. It was not to be supposed that the stronger communities, populous and well governed, should succumb without a struggle to the tyranny of the new-comers.

The middle of the seventeenth century was filled with a succession of conflicts and revolts, arising from these circumstances. Many of these were local and swiftly suppressed; frequently being betrayed before really commenced, and requiring no particular notice here. In 1640 a special exercise of religious persecution in the whipping, imprisonment, and hanging of forty natives, because they would not be converted from their old faith, aroused the Indians to revolt; but only to be reduced to more complete subjection. Very shortly afterwards the Jemez nation took up arms, and obtained the promise of assistance from their old enemies, the Apaches, but were unsuccessful; and the Spanish Governor, Gen. Arguello, punished them by the imprisonment of twenty-nine of their leading chiefs. A more important attempt was made in 1650, when the whole Tegua nation, including the pueblos of Jemez, Cochiti, San Felipe, Sandia, Alameda, and Isleta, united in a project to kill or drive away the entire Spanish population, and especially the priests; the Apaches being also implicated, as the new danger of foreign domination seemed to heal for the time the old enmity between the industrious inhabitants of the pueblos and the nomadic tribes which had been accustomed to subsist on the stolen products of their labors. The plan was to make a simultaneous attack on the Spanish settlements on the evening of Holy Thursday, when the people would be at church and unsuspicious of danger; and it bid fair to be successful, but for its untimely discovery, and the energetic measures of Gov. Concha, who arrested and imprisoned the leaders, of whom nine were subsequently hung, and the remainder sold into slavery. While Gen. Villanueva was Governor, the Piros Pueblos rose and killed a number of Spaniards, but were in turn overpowered; and soon after, the Pueblos of the Salt Lake country in the south-east, under Estevan Clemente, their Governor, organized a general revolt, which however was discovered in advance and its execution prevented. These unsuccessful attempts however taught the Indians that the only hope of success was in united action by all of the native nations; and preparations for this were quietly discussed and arranged through a considerable series of years, at the time of the annual festivals, when the people of the different pueblos were brought together. Once it seemed as if the time for the rising had come—the people of Taos taking the lead in the work—but through the refusal of the distant Moqui Indians to unite in the revolt, it was for a time abandoned. The Spaniards, however, were kept in a condition of constant fear, as it was impossible to know at what time a formidable rising and general massacre might take place.

The bitter feeling of the natives was heightened by a singular transaction in 1675. According to the superstitious ideas of the day, Friar Andres Duran, Superior of the great Franciscan Monastery at San Yldefonso, together with some of his relations, believed themselves to be bewitched, and accused the Tegua nation of being guilty of causing the affliction. Such an attack by the emissaries of Satan on the very head of the missionary organization of the territory was a serious matter, and the Governor, Don Juan Francisco Frecencio, organized a special tribunal, consisting of Francisco Javier, the the Civil and Military Secretary, and Luis de Quintana, as judges, with Diego Lopez as interpreter, to investigate the charge. The result was the conviction of forty-seven Indians, of whom forty-three were whipped and enslaved, and the remainder hung; the executions being distributed between Jemez, Nambé, and San Felipe, in order to be a warning to future wrong-doers. This action naturally incensed the Teguas to the highest degree. Seventy of them, led by Popé, a San Juan Indian, who had begun to be prominent for his enterprise and wisdom, marched to Santa Fé to endeavor to ransom the prisoners; and a conspiracy was formed to assassinate the Governor, but nothing was accomplished at the time. Meanwhile the cruelty of the slavery in the mines increased, the religious persecution continued, and everything united to drive the natives into the great revolt which occurred in 1680.

During the period from 1600 to 1680 a considerable number of Governors ruled in New Mexico, the appointments being made by the Viceroy of New Spain. Unfortunately, in consequence of the destruction of the records at the time of the Pueblo Revolution, no perfect statement even of their names can be made. In the year 1600 Don Pedro de Peralta was appointed Governor, apparently superseding Oñate, who only the year before had led the expedition to Quivira. But it is evident that Oñate was soon restored, for the Quiviran delegation in 1606 was received by him; in 1611 he made his second exploration to the eastward, and as late as 1618 we are told that the expedition of Don Vicente de Saldivar, of which more will be said presently, was undertaken "by order of his uncle, the Adelantado Don Juan de Oñate." The celebrated Moro, or Inscription Rock, near Zuñi, bears on its surface the memorial of a Governor who otherwise might have remained unknown, in the following words: "Bartolome Narrso, Governor and Captain-General of the Provinces of New Mexico, passed by this place on his return from the Pueblo of Zuñi, on the 29th of July, 1620, having put them at peace, etc." How long this Narrso continued to govern we do not know; but it is evident from some old documents that in 1640 General Arguello was Governor, and General Concha in 1650. One of the oldest of the archives, dated 1683, mentions Enrique de Abela y Pacheco, as having governed the province in 1656. He must have been followed soon after by Bernardo Lopez de Mendizaval, as the latter had time enough before 1660 to render himself obnoxious to the Inquisition, whose complaint was sufficiently influential to effect his removal in that year. The Count of Peñalosa, a more full account of whom we will soon present in connection with his expedition to Quivira, was appointed Governor in 1660, but did not arrive till late in the spring of 1661. He also had the misfortune to come in collision with the Inquisition, whose chief official was assuming such dictatorial powers that Peñalosa finally felt compelled to arrest him and hold him as a prisoner for a week in the Palace; for which the Inquisition repaid him with interest a short time after, causing him to be deprived of his office and suffer a long imprisonment and enormous fine. Soon after General Villanueva was Governor, and in 1675 Don Juan Francisco Frecenio was appointed. Altogether, between 1640 and 1680, fourteen persons exercised the gubernatorial authority, but the above names are all that are certainly known, except that of Antonio Otermin, who was Governor at the time of the breaking out of the Pueblo rebellion in 1680.

During this period various expeditions were undertaken from time to time with a view to the exploration of the country, or the extension of the knowledge of Christianity among the natives. To two of these (that of Saldivar in 1618, and that of Peñalosa in 1662) separate chapters will be devoted, on account of the quaintness of the record of the former, and the important historic interest of the latter. At one time (the exact date not being preserved) two Franciscans, Father Pedro Ortega, Guardian of Santa Fé, and Father Alonzo Yanis, advanced 100 leagues into the Apache country, and then went 50 leagues east, and 50 north, reaching finally a very large river, which they called San Francisco; but their Apache guides were afraid to proceed any further, and the zealous priests returned. Another expedition eastward from Santa Fé was that of the Missionary Fathers Juan de Salas and Diego Lopez, to the Xumana nation. Benavides, who narrates the miraculous conversion of this tribe, fixes the locality of this people as follows: "Setting out from the city of Santa Fé, the center of New Mexico, and passing through the Apache nation of the Vaqueros (Buffalo-hunters), you come to the Xumana nation, whose conversion was so miraculous that it is just to relate how it was." Nothing else worthy of special mention has come down to us in the meagre chronicles of that period. Everything was slowly but surely drifting toward a great revolt by the ill-treated Pueblos. After giving narratives of the expeditions of Saldivar and Peñalosa, we will see how formidable that revolt was when it actually occurred.

CHAPTER X.

THE EXPEDITION OF SALDIVAR.

In 1618 an expedition, of which a brief account has come down to us, was made by Vicente de Saldivar, Maestre de Campo, and nephew of Don Juan de Oñate, with forty-seven men. He was accompanied, as usual on such expeditions, by an ecclesiastic, not only for the spiritual welfare of the men and the conversion of such natives as it might be possible to bring under Christian influences, but also as a kind of historian of the expedition. Nothing was really accomplished, on account of the fears aroused by the stories of a nation of giants soon to be encountered if the expedition proceeded farther, and it is impossible to tell the exact direction taken on the march. The Rio de Buena Esperanza, or Del Tison, has generally been considered to be the Gila, but much difficulty often arises from the same name being applied by different narrators to various rivers or cities, or sometimes by distinct rivers reached by different travellers being supposed by them to be parts of the same, and so miscalled by the same name. In one narrative the Colorado of the West near the Grand Cañon is called "Tison," and the description of the giants is similar to what was said of a tribe on that river. This theory that the Colorado is intended is the more plausible on account of the word "Moq," which would evidently mean the land of the Moquis. The narrative of this expedition is so brief, and at the same time so quaint and characteristic of the times, that we give a translation in full,—

"In the year 1618 the Maestre de Campo Vicente de Saldivar set forth on a journey of discovery, with forty-seven well appointed soldiers, accompanied by the Padre Friar Lazaro Ximenes, of the order of our Seraphic Padre San Francisco, and passing through these same populated and civilized nations to the end of Moq, and journeying through those unpeopled countries fifteen more days, they arrived at the Rio de Buena Esperanza (Goodhope River), or Tison River, in which place they found themselves in latitude thirty six and one-half degrees; and journeying up for two days towards the north with a very good guide who offered to conduct them, they arrived at a little village, and asking information of the country in the interior, they told such great things of it as those in the west on the coasts of the South Sea and California had told them, and as had been described to us by those in the east at the Quivira, which greatly encouraged all to continue their journey; but as among other things they told them that in the country beyond they would find a gigantic and terrible people, so enormous and wonderful that one of our men on horseback was small in comparison, and who shot exceedingly large arrows, it appeared to Saldivar that he could not raise sufficient force to encounter such a multitude of barbarians, and so he determined to return, fearing some misfortune such as was experienced by Captain Humaña and others; and although Friar Lazaro and the greater part of the soldiers opposed this determination they could not prevail, and although twenty-five of them begged permission to enter and explore the land, the Maestre de Campo was not willing to permit it, fearing they would all be lost; but commanded that they should go no further, but turn about; and while this determination was being carried into effect and the baggage being packed, the earth at that point exhibited great feeling and sorrow by a terrific and frightful earthquake, which appeared to play even with the most massive mountains, throwing to the ground the laden animals as well as the men, without leaving anything in its place, thus manifesting in a mysterious manner, by this earthquake, the cowardice of heart of those who turned back from the gates of that fertile, rich, and extensive country, which is so good that it is generally believed that all that to this time, has been conquered and colonized under the name of America is dull in comparison with what is contained in this new part of the New World, which is menaced by conquest by the French who are bounded by it, and by the English and Dutch who desire it so greatly, although neither the one nor the other can obtain it, because they do not understand the art of conquest, which is reserved to the valor and discretion of our nation and the Portuguese, although ours did not then dare to go to see it even to be undeceived. They say that Padre Lazaro then exclaimed in a loud voice with indescribable grief, 'Oh Spaniards, what sorrow the earth feels at our lack of courage, and we do not feel it ourselves!'"

CHAPTER XI.

THE EXPEDITION OF PEÑALOSA TO QUIVIRA.

THE expedition of Don Diego de Peñalosa, though comparatively little known, was certainly the most ambitious, as it came near being the most important in results, of all the expeditions of the Spaniards of New Mexico in the period which succeeded the conquest. By both birth and experience he was just the man calculated to organize and lead in adventurous exploits, which promised rich results in honor, or power, or gold. In a document apparently drawn up by himself, published by Margry, and reproduced in Shea's "Peñalosa," it is stated that Pedro Arias de Avila, first governor of Terra Firma, was his great-great-grandfather; Diego de Ocampo, admiral of the South Sea, and Pedro de Valdivia, who, at his own cost, conquered the Kingdom of Chile, were his great-grandfathers; the Commander Diego de Peñalosa, his grandfather, held many important offices, both civil and military, in Peru; his father, Don Alonzo, was governor of the provinces of Arequipa and Aricaxa, etc., and a knight of Calatrava; and he himself had been Alcalde and Justicia Mayor of La Paz, Governor of Omasuyos, Alcalde of Cuzco, and finally Provincial Alcalde of the city of La Paz and its five dependent provinces, which last office cost him 50,000 crowns.

A quarrel with the brother of the Viceroy of Peru led him to leave that country for Spain; but misfortune attended the journey, for he was wrecked in the Pacific, losing 40,000 crowns, and saving only his pearls and precious stones; and then concluding to visit his uncle, the Bishop of Nicaragua, he was again wrecked and with difficulty reached the cathedral city of that ecclesiastic, in an impoverished condition. The Bishop, however, provided him with everything suitable to his wealth and rank, and thus equipped he proceeded to Mexico, where the Viceroy of New Spain, the Duke of Albuquerque, received him with great favor, appointed him to various important offices, and so loaded him with honors that he abandoned the design of proceeding to the mother country. This favor at the vice-regal court continued not only during the whole official term of Albuquerque, but under his successor Juan de Leiva y de la Cerda, Marquis and Count de Baños, who appointed him in 1660 Governor of New Mexico, in place of Don Bernardo Lopez Mendizaval, who had been complained of by the officials of the Inquisition.

Proceeding to his new dominion by easy stages, stopping two months at Zacatecas and one at Parral, he arrived at Santa Fé in the early summer of 1661, and by his energy and tact soon quieted the troubles that had arisen under his predecessor; and after a vigorous campaign against the marauding Apaches, defeated that restive tribe, and forced them to keep the peace. Seeking to extend the area of Spanish authority, and always fond of adventure and fearless of danger, he then proceeded to organize an expedition to penetrate the country to the north-east, of which nothing definite was known, save the rumors and traditions of cities of great extent, splendor, and riches, and the exaggerated reports brought by the early explorers, who had endeavored, unsuccessfully, to solve entirely the problem of the unknown land beyond the plain. One hundred and twenty years had passed since Coronado had set out on a similar quest, and over half a century since the last expedition, under Oñate; and the vague traditions of what they saw only served to stimulate the curiosity and the ambition of the new generation of Spaniards.

In this project he was encouraged by the adulation of Friar Nicolas de Freytas, Guardian of the ancient

convent of San Yldefonso (the first established in New
Mexico), who exclaims, in writing of the unsuccessful
exploits of Vicente de Saldivar: "But I believe and
hold as undoubted, that as our good God and Lord reserved the conquest of the Terra Firma for the illustrious Pedro Arias de Avila; and that of Peru for the
most fortunate Francisco Pizarro; and that of Chile for
the celebrated Pedro Gutierrez de Valdivia; and that of
the South Sea for the famous Don Diego de Ocampo;
and that of Mexico for the renowned Hernando Cortez;
so he keeps this for the excellent Don Diego Dionisio de
Peñalosa, who—as great-grandson of the three greatest
knights (De Avila, Valdivia, and Ocampo), and best
soldiers of the five just named, and husband of the
granddaughter of the ever-victorious Marquis of the
Valley, Cortez—appears to reproduce the valor of those
noble heroes."

Throughout the winter the preparations proceeded
with energy, enlisting the interest and support of the
most important people of New Mexico; and finally the
expedition commenced its march from the Capital, on
the 6th of March, 1662. Seldom has Santa Fé seen a
more brilliant spectacle. Eighty Spaniards formed the
nucleus of the force; all equipped in the best style of
the times—and under the immediate command of Don
Miguel de Noriega, who had for his lieutenant Tomé
Dominguez de Mendoza; and as sergeant-majors, Fernando Duran y Chavez and Juan Lucero Godoy. With
them were no less than 1,000 native Indian infantry, armed with bows and arrows; and the whole
provided with full camp equipage — including 800
horses, 300 mules, 36 wagons and carts containing
provisions and munitions of war, and 6 small cannon.
There was also, apparently for the comfort of the Commander-in-chief, a large carriage, a litter, and two hand-chairs; the whole forming a brilliant array, as it started
full of ambition and high hopes on its long journey in

search of the Quivira, and the rich kingdoms of the East.

Accompanying Peñalosa as chaplains to himself and the army, and as missionaries to the heathen who should be found, were the two Franciscan Fathers, Friar Miguel de Guevara, Guardian of the Convent of Santa Fé, and Friar Nicolas de Freytas above mentioned, Guardian of the Convent of San Yldefonso. The latter was the historian of the expedition, and has left us a most graphic account thereof, the only difficulty being that like many other narratives of that time, especially when written with a view to bring honors to the conquerors, or induce new expeditions to follow, the writer indulges so freely in superlatives and exaggerations that it is difficult to distinguish the exact facts.

He tells us that the army marched for three full months in an easterly direction, over beautiful and fertile plains, so level that no mountain or hill was ever seen, and covered with immense herds of buffaloes, or cows of Cibola, which increased in number as they proceeded. They crossed many very beautiful rivers and found fine meadow-lands and springs, as well as forests and abundance of fruit-trees of various kinds, including delicious plums and mulberries. Grape-vines abounded bearing great clusters of luscious fruit, even exceeding that of Spain in flavor, and there was an infinity of strawberries. Indeed, the great prairies traversed are described as a kind of earthly paradise, of which the narrator says that neither in all the Indies of Peru and New Spain, nor in Europe, have any other such been seen, so pleasant and delightful; and that on the expedition were men from Europe, Asia, Africa, and America, and all with one voice declared that they had never seen so fertile, pleasant, and agreeable a country as that.

Two hundred leagues (about 500 English miles) they had thus travelled, always through these charming plains, when they arrived at a great river called "Mischipi," where they met a large army of Indians of the Escanxaques Nation, about 3,000 in number, on the march to attack the nearest city of the Quivirans, who were the hereditary enemies of the Escanxaques. Peñalosa entered into friendly relations with the Indians and the two armies marched on, side by side, up along the banks of the Mischipi, which flowed rapidly through fields so fertile that they produced in places two crops a year After one day's travel, the course of the river turned to the north, and in the evening 600 of the Indians started out on a grand buffalo hunt, from which they returned in less than three hours, bringing one, two or three cow's-tongues each, as evidence of their success and the vast number of the animals on the plains.

Four leagues above this point they came in sight of a great range of mountains which skirted the east side of the river, and soon after had their first view of the celebrated city of Quivira, the goal of their expedition, which they found situated on a beautiful prairie, on a branch of the Mischipi, which flowed from the mountains till it joined the main stream. Here without crossing the river, Peñalosa encamped, and with great difficulty restrained the Escanxaques from pressing on to an immediate attack upon the city, which, since their alliance with the Spaniards, they felt to be within their power.

Crowds of people in enormous numbers were seen in front of the city, and soon a deputation of seventy chiefs (caciques) came to visit the Spanish commander and welcome him to the country; at the same time they evinced considerable uneasiness at finding him in company with their inveterate enemies, the Escanxaques. Peñalosa treated them with great consideration, making them presents of such things as pleased their fancy, and impressing upon them his desire for friendly intercourse, and the importance of such commerce to themselves.

He also endeavored to instill a first lesson in religion by causing an altar to be erected, the Salve and Litany to be sung, and other ceremonies performed. In return, they delivered presents of provisions of various kinds, and skins and furs in great abundance, saying that these were but an earnest of the hospitality they would show when he should cross the river and enter their city on the next day.

The Caciques then retired, with the exception of two, whom Peñalosa induced to stay, that he might converse more fully with them regarding the country and its inhabitants. These chiefs gave a most inviting account of the land across the river, telling that the city of Quivira was so large that the end of it would require more than two days to reach, and that the country between the Mischipi and the range of mountains then in sight was well watered by numerous streams flowing from the hills to the river, on which were countless cities and towns of their nation, some being larger even than Quivira itself. They then went on to say that from the eastern slopes of the range ran other streams, which flowed into a very large salt-water lake, the ultimate extent of which they did not know (but which Friar Nicolas says, was doubtless the Atlantic Ocean), and that that country was even more thickly populated than the land of Quivira, and contained greater cities, the whole being ruled over by one mighty king; and that perpetual war existed between the nation on the east of the mountain—called the Ahijaos—and their own. They also spoke of powerful nations to the north, and of another great lake, which was surrounded by splendid cities. So interested was Peñalosa in hearing of these magnificent fields for future enterprise and valor, that the conversation continued till midnight, when the Chiefs were conducted to a place to sleep. But they, fearful at their proximity to their Indian enemies, and, as the sequel proved, with a more correct idea of their character than had Peñalosa himself, quickly escaped across the river,—and none too soon; for before morning the Escanxaques, without disturbing the Spanish army, stealthily attacked the city, killing and burning as they went, and causing such consternation that the inhabitants fled, leaving not even one behind. As soon as this was discovered, and before dawn, Peñalosa pressed across with his army, anxious to save the city from pillage or conflagration.

The chronicler describes Quivira as charmingly situated on both banks of the eastern branch of the Mischipi, with streets of great length, and highways entering at regular intervals from the surrounding country. The houses were generally circular, and two, three, and even four stories in height, the frame-work being of a very strong, solid, and knotty cane, and the roofs made most skillfully of straw. The Spanish army marched for two leagues through the town, without coming to its terminus, when the commander sent a company of twenty-five soldiers, under Francisco de Madrid, to explore further, but even they failed to find the end of this wonderful city; but all could see that the country between the mountains and the river—the distance being six or seven leagues—was like a paradise for fertility and beauty.

Then Don Diego, finding that all the inhabitants had fled, and not wishing at that time to undertake an expedition over the mountains, concluded to return; but found himself confronted by a new danger, for the Escanxaques having been joined by a large body of their countrymen, so that they now amounted to 7,000, and exasperated at having been frustrated in their design to sack the city, and not recognizing their obligation towards their late allies, commenced hostilities; and a fierce battle ensued, in which the Spaniards suffered largely, on account of the shower of arrows which assailed them, but finally by the display of great valor and the "superiority of bullets over arrows," defeated their enemies with great slaughter, killing, we are told, more than 3,000 of them in three hours, and putting the remainder to flight. This battle occurred on the 11th of June, and then the expedition returned by the route which it had previously taken, to New Mexico.

This is the story of the most chivalrous and ambitious of all the attempt to penetrate into the interior of the continent. What point was really reached is a matter not yet certainly determined. Scarcely a more interesting question exists in the early history of America than the exact location of this "Quivira," which was so famous in the sixteenth and seventeenth centuries, and was the goal of so many hopes among the adventurous and ambitious cavaliers of that day. All that we can glean positively from this narrative of Friar Nicolas is that Peñalosa proceeded easterly across the plains for three months, travelling about 500 miles without seeing a mountain, and then reached the right bank of a great river, running south-east; that a day's journey farther up was a bend in the river, which above that ran directly south, and that about four leagues beyond, on the east side of the river, where an important branch came in from the mountains, was the city of Quivira, situated on both sides of the tributary stream; and that a range of mountains ran from north-west to south-east about six or seven leagues from the river. The distance from Santa Fé would answer very well for a point either on the Arkansas or the Missouri, and both rivers have tributaries from the east, which would fill the description given of the branch on which Quivira was situated. But it is difficult to understand with regard to the range of mountains near the river to the eastward, unless it is considered to be a great exaggeration of the bluffs which separate the bottom-lands in several places from the interior uplands.

Twice we have records of bands of Indians from Quivira coming to Santa Fé. Once in 1606, as already narrated, a few years after Oñate's expedition to their city, some 800 men of Quivira came to ask that Governor to aid them in repelling the fierce attacks of the Ayjaos, their enemies, across the range of mountains. They gave glowing descriptions of the riches of their adversaries, and the amount of gold to be found in their country; probably heightened with the view of inducing the Spaniards to invade that country, and with a knowledge of the peculiar attractions of the precious metal to European adventurers. And again, in the latter part of 1662, very shortly after the return of Peñalosa, there came across the plains to Santa Fé another expedition, consisting of more than 700 Quivirans, headed by a powerful chief, to bring thanks to the Spaniards for having defeated the Escanxaques; and apparently with the same object as before, to give so highly colored an account of the land of the Ayjaos as to induce a Mexican expedition against them. These Quivirans were accompanied by trains of dogs carrying furs and skins as a present; and two of the Indians were left by the chief with Peñalosa, in order to show him a shorter route than he had before pursued, in case he would return to Quivira the next year.

This shorter route seems to have been by Taos, as Freytas says that the Quivirans told them that the most direct road was by that town, and adds his own belief, that "the nine large towns which are seventy leagues from here, in a direct line from the Tahos towards the north, are the beginning of these unknown kingdoms, and that from them the settled country continues, and further on the settlements become more numerous." This seems to lead conclusively to the opinion, that Quivira was farther north than any locality of the proper distance on the Arkansas, and points to the Missouri, as being the Mischipi of the narrative. Seales' map of America, printed in Churchill's Voyages, accompanying the narrative of Dr. John Francis Gemelli

Careri's travels in New Spain (Vol. III, p. 480), puts the "Essanapes Country" north-east of the Missouri and Kansas, and even north of the supposed "Morte or Longue" River, much of which was really the Missouri.

Taking every source of information into consideration, the conclusion would therefore be that Quivira was situated near the east bank of the Missouri River, somewhere between the present cities of St. Joseph and Council Bluffs, on an eastern branch, which may have been the Nodaway or the Nishabotony. It is almost certain that Peñalosa could not have gone as far north as the Platte, or mention would have been made of so important a stream, unless, indeed, the Spaniards considered the Platte the main stream, in which case the Missouri may have been the branch from the north-east, on which Quivira was situated, and the heights in the vicinity of Council Bluffs, the range of mountains seen in the distance.

The subsequent history of Peñalosa may be briefly stated. After returning from his expedition he engaged in erecting public buildings, and founding new towns; but he soon came, like his predecessor, into collision with the dictatorial agents of the Inquisition, and finally arrested the Commissary-General and imprisoned him for a week in the Palace at Santa Fé. As soon as he could arrange it, he returned to the City of Mexico in order to interest the Viceroy in a grand scheme of conquest to follow up his discoveries at Quivira; but the agents of the Inquisition followed him, had him arrested, and punished by imprisonment and fine. He then determined to proceed to Spain to get redress; but being carried to the Canary Islands, his only means of passage was in a vessel to England. There the Spanish ambassador regarded him with suspicion—which was increased by his attempts to proceed to Spain by way of France. At length, apparently exasperated by lack of appreciation on the part of his own countrymen, he determined to apply to the French Government; and presented to it a proposition for the establishment of a colony at the mouth of the Rio Grande, and the conquest of a large district of country, by expeditions from that point. Nothing came of it, however, and the Ex-Governor died at Paris in 1687. Had he succeeded in enlisting the interest which was necessary for a new expedition to, and conquest of, the regions of Quivira and the North-east, the history of the continent might have been materially changed; and the Mississippi Valley might have been peopled from Spain, instead of by the French and English.

CHAPTER XII.

THE REVOLUTION OF 1680.

FROM the time of his first leadership in 1675, Popé was untiring in his efforts to unite the whole native population in a war of extermination against the Spaniards. He was a man of great ability and natural resources, thoroughly acquainted with the feelings of his countrymen and the best methods of influencing them, and endowed with an eloquence which seldom failed to effect its purpose. He devoted himself to the work of arousing the people to resistance, and traversed the country from pueblo to pueblo to induce concert of action and forgetfulness of local jealousies. Knowing their reverence for the supernatural, he claimed to be specially commissioned from heaven to drive the Spaniards from the land and restore the people to their ancient peace and happiness; and at the same time he stated that he had aid from the lower regions as well, three spirits named Caidit, Tilim, and Tlesime, enveloped in flames which shot from every extremity of their bodies, having appeared to him in the estufa at Taos, and given him counsel as to the revolution. Leading Indians from other nations and pueblos aided Popé in this work of preparation; prominent among them being Catité, of the Queres nation, Jaca, of Taos, and Francisco, of San Yldefonso; and he also had an efficient lieutenant in a neighbor of his own pueblo, named Tacu. The precise cause which led to the fixing of the time for the outbreak is a little obscure. The tradition which seems too universal not to be true tells us that the caving in of the shaft of a mine, in which a large number of Indians had been forced to labor, and the consequent burying alive and destruction of many of them, was the "last straw" which exhausted the long-tried patience of the natives, and precipitated the revolt.

Popé sent swift messengers to the pueblos conveying a rope made of the fibre of the Amole, in which were a number of knots corresponding to the days before the time fixed for the uprising, and bearing a message of invitation to join in the work, and of threatening to those who refused. Every effort was made to insure absolute secrecy, and a freedom from the treachery which had wrecked former attempts. Not a woman was entrusted with the secret, and a continued watch was maintained on every man suspected of being unfaithful. So determined were they to achieve success this time that Popé killed with his own hands his son-in-law, Nicolas Bua, Governor of the pueblo of San Juan, who had given cause for suspicion of his loyalty. The day appointed was August 10, 1680, and as it approached, the fullest preparations consistent with secrecy were made in all the pueblos. But all of these precautions were unsuccessful, for two days before the prearranged time, two Indians of Tesuque, whose nearness to the Capital made them specially intimate with the Spaniards, betrayed the entire plot to the Governor, Don Antonio Otermin.

News of this treachery was immediately conveyed to the Pueblo leaders, and they determined that their only chance of success was in an immediate attack on the Spaniards, without waiting for the arrival of the day agreed on; and that very night in all the pueblos to which the news had reached, a simultaneous attack was made on the Christians and all were slaughtered without regard to age or sex, except a few girls, reserved for wives of the young braves. The wisdom of this decision to anticipate the day selected was soon seen in the consternation of the Spanish authorities and people at

Santa Fé, who were entirely unprepared for the sudden uprising. The Governor took every measure possible for the defense of the city, and sent messengers to all the Spanish settlements, directing the people at the north to concentrate at the capital; and those at the south to gather at Isleta, which was to be fortified by the Lieutenant Governor. The Spaniards lost no time in seeking these places of safety, some succeeding in reaching them, but many others, being overtaken on the road or found at their houses before the news had reached them, were killed without mercy. The people of the northern villages, finding it dangerous to attempt to reach Santa Fé, collected at Santa Cruz, which they fortified as thoroughly as possible in the hope of resisting any attack, but on the 11th the Pueblos carried the town by storm and massacred all the people they could find, and then proceeded on the march toward Santa Fé.

All the Indians in the Territory from Pecos to Moqui were thoroughly united in the revolution, and soon news came to the Governor that armies were concentrating upon the capital from all directions. Spies sent to the Galisteo brought tidings of the approach of the Tanos Indians, while the Teguas with their Apache allies were marching from the north. Everything possible was done by the Spaniards to provide for their defense. The houses in the outskirts were abandoned, all the people gathering in the plaza and the buildings which bordered upon it; the entrances to the plaza were fortified, the palace put into condition to stand a siege and all the citizens were supplied with arms and ammunition. It was perfectly understood that the war on the part of the Pueblos was one of extermination, so that the condition of the Christians was critical in the extreme. The natives were flushed with success and confident of victory. They declared that the God of the white man was dead, but that their God, the Sun, could not die. Religious feeling was a very strong element among the causes which led to the revolution, and a bitter hatred to the Christianity of the Spaniards was evinced in almost every act during the struggle.

Scarcely were the hasty fortifications at Santa Fé completed, when the Taños Indians were seen approaching from the south, coming so near as to occupy the abandoned houses in the suburbs. Governor Otermin wisely endeavored to treat with them before their allies from the north should appear, and so sent a deputation to confer with them, but without result. The Indians said that they had brought with them two crosses, one red and one white, signifying war and peace—that the Spaniards might take their choice; but if they chose "peace," they must immediately leave the country to its original possessors. Not being prepared for such an abandonment, and negotiation having failed, the Governor concluded to make an attack and endeavor to drive these enemies from the field before the others approached; and accordingly, a vigorous sortie was made by the garrison. But it was met with equal gallantry by the Indians, and soon all the available Spaniards had to join in the battle, which was fiercely contested throughout the entire day. The native loss far exceeded that of the Christians; but their superior numbers enabled them to hold their ground, and toward evening the appearance of the Teguan army on the hills to the north forced the Spaniards to return to their fortifications and prepare for the combined attack, to which they might now be subjected at any moment.

The Indians, however, did not seem disposed to risk an open assault, but contented themselves with the safer and surer method of a regular siege. They cut off the water supply of the city, and invested it so closely as to produce great distress. The number of the Spaniards was upwards of 1,000, but they included men, women, and children, and the available force of fighting men did not reach 200, and was being daily reduced from various causes; while the armies of the Pueblos were continually increased by the arrival of fresh parties from the various villages, until they amounted to nearly 3,000 men. The situation became more and more desperate as time passed, and finally a sortie was determined on as presenting the only chance of relief, and that only as being less dangerous than the sure destruction by continued siege. This was attempted on the morning of August 19th, and was so gallantly conducted that the lines of the enemy were broken, a large number slain, and no less than forty-seven taken prisoners, the Indians retiring to the east and north of the town. Both sides seem to have been equally determined in this conflict, as we are told that all the prisoners after a brief examination were executed in the Plaza. A hasty council of war was held, and after some discussion it was concluded that notwithstanding their temporary success, the safest course, considering their reduced condition and the scarcity of provisions, was to evacuate the town while the road was open. No time was lost in carrying this determination into effect. Preparations were made during the night, and at day-break of the next day (August 21), they left the capital to its fate and commenced the long march toward the south. Not enough horses remained to carry even the sick and wounded; so that all the inhabitants, including women and children, had to proceed on foot, carrying such articles as they needed in bundles, like the pilgrims of old. Fortunately, they were not attacked or in any way molested, the Indians, who watched them from the adjacent hills, being entirely satisfied so long as the country was to be abandoned. They followed the retreating Spaniards at a distance for about seventy miles, to see that they continued their march towards Mexico, and then returned to enjoy the hoped-for fruits of their victory, in the peaceable occupation of the country and the practice of the faith of their forefathers.

At Alamillo the Governor met his adjutant, Pedro Leiva, with a re-inforcement of forty men, but continued to travel down the river, hoping to find the Christians of the southern villages congregated at Isleta. In this, however, he was disappointed, as they had already marched, under the Lieutenant-Governor, to El Paso. All along the route the towns were deserted and laid waste, and all provisions, including standing corn, had been destroyed or carried away. This occasioned great distress, and finally the company became so enfeebled that it could proceed no further, and was forced to send south for assistance. Father Ayeta, of El Paso, responded with four wagon-loads of corn, and the Lieutenant-Governor with a portion of his own scanty store; and thus, partially relieved, they continued on, joining the company which had collected at Isleta, and finally making a winter encampment at San Lorenzo, about thirty miles north of El Paso, where there was abundant wood and water. Here they built rude houses, all, from the Governor to the small children, taking their parts in the work; and remained till spring, losing a large portion of their number, who fled from the privations of the camp to seek an asylum in villages of Chihuahua and Sonora, and subsisting frequently on wild fruits, mesquite, beans, and mescal; their wretchedness being enhanced by the constant fear of attack by neighboring Indians.

The unfortunate priests, who were left in the midst of the Indians, met with horrible fates. Not one escaped martyrdom. At Zuñi, three Franciscans had been stationed—Fathers Analiza, Espinosa, and Calsada. When the news of the Spanish retreat reached that town, the people dragged these priests from their cells, stripped and stoned them, and afterwards compelled the servant of Analiza to finish the work by shooting them. Having thus whetted their appetite for cruelty and vengeance, the Indians started to carry the news of their independence to Moqui, and signalized their arrival by the barbarous murder of the two missionaries who were living there, Padre Juan de Vallada and Brother Jesus de Lombarde. Their bodies were left unburied, as a prey for the wild beasts. At Jemez, they indulged in every refinement of cruelty. The old priest, Jesus Morador, was seized in his bed at night, stripped naked and mounted on a hog, and thus paraded through the streets, while the crowd shouted and yelled around. Not satisfied with this, they then forced him to carry them as a beast would, crawling on his hands and feet, until, from repeated beating and the cruel tortures of sharp spurs, he fell dead in their midst. A similar chapter of horrors was enacted at Acoma, where the three priests, Fathers Maldonado, Figeroa, and Mora, were stripped, tied together with hair rope, and so driven through the streets, and finally stoned to death. So utterly did the mild nature of the Pueblo Indians appear to have been changed in half a century! and so terribly did the persecutions which the misdirected zeal of some of the ecclesiastics inaugurated, react on others, many of whom were men of great kindness and benevolence, and all of whom had shown marked self-sacrifice and zeal !

Thus ended the first act in the drama of a renewal of aboriginal control. About 100 Spaniards had been killed thus far during the conflict, and with them a number of christianized Indians who adhered to their new religion. The priests had been special objects of hatred to the revolutionists, and no less than eighteen of them had fallen a sacrifice. Of the Indians a far greater number had been killed, but the survivors had the satisfaction of seeing their object accomplished. Not a Christian remained free within the limits of New Mexico, and those who had been dominant a few months before were now wretched and half-starved fugitives, huddled together in the rude huts of San Lorenzo.

CHAPTER XIII.

THE PUEBLO GOVERNMENT—1680 TO 1692.

AS soon as the Spaniards had retreated from the country, the Pueblo Indians gave themselves up for a time to rejoicing, and to the destruction of everything which could remind them of the Europeans, their religion, and their domination. The army which had besieged Santa Fé quickly entered that city, took possession of the palace as the seat of government, and commenced the work of demolition. The churches and the monastery of the Franciscans were burned with all their contents, amid the almost frantic acclamations of the natives. The gorgeous vestments of the priests had been dragged out before the conflagration, and now were worn in derision by Indians, who rode through the streets at full speed, shouting for joy. The official documents and books in the palace were brought forth, and made fuel for a bonfire in the center of the plaza; and here also they danced the *cachina*, with all the accompanying religious ceremonies of the olden time. Everything imaginable was done to show their detestation of the Christain faith, and their determination utterly to eradicate even its memory. Those who had been baptized were washed with amole in the Rio Chiquito, in order to be cleansed from the infection of Christianity. All baptismal names were discarded, marriages celebrated by Christian priests were annulled, the very mention of the names Jesus and Mary was made an offense, and estufas were constructed to take the place of the ruined churches.

The chief authority was conferred on Popé, who had been the leader throughout all the preparation for the revolution, and who now established himself at Santa

Fé. Believing that the next spring would see a renewed attempt to establish the Spanish power, with prudent foresight he endeavored to strengthen the bonds between the different Pueblo nations, and even to effect a permanent alliance with the Apaches, by proposing marriages with that tribe. To attain these objects, and at the same time to aid in establishing the new order of things, he made a kind of royal progress through the whole territory, journeying on horseback from pueblo to pueblo, and everywhere receiving the highest honors. He was preceded by envoys to give notice of his approach, and was generally accompanied by Catité, Jaca, and Cupavo, who had been his most faithful and active Lieutenants. His commands were implicitly obeyed, and for a time he possessed almost absolute authority; but as usual in cases of sudden elevation, his vanity and arrogance soon became almost insupportable, and the Pueblos were forced to place limitations on the exercise of his power. His primary object during this grand tour appears to have been, as at Santa Fé, to obliterate all remembrance of the days of their thraldom, and to re-establish every ancient custom. The use of the Spanish language was strictly prohibited, even the planting of grains and seeds introduced by the invaders was forbidden; all churches and monasteries were to be burned, and every crucifix, cross, picture, or other article used in the Christian ceremonials, was to be absolutely destroyed. At the same time the mines in which the people had suffered such brutal slavery were to be filled up, and their very locations obliterated as far as possible. Popé still assumed to have supernatural assistance, and like other self-called prophets, promulgated from time to time communications from the higher powers, as seemed desirable for the development of his purposes. He possessed much administrative ability, coupled with energy and tact, and even with the drawbacks presented by his occasional selfishness and cruelty, was undoubtedly the best leader whom the natives possessed. For a short time, when incensed at some special instance of his tyranny, they substituted Cupavo for him in the seat of power, but were glad after a little experience to recall their old and tried leader.

Meanwhile Governor Otermin had not been idle. As soon as the spring opened in 1681, he had commenced preparations for the reconquest of his dominion; but it was not till fall that he received the special authorization required from the Viceroy of New Spain. Even then he encountered great difficulties from the scarcity of provisions and ammunition, and for lack of other armor, was finally compelled to protect his men with shields and other defenses made of ox-hide. At last, after much delay, he organized an army of about 1,000 soldiers, mostly cavalry, including all the able-bodied men who had been driven from their New Mexican homes, and who for greater efficiency left their families at San Lorenzo. A number of friendly Indians also constituted a part of his force. When fully equipped, the army started on its march, on the 5th of November, and crossed the Rio Grande at the well-known ford, at Paso del Norte. They pushed on by rapid marches up the river, crossed the Jornada del Muerto, and on November 27th arrived at a point opposite the village of Senecu, which was the most southerly of the Pueblo towns. A party was sent across the river to examine this place, and found it deserted and in ruins, with the appearance of having been captured in war and pillaged. The priests collected the few remains of church ornaments and crosses and burned them; and the work of the destruction of the town was then completed by fire. The next day the army passed the ruins of San Pascual, and on the succeeding one the Governor crossed the Rio Grande to visit the town of Our Lady of Succor, (Socorro). This town was also deserted, and showed evidences of having been taken by assault. The plaza was barricaded by a strong wall, many of the houses were half in ruins, and the images and crosses which had been concealed in the church were broken and destroyed. Though the town itself presented no attractions, Otermin was charmed by its beautiful situation, and paid a special visit to the warm spring, now so well known, at the foot of the mountain.

Thus the army marched up the valley, finding nothing but deserted villages and ruins, until they reached Isleta. Here there were a number of inhabitants, but they were surprised at the appearance of the Spaniards, and made very little resistance. When assembled in the plaza and questioned by the General, they denied having taken any part in the destruction of the church and sacred vessels, saying that that had been done by the army from the northern pueblos, which had come soon after the Spanish retreat, burned the church, and commanded every one to return to the old religion. Otermin commanded crosses to be erected in the plaza and the houses, and a procession was then formed to meet Father Ayeta, the principal priest of the expedition, who was now approaching. He came singing an anthem, to which the Indians responded; and the next day religious services were held in the plaza, at which the priest urged the people to return to Christianity, and granted them absolution for past offenses. A number of children were then baptized, the first one being christened "Carlos," after the reigning King of Spain; the Governor himself standing as sponsor. At the conclusion of the ceremonies, which lasted two days, Otermin graciously pardoned the people for all crimes against the King; and the Indians, having thus received both heavenly and earthly absolution, promised to remain good Christians and loyal subjects for the future.

From this point the Governor dispatched Don Juan Dominguez de Mendoza, the general of cavalry, with seventy Spaniards and a company of friendly Indians, to march in advance and reconnoitre the country to the north, while the main army remained for several days at Isleta recruiting its strength and endeavoring to collect grain and food from the surrounding country. It appeared that during the summer there had been a severe drought, which had destroyed most of the crops —especially in the north—so that great destitution and suffering prevailed. This had caused the abandonment of some of the pueblos, whose inhabitants had left their houses in search of food; and was also the occasion of conflicts between the different nations and towns, each of which was endeavoring to procure a supply at the expense of its neighbor. All these circumstances conduced to make the advance of the Spaniards much easier than it otherwise would have been, and caused them in some places to be hailed as deliverers, rather than resisted as enemies.

Mendoza marched rapidly up the valley, but for a long distance found little save abandoned pueblos, the inhabitants of which had fled at his approach. This was the case at Sandia, Alameda, and Puara; and also at San Felipe and Santo Domingo. In all the pueblos the churches and religious houses had been destroyed, and the images and ornaments broken or concealed; while estufas had been constructed, and the Spaniards found many articles connected with the restoration of the heathen ceremonies of the natives.

Passing Santo Domingo, Mendoza marched to Cochití, and here for the first time encountered a considerable number of Indians. They had abandoned the pueblo, apparently very hastily, but were seen in large force on the hills around. The Spaniards entered the town in the evening, and the next morning marched out to attack the enemy. The Indians also descended from the hills under command of Catité, sounding their war-cry, and apparently eager for the conflict. A conference however was arranged, the crafty Pueblo Chieftain expressing a desire for peace; and finally it was agreed that the Indians should be pardoned for all past offenses, and return to their allegiance both to the Church and the King; and the officers embraced each other as a token of enduring friendship. That night however large re-inforcements were received by the natives, and in the morning their army again advanced, nearly 1,000 strong, arranged in a semi-circle, with the apparent intent of surrounding and capturing the Spaniards. But again negotiation took the place of battle, and finally a treaty was concluded which was to be a protection, not only to the Indians there present, but to all connected with them who should return to their villages and abandon idolatry.

The army under Catité embraced representatives of the three great nations, the Teguas, Taños, and Queres, and of nearly all of the Pueblos, but time was asked by that Chieftain to bring together the Indians of Cochití, Santo Domingo, and San Felipe, many of whom were still in the mountains; and other Caciques desired also to notify their respective pueblos of the return of peace, and have them more fully represented. It was arranged therefore that at the end of two days there should be a great assemblage at which the Spanish authority should be formally recognized, and all the Indians again be received into the bosom of the Church. The native army then withdrew; but as it did not return at the appointed time, Mendoza began to suspect some treachery, and soon after had his fears verified by the reports of spies, from which it appeared that at the time of the conference the snow had wet the bow-strings of the Indians and so rendered them unserviceable, and that the delay asked for was in order to remedy this difficulty, and also to concentrate warriors near San Felipe, who might destroy the Spaniards on their downward march. On learning these facts Mendoza hastily broke camp and returned to the main army, meeting the Governor near the Pueblo of Sandia. At this point Otermin had remained for several days, while a formal investigation was being made of the facts connected with the rebellion of the year before.

Meanwhile the winter had commenced in earnest; snow was constantly falling, and the suffering of the soldiers was very severe. The pasturage in the vicinity was exhausted, and the store of provisions was alarmingly low. The Indians were constantly increasing in numbers by the arrival of fresh bands from the more distant pueblos, and a detachment on horseback, under Luis of Picuris, was scouring the country south of the Spanish camp. Under these circumstances a council of war was held, at which each military officer, and Father Ayeta, presented their views in writing; and while some favored an advance, and some an entire abandonment of the country, the compromise was decided upon of retiring to the friendly Pueblo of Isleta for winter-quarters. On arriving there, however, it was found that the troops were so exhausted, and the horses in such bad condition (less than one-seventh of the original number being fit for service), that the General determined to continue the march down the river to El Paso, in order to prepare fully for the campaign of the next year. Since they had left Isleta, six weeks before, over 100 of its inhabitants had deserted the town to join the Indian army; and the remainder, consisting of 385 who had been christianized, begged to accompany the army to Mexico, as they feared to be left at their old home without protection. This request was granted; and after the desertion of the town it was burned, with all the stores that had been collected there, in order to prevent their being of service to the enemy. The army left Isleta on the day after New-year's, 1682, and arrived at El Paso after a laborious march of nine days; leaving the territory for the second time to the sole occupancy of the native population.

Otermin had expected to recruit his army during the spring and return to New Mexico before many months, but in this he was disappointed; and his lack of success in the reduction of the country appears to have been so unsatisfactory to the Viceroy that he was removed from office and Don Bartolomé de Estrada Ramirez appointed in his place. No record is to be found of any attempt, by this official, to take actual possession of his province, and probably after ascertaining the danger and difficulties of the position, he concluded to be satisfied with the titular honor of the Governorship; for a year afterwards, in 1684, Don Domingo Jironza Petriz de Cruzate was made Governor and Captain-General. Cruzate organized an expedition in the succeeding year to penetrate the country, and started from Paso del Norte, where the remainder of the old inhabitants of New Mexico were still living, for the march up the Rio Grande. He reached the Pueblo of Senecu (now abandoned, but then south of Socorro), and addressed the people, who were all assembled in the plaza, on their duties to God and the King, and also gave them some sanitary advice, as, for instance, that it was more healthful to sleep in the second story of the buildings. Nothing, however, was accomplished towards the reconquest of the country during this year; and although Cruzate made various attempts to effect that object, and in 1688 again entered the territory, with a considerable force, and no less than seventy Franciscan Friars, and on one expedition certainly marched as far as Zia, which he captured, yet he was always unsuccessful, and the Indians were left in almost undisturbed possession of the land.

Far from employing this period, however, to consolidate their strength or prepare to resist new invasion, scarcely were the Spaniards expelled, when dissensions arose between the various nations, and a state of war existed in one or another part of New Mexico during almost the entire period of the Pueblo control. The consequent interruptions to the planting of corn, and the frequent destruction of supplies during hostile invasion, caused much destitution and suffering; and combined with the destruction of towns by siege or burning, led to the abandonment of a considerable number of the pueblos. In fact, the half century of Spanish control seems to have unfitted the natives for self-government, and the nations which had generally lived so prosperously and peacefully as neighbors, down to the coming of Coronado, now seemed determined to effect each other's destruction; and thus prepared the way for an easy reconquest by the Spaniards.

CHAPTER XIV.

THE RECONQUEST BY VARGAS.

CRUZATE having failed to take possession of the province with which he had been entrusted, the Viceroy of New Spain, in the spring of 1692, appointed Don Diego de Vargas Zapata Lujan as Governor, with the avowed desire of having New Mexico reconquered as speedily as possible. Vargas was a man of great energy and decision of character, and lost no time in preparing for the work before him. He left his home immediately for Paso del Norte, and although he was greatly disappointed at the amount of force which he was enabled to muster for the campaign, which barely amounted to 300 in all, including 100 friendly Indians, yet he determined to undertake the work without more delay, and commenced his march on the last day of August. He passed rapidly up the valley of the Rio Grande, finding nearly all the old pueblos in a half-ruined condition, but only stopping for necessary rest and sleep, as he decided to strike his blows before the enemy was prepared; and in less than a fortnight (September 12th) was in sight of Santa Fé.

Meanwhile the Indians had been watching his movements, not knowing what point was first to be attacked, but as soon as it was evident that it was the capital, began concentrating towards Santa Fé, and as Vargas approached the city, he saw numerous companies from the adjacent pueblos hastening to its relief Early the next morning a battle commenced, which was waged with great determination for eleven hours, when at length the Pueblos gave way, and Vargas entered the city. This signal success had an important effect, for judging, from the speed with which the capital was captured, that nothing was to be gained by resistance, twelve adjacent pueblos surrendered and were immediately occupied. Vargas however well understood that with so small a force it would be impossible to hold so extensive a country, and wrote to the Viceroy from Santa Fé in the very height of his success, that in order to retain possession of the country, it would be necessary to establish permanent garrisons; "and to send less than 500 families and 100 soldiers would be like throwing a grain of salt into the sea."

The Governor however, did not wait for any re-inforcements; but with characteristic energy, started almost immediately for the Pueblo of Taos, which was considered the most determined in its opposition to Spanish rule. So rapid was his march that although a considerable halt was made near San Juan, in order to receive with proper ceremony the warriors of that pueblo, who were counted as allies, the army reached the Taos Valley on the third day (October 7th), and speedily surrounded the two great buildings. Not an Indian appeared; and on entering, they found that they were entirely deserted—the inhabitants having retired to a gorge in the adjacent mountains. Sending Luis (an influential, friendly Indian, of Picuris) in advance, Vargas succeeded in arranging a conference, and after a short time induced the Pueblos to return to their homes, promising loyalty to state and church; the General, on his part, agreeing to overlook the past, and providing them with a priest, who absolved the whole community, and then proceeded to receive into the church, by baptism, no less than ninety-six of their number. The Governor also succeeded in adjusting the feud existing between Taos and the pueblos to the south; and induced a number of the best of the young men to promise to join his standard in an expedition soon to be undertaken against the Indians of Zuñi. All this accomplished, Vargas returned to Santa Fé by the way of Picuris, and arrived on the 13th; having been absent from the capital but eight days, and not losing a single man.

No sooner had he returned, however, than with wonderful energy he prepared for another expedition, which was to be of a more extensive character. As he expected to be absent some time, he appointed Luis, of Picuris (whom we have heard of several times before, and who appears to have been a man of superior ability), as Governor of all the pueblos under Spanish control; and administered to him the oath of office upon a cross, in presence of the chief men of the different towns Intending to make his first visit to Pecos, and then proceed westward, he dispatched part of his troops, with two pieces of artillery, to Santo Domingo, to await him there; and then, after remaining only three days in the capital, set out early on the morning of October 17th, and reached Pecos by 2 o'clock. Here the people were prepared to receive him very favorably; and had erected a large cross and arches at the entrance of their town by way of greeting. They were absolved by the two priests (Fathers Corven and Barras) who accompanied the army, and 248 were baptized. The next morning Vargas, at the request of the people, appointed officers for the pueblo, and then left for the west; arriving at night at the ruined Pueblo of Galisteo, which had been entirely abandoned. Three leagues farther on, the next day, they passed San Marcos, once a populous town, but now deserted; and toward evening came to Santo Domingo, where they found the other detachment. Here the Governor held a council with the caciques of a number of the neighboring pueblos; who were then presented with crosses, rosaries, and other gifts, and sent to their respective villages, with instructions to prepare to receive the army. On the 21st he marched from Santo Domingo to Cochití, where he met the inhabitants of that town, together with those of San Marcos and San Felipe, who had deserted their pueblos for fear of the other Indians, who had combined against them. They were assured of protection, and promised to return to their homes.

From here, with a detachment of troops, Vargas proceeded to Zia, where he found the old pueblo in the ruinous condition in which it had been left after its capture by Cruzate, the people having built a new town near by. Crosses and arches had been prepared, as at Pecos, and the people received him with acclamations. The Governor recommended that they should re-occupy the old pueblo, and gave them some steel axes to assist in the work; and then, after witnessing a grand dance, rode on to Jemez. Here, as at Zia, the old pueblo had been abandoned, and a new one established on an elevation three leagues beyond, where the position was almost impregnable, and had been rendered still stronger by the erection of thick walls and redoubts, the town being built around two plazas, each of which had only one narrow entrance. Although about 600 warriors were in arms, and Vargas was in continual dread of an attack, no opposition was made to his approach, and he was treated with great hospitality by the chiefs. In each village the same ceremonies of absolution were performed, followed by the baptism of large numbers of Indians. From Jemez the Governor marched to Santa Ana, and as this completed the pacification of all the country in the Rio Grande Valley, he sent a detachment of troops, with a number of citizens, to El Paso to bring back into the territory the families of the old residents which had so long been awaiting at that point the time when they could safely return.

So rapid had been the movements of Vargas that much of the fall still remained for active operations, and he determined to visit the whole province if possible, before the end of the season. He set out therefore from

Santa Ana on the 30th of October, with eighty-nine soldiers and thirty Indian scouts, and marched first to Isleta, which he found in ruins, with the exception of the church, and on the 3d of November reached Acoma. Here considerable time was occupied in sending messages and holding councils, the inhabitants having been warned by their friends, the Navajoes, not to put any trust in the professions and promises of Vargas; and the Spaniards, on the other hand, being unable, if they so desired, to assault the town, on account of the great strength of its position. At length, however, the Governor succeeded in gaining the confidence of the natives. Vargas and the Pueblo chief, Mateo, publicly embraced each other, and a large cross was erected, and the usual absolution and general baptism took place.

From here the Spaniards started on their arduous march across the desert to Zuñi, sending in advance a messenger bearing a cross and a rosary, to explain their peaceful intentions; and when near their journey's end, were met by twelve envoys, who brought messages of good-will and welcome from the chiefs of the pueblo. Vargas found the ascent of the mesa, on which the town was situated, so sharp that it could only be made on foot; but he was rewarded on reaching the summit by seeing the inhabitants assembled in the plaza to receive him with honor, and by no less than 294 presenting themselves for baptism. The Governor and priests were entertained by the chiefs of the pueblo in the most cordial manner, and were in every way gratified at their reception by this intelligent and powerful nation.

Vargas was desirous of extending his expedition still farther west, to the Moqui country, and even beyond, where mines of cinnabar and red ochre were said to exist. He learned, however, that the Moqui chiefs were suspicious of his intentions, and had little confidence in the friendly letter he had dispatched to them from Jemez; having been rendered distrustful by the reports of the same Navajoes who had similarly affected the people of Acoma. He therefore wrote a second letter, in which he stated that he had already pardoned them for their action in the rebellion, and asked them to meet him in a friendly spirit at their villages. Having allowed a little time for this message to have an effect, he started from Zuñi with sixty-three soldiers and two priests, on November 15. The first of the pueblos reached was Aguatubi, five days distant, where the Spaniards were at first met with apparent hostility; 700 or 800 Indians, well armed, surrounding the little band, and singing their war-songs. The tact of Vargas, however, extricated him from this difficulty, as it had from many previous dangers, and the chief named Miguel directed his people to lay aside their weapons and receive the Spaniards as brothers. It afterward appeared that when the letter of Vargas from Zuñi was received at this pueblo, word was sent to the other towns of the Moquis, Gualpi, Jongopabi, Monsonabi, and Oraybi, and a great council of the natives was held, at which a chief of Gualpi, named Antonio, was the leading spirit, and where it was determined to resist the Spanish invasion by every available means. Miguel claimed to have opposed this course of action, and urged that a friendly reception be accorded to Vargas, who had come a long distance on a mission of peace. The hostility at first manifested was attributable to the decision of that council, but afterward the more pacific policy of Miguel and his friends prevailed. Had the attitude of the Indians not been changed, it would certainly have been impossible for the Spaniards to have entered the town, as the passage was only sufficiently wide for one man to pass at a time, and it was well defended by fortifications. Even as it was, Vargas was continually fearful of treachery, and declined to enter the houses to eat, or even to encamp at night in the plaza; but nothing occurred to justify his apprehensions.

The people erected the usual cross in the center of the plaza, 122 were baptized, and Vargas acted as sponsor for two children of Miguel, whom he confirmed in his authority as Governor of the pueblo.

Leaving fifteen men in charge of the animals, the Governor with forty-five soldiers pressed on to Gualpi, the next town of the Moqui nation, where he was well received and entertained by the same Antonio whose feelings had been so hostile a few days before. Here and at Monsonabi and Jongopabi—in the former of which Pedro, the messenger who had been sent from Jemez, was found in the midst of the people in the plaza, holding aloft a large cross—Vargas made the usual address explanatory of his peaceful intentions toward all who respect the authority of the King and the Church, and the people were absolved and baptized; nothing unusual occurring to vary the ceremonies. The horses of the Spaniards were now nearly broken down from fatigue, and it appearing that the mines were on the other side of the Colorado River, whose deep cañon was almost impassable, Vargas determined to return to Zuñi, having also to abandon his contemplated visit to Oraybe on account of the scarcity of water on the road. At Zuñi he heard of a short route by which he could reach the Rio Grande near Socorro, and having determined for some reason which is unexplained—and certainly seems singular after his wonderfully successful and rapid pacification of the whole province—to march to El Paso instead of returning to Santa Fé, he availed himself of this information, and after travelling through a country covered with broken lava (malpais) and infested with wandering bands of Apaches, reached Socorro on the 9th of December. Soon after leaving Zuñi he passed by the Moro, now known as the "Inscription Rock," and there left a memorial, which is reproduced in Simpson's Report, plate seventy-one, and reads as follows: "Here served General Don Diego de

Vargas in the conquest of Santa Fé and New Mexico, for the royal crown, at his own cost, 1692." From Socorro to El Paso the little army marched in a very leisurely way as compared with their previous rapid movements, arriving at the latter place on December 20th, somewhat less than four months from the time of leaving it. During the progress of this expedition nearly every pueblo of importance had been visited; from Pecos in the extreme east to Moqui in the west, 2,214 natives had been baptized, and no less than seventy-four Spanish women and children, who had been captives since the beginning of the revolution, were released.

The probable object of Vargas in proceeding to El Paso was to arrange for the immigration into New Mexico of a sufficient number of families to colonize it permanently, in accordance with the report which he made to the Viceroy soon after his arrival at Santa Fé. At all events, he proceeded to devote himself to the work of collecting a large number of families for that purpose; the refugees from New Mexico, who had not yet set out on the return to their old home, being used as a nucleus. Much more time was thus occupied than had at first been expected, so that it was not until the 11th of October, 1693, that the company was ready to commence its march. The whole number, including both colonists and escort, reached 1,500 persons, and they carried with them over 3,000 horses and mules. Each family had been supplied with a certain amount of money, generally from $10 to $40, to purchase supplies; over $42,000 having been furnished to Vargas by the vice-regal authorities for that purpose. Don Juan Paes Hurtado, who was afterwards Governor of New Mexico at various times between 1704 and 1735, was appointed to take charge of the immigration. This unwieldy company, consisting largely of women and children, slowly proceeded up the valley, suffering much from lack of sufficient supplies, and from the scarcity of water in certain parts of their route. It is said that at least thirty persons perished from these causes, and from exposure to the cold, to which they were unaccustomed.

Vargas had hoped to find the Pueblo Indians in the same pacific and hospitable frame of mind in which he had left them, but such was far from the case. No sooner had the Spaniards left the country the year before than the Governor's interpreter, Pedro de Tapia, began circulating a report that the moderation of Vargas was all assumed, and that he intended to return some day and order the execution of all the leading men who had taken part in the revolution. This idea spread rapidly, and soon to a great extent undid the good results of the Governor's conciliatory policy. When the natives heard that he was again approaching, they feared that it was with a view to carry into effect the threatened punishment, and a great council was held at Santa Fé, at which the majority determined to resist his advance, and began making preparations to arm all of the natives for that purpose. Vargas learned of this condition of affairs from scouts whom he had sent out in advance, and in consequence marched with great caution. It turned out, however, that in many of the pueblos there was a division of opinion on the subject, which prevented the prompt action that might have been fatal to the Spaniards, and greatly facilitated their march. The pueblos of Santa Ana, Zia, and Cochití gave evidence of a friendly disposition and on the 1st of December, at Santo Domingo, Vargas met the Governors of Tesuque, San Lazaro, and San Yldefonso, together with Don Luis, whom he had appointed to the chief government the year before, and contradicted the report of the interpreter in such a convincing manner as to renew their confidence, and Luis went on a mission to Santa Fé to procure provisions and endeavor to induce the inhabitants to allow the Spaniards to enter. On the evening of the 11th, Vargas, who had encamped at the Ranch of Roque Madrid, five miles south-west of the town, was met by a deputation including the Governors of Santa Fé and Tesuque, who expressed the best of feeling, and in token of friendship brought a quantity of tortillas. They said that the story of the Interpreter had done much harm, but that the older men and women had never believed it.

On the 16th the Spanish army marched into Santa Fé, bearing the same banner which had been carried by Oñate when he entered the city just a century before. The occasion was one of much pomp and ceremony. The inhabitants were assembled in the plaza, the men on one side and the women on the other; the soldiers opened ranks to allow the priests to pass through, the latter, in gorgeous vestments, saying the Te Deum and chanting the Litany; and the Governor then delivered an address. When all was concluded the troops and immigrants were marched to the hill immediately north of the city, where a camp was prepared, and where they remained until Christmas day; the Tanos Indians being left in possession of the Palace, and the other natives, of the houses in the town. The weather meanwhile became very cold; men sent out for timber to repair the church of San Miguel were unable to work on account of the severity of the season, and the priests and the council asked permission to occupy houses in the city, instead of remaining in the camp. Vargas therefore directed the Tanos Indians to vacate the Palace and return to their pueblos on the Galisteo; but this created a great commotion, and on the 24th of December, at a council held by them, it was determined not to allow the Spaniards to enter the city. When Vargas heard of this, he prepared to make an assault, but waited for one day, in hopes that better counsels would prevail among the Pueblos. On the 26th, however, a fierce battle was waged during the whole day. The defenses were strong and the place could only be taken by scaling the walls. The Indians fought vigorously with bows and arrows, and used boiling water to prevent an attack close to the walls. In the afternoon re-inforcements from other pueblos appeared, and only after successive cavalry charges were driven back. At night both sides, exhausted, were glad to have the conflict cease. But the Indians had suffered heavily; ninety of their number were killed, and they were discouraged at the retreat of their allies. The next morning, therefore, no opposition was made to the entry of the Spaniards, and formal possession of the city was taken by the Governor. Four hundred women and children who were captured, were divided among the Spanish families in practical slavery. Seventy warriors were executed, and their property, consisting principally of corn and beans, confiscated.

While the capture of the capital was a great blow to the hostile Pueblos, yet they did not yet despair of success. They camped on the surrounding hills, and attacked any parties who dared to go beyond the walls. The Spaniards were practically kept in a state of siege, and what added to their difficulties as spring advanced, was the scarcity of provisions. This annoying and dangerous condition of things continued until Vargas determined to take the field and punish the Indians for their hostility. Starting therefore from Santa Fé in the beginning of March (1694), he marched directly to San Yldefonso, the high mesa north of which was the rendezvous of the northern Pueblos during periods of war. A terrible snow-storm forced him to seek shelter in the houses of the pueblo; but after three days he made an attack on the stronghold, when however the steepness of the ascent gave the defenders such an advantage that the Spaniards had to retire. A few days afterwards he made a second attack, from both sides of the mesa at once, but was again unsuccessful; and then in turn the Indians attacked his force in the night-time, at the pueblo, but the positions now being reversed, they were compelled to retire. In all three conflicts the Indian loss far exceeded that of the Spaniards, but the position on the mesa being practically impregnable while defended by such large numbers as now occupied it, Vargas finally concluded, on March 19th, to withdraw to Santa Fé, having been successful in one great object of his expedition, that of obtaining cattle and provisions.

He had scarcely reached the capital, when a deputation arrived from the friendly pueblos of Zia and Santa Ana, asking for assistance, as they were threatened with attack. Vargas persuaded them that the best assurance of safety was to defeat their enemies in the field, and was consequently joined by a considerable body of allies, with whom he again marched his little army to San Yldefonso, and this time, after an obstinate fight, succeeded in gaining the heights, dispersing the Indians, and taking possession of the camp, with over 300 prisoners, mostly women and children, and 900 sheep, besides horses and mules. The sheep were turned over to the Indian allies, thirteen warriors who were taken were shot, and Vargas refused to give up the women and children until the leader of the natives, named Zepe, and his principal officers, were surrendered to him. Various skirmishes ensued, in which about half of the prisoners escaped, and then Vargas was obliged to hasten back to Santa Fé by news of an attack on that town, leaving Captain Roque Madrid in command of a detachment left at San Yldefonso.

Planting-time had now come, and both Indians and Spaniards ceased hostilities for a space to attend to agriculture, the lands around Santa Fé being apportioned among the soldiers for this purpose. Early in April the Governor visited Cochit to endeavor toí arrange that the people of the adjacent pueblos, at Santo Domingo, San Felipe, etc., should re-inhabit their old villages and plant their land, in which he was fairly successful, although his escort suffered somewhat from a night attack unexpectedly made on them while there. Nor did the Indians at all give up hopes of repossessing the capital, but made assaults on it from time to time, especially when the Governor was away and the garrison weakened; two of these attacks being on April 19th and May 25th, respectively. They also returned to their stronghold at the mesa of San Yldefonso, and successive attempts of Vargas to dislodge them in May were unsuccessful. In the middle of June he again marched from Santa Fé to the mesa, but finding that the enemy's force was largely made up of Taos and Picuris Indians, he concluded to proceed directly to those pueblos in order to inflict chastisement. Both towns were found deserted, the inhabitants having fled to the mountains. Vargas commanded the people of Taos to return to their homes within a certain limited period, and negotiations proceeded for some time between the Governor of Pecos, acting for the Spaniards, and Pacheco, the Governor of Taos; but the Indians failing to return, the pueblo was given up to pillage by the soldiers on July 5th, and a considerable amount of corn secured. As a large body of the enemy had collected in the mountains to attack him on his march back to Santa Fé, Vargas returned through the country of the Utes, who were friendly with the Spaniards. The route led him to cross the Rio Grande near the Colorado, north of Taos, and then march to the Ojo Caliente River, and down that stream and the Chama to the junction of the latter with the Rio Grande. At San Yldefonso he found so many Indians that he did not attack the mesa, but proceeded direct to Santa Fé, arriving on July 14th, after having marched 120 leagues in seventeen days.

The river having fallen now, so as to make its crossing easy, the Governor without any delay started on another expedition to the west, to punish the Indians of Jemez for their attacks on the pueblos of Santa Ana and Zia, and to obtain corn for the people of Santa Fé. After crossing the Rio Grande, Vargas was joined by a large number of Indian allies, and with them marched rapidly to Jemez, where the old pueblo was found abandoned, the people having moved to the top of an adjacent hill, where they were building a new town. Here a fierce battle took place, the Spaniards with their allies assaulting the place, and the Jemez Indians defending it with great obstinacy. At length however they were overcome, nearly 100 being killed, and 370 women and children captured. While here the Governor had a special search made for the burial-place of the priest, Juan de Jesus, who had been killed, as previously related, at the opening of the rebellion; and after some difficulty his remains were found and conveyed to Santa Fé, where they were re-interred in the parish church with much ceremony on the 11th of August, exactly fourteen years after his martyrdom at Jemez. Soon after this, peace was made with the remaining Indians of Jemez, the prisoners restored, and the pueblo rebuilt. This may be considered as the end of the general and organized opposition to Spanish rule by the Pueblos, included in the period of the great rebellion, although some individual towns were not entirely reduced to submission until a short time later.

In 1696 a severe famine afflicted the territory, and especially the Spanish towns, being caused, as was alleged, by the cupidity of Governor Vargas, who retained for his own use a large proportion of the corn sent from Mexico for the support of the colonists; and the Indians of fourteen Pueblos took advantage of the occasion again to rise and endeavor to expel their rulers. A desolating war ensued, which resulted in the destruction or abandonment of many of the pueblos, and the death of at least 2,000 Indians, mostly from sickness and exposure. Others left their old homes and joined the wandering tribes of the plains, rather than submi to Spanish civil and ecclesiastical rule; so that the result was a great diminution in the pueblo population and the number of their villages. The Spaniards, meanwhile, constantly increased in population, and the working in the mines, which had been so prolific a cause of suffering and discontent, not being renewed, the incentive as well as the provocation to rebellion, to a large extent, ceased; and the end of the seventeenth century saw the country entirely at rest.

CHAPTER XV.

THE EIGHTEENTH CENTURY.

THE eighteenth century was for New Mexico a season of comparative quiet. The Pueblo Indians, demoralized by divisions, and tired of revolts which never proved permanently successful, made no trouble during the entire period. With the wild tribes, however, there were almost continual hostilities. They made annual forays upon the more exposed settlements, carrying off the corn and vegetables, which were the results of a year of labor; or the cattle and sheep, which formed the principal property of the people. They frequently attacked the smaller villages — and sometimes, when in force, the larger ones; and many of the towns to-day contain the ruins of the forts and *torreons* built for defense at such times.

Through this century the Comanches were the most troublesome of these tribes; an almost constant warfare continuing between them and the Spaniards. While it consisted mainly of sudden incursions and unexpected attacks, after the manner of most Indian warfare, yet at times there were important battles between the Spanish troops and New Mexican volunteers on the one side and the united bands of Indians on the other. Such were the action at Green Horn, near the middle of the century, and that of El Rito Don Carlos in 1783. The most important and decisive of these battles was that fought at a place called Rabbit Ear two years later. The Comanches had just swept through part of the valley in the Rio Abajo, and made an attack on the town of Tomé, one of the most important in Valencia County, from which they had carried off a number of animals and a quantity of goods, and made prisoners of two sisters of the Pino family, besides killing a number of citizens. Great indignation and excitement prevailed; and the territorial troops and volunteers quickly gathered to the number of 250, and under Lieutenant Guerrero, started in pursuit of the Indians. The latter were found having a grand council, accompanied by a war-dance around the scalps which they had taken as trophies of their success. They were immediately attacked, and a desperate battle ensued for the space of three hours; when the Indians were forced to retreat, losing a large number in killed and wounded, and all their booty and animals, including their own horses. The prisoners were rescued amid the rejoicing of their old friends and neighbors. The Comanches, however, rallied after a short time, and in turn attacked the Mexicans, recovering most of their horses, and forcing the troops to retreat. They lost so many men, however, in these two battles, that they soon after agreed to a peace, and were not troublesome for a considerable time thereafter.

During this century a long succession of Governors ruled in New Mexico, usually with the title of Governor and Captain-General; with sometimes special additions. There is in most cases no record of the time of appointment, so that the dates of their official terms have had to be obtained from various documents executed by their authority and found among the archives at Santa Fé. In 1862 a list was prepared for the report of the Surveyor-General, John A. Clark, by the veteran Chief Clerk, David J. Miller, and from that and some other information of more recent date the succession can now be presented with substantial accuracy. Going back for a moment to the time of Vargas, we find that in 1695 charges were presented against him by the civil authorities of Santa Fé, and the regiment stationed there, for peculation in using government funds and property for his own purposes.

GASPAR DE SANDOVAL ZERDA SILVA Y MENDOZA.—This cavalier was probably appointed Governor pending the investigation, as he appears as such in 1695 and again in 1722. In 1697 Vargas was formally removed from office, and was succeeded by—

PEDRO RODRIGUEZ CUBERO.—His rule continued until 1703, when Vargas was restored to power as Military Commandant of the Province, from which it would appear that he must have been acquitted of the charges against him.

THE DUKE OF ALBUQUERQUE appears to have governed at certain times between 1703 and 1710. The town of Albuquerque is named after him.

JUAN PAEZ HURTADO was Lieutenant-Governor in 1704; commissioned by the Marquis de la Peñuela, the Viceroy, as Governor and Captain-General in 1712; and as Inspector-General in 1716. He was again Lieutenant-Governor in 1735, and in 1736 went on an expedition to the western country, as the following sentence on Inscription Rock near Zuñi proves: "On the 14th day of July, of the year 1736, Gen. Juan Paez Hurtado, Inspector, passed by this place, and in his company Corporal Joseph Armenta, Antonio Sandoval Martinez, Alonzo Barela, Marcos Duran, Francisco Barela, Luis Pacheco, Antonio de Salas, Roque Gomas."

FRANCISCO CUERBO Y VALDEZ, Governor *ad interim* in 1705, 1706, and 1707.—He was "Knight of the Order of Santiago, official judge, royal treasurer, factor of the royal domain, treasurer of the city of Guadalajara, etc."

JOSÉ CHACON MEDINA SALAZAR Y VILLASEÑOR, Marquis of Peñuela, Governor from 1708 to 1712.—It was under his administration that the rebuilding of the church of San Miguel in Santa Fé, which had been destroyed in the Pueblo rebellion, was completed; as appears from the carved viga, on which the inscription is as follows: " El Señor Marquez de la Peñuela hizo esta fabrica; el Alferes Real Don Agustin Flores Vergara su criado. Año de 1710."—"His Lordship, the Marquis de la Peñuela, erected this building; the Royal Ensign Don Augustin Flores Vergara, his servant. A. D. 1710." At this period all the principal churches in the "kingdom" were rebuilt, including many that are now standing. The register of deaths, "Libro de Difuntos," of the mission of San Diego, of Jemez, commences in August, 1720, when Francisco Carlos Joseph Delgado, "Preacher of the Holy Office of the Inquisition," was the priest in charge.

The great church at Santa Cruz, which was the center of an enormous parish in the north, has records anterior to 1720; and its Register of Marriages, with a curious pen-picture of the marriage of the Blessed Virgin to Saint Joseph as a frontispiece, bears date 1726, the first part being written by Padre Predicador Fray Manuel de Sopeña. The baptismal register in the church at Albuquerque commences in 1743. Governor Peñuela was an active official in many ways, and during his administration made three campaigns into the Navajo country, to subdue those Indians. He was afterwards Viceroy of New Spain.

FERNANDO DE ALENCASTER NOREÑO Y SILVA, Duke of Lenares, Marquis of Valdefuentes and of Govea, Count of Portoalegre, Grand Commander of the Order of Santiago of Portugal, etc., was Governor in 1712. He was afterwards made Viceroy of New Spain, and held that office in 1714 and 1715.

JUAN IGNACIO FLORES MOGOLLON was commissioned as Civil and Military Governor by Philip V., at Madrid, September 27, 1707, for five years, and qualified October 9; but did not arrive in Mexico till long after, being recommissioned by the Viceroy, February 9, 1712, and installed in office in Santa Fé, October 5, 1712. His salary, as fixed by the King, was $2,000 per annum. He was accused of malfeasance in office, but the case did not come on for trial until after a delay of some years. By the King's command he was relieved from his position, October 5, 1715, after serving exactly three years. His trial was had at Santa Fé in 1721, long after he had left New Mexico; and his sentence was sent to the Viceroy for confirmation, the costs being adjudged against him. The officer charged with their collection reported that neither the accused nor any of his property could be found.

ANTONIO VALVERDE COSSIO was appointed Governor, *ad interim*, for a period in 1714, and again in 1718.

FELIX MARTINEZ, was appointed by the Viceroy to succeed Governor Mogollon, and qualified at Santa Fé, December 1, 1715. In the succeeding year he led an expedition to the western confines of the kingdom as far as the Moqui province, in order to bring those freedom-loving cities into subjection. On the north wall of the Inscription Rock, which is an invaluable historical tablet, appears the record of his passage, as follows: " In the year 1716, upon the 26th day of August, passed by this place Don Felix Martinez, Governor and Captain-General of this kingdom, for the purpose of reducing and uniting Moqui." On another part of the rock are the inscriptions of some of the companions of the Governor on this expedition, as follows: "Juan Garcia de la Revas, Chief Alcalde, and the first elected, of the town of Santa Fé, in the year 1716, on the 26th of August. By the hand of Bartolo Fernandez, Antonio Fernandez." In 1719 an expedition under Villaza started from Santa Fé, guided by a Frenchman, and succeeded in reaching the banks of the Missouri River, opposite the towns of the Pawnees (called Pananas); but the Indians crossed in the night, surprised the Spaniards, killed the commander and guide, and also Father Juan Dominguez, the chaplain.

JUAN DE ESTRADA Y AUSTRIA, His Majesty's Residuary Judge, Acting-Governor and Captain-General, during the trial of Ex-Governor Mogollon, 1721

JUAN DOMINGO DE BUSTAMANTE.—He was Governor

for nearly or all the period from 1721 to 1731, and again in 1738.

Gervacio Cruzat y Gongora was Governor from 1731 to 1737. In the latter year the Bishop of Durango, whose diocese included New Mexico, made the first episcopal visitation ever had in the territory. He visited all parts of New Mexico, going even as far west as Zuñi, and left on the Inscription Rock the following memorial: "On the 28th day of September, of the year 1737, arrived at this place the Illustrious Don Martin de Liza Cochea, Bishop of Durango; and on the 29th left for Zuñi." On this trip he was accompanied by the Batchelor Don Juan Ignacio de Arrasain, whose name appears on the rock, on the same date.

Henrique de Olavide y Michelena.—1738.

Gaspar Domingo y Mendoza.—He was Governor from 1739 to 1743.

Joaquin Codallos y Rebal was Governor from 1744 to 1749, except in 1747 when—

Francisco Huemes y Horcasitas was Governor *ad interim*.

Tomas Veles Cachupin was Governor for many years, embracing the periods from 1749 to 1754, and probably to 1758; from 1762 to 1767, and again in 1773.

Manuel Portillo Urrisola appears to have been Governor for a short time in 1761, and—

Francisco Antonio Marin del Valle was Acting-Governor in that year and 1762. He and his wife presented to the Church the great carved stone Reredos now in the cathedral at Santa Fé, as appears from the inscription thereon.

Pedro Fermin de Mendinueta held office several times, and was the last of the officials having the title of "Captain-General." He was a Colonel in the Royal army, and Knight of the Order of Santiago; and was first Governor in 1759, then for a short term in 1762, when he was succeeded by Cachupin, and afterwards succeeded the latter in 1767, and held the position until

1778, except a brief interval in 1773, when Cachupin again acted.

JUAN BAUTISTA DE ANSA was appointed as "Civil and Military Governor" in 1780, and held office until 1787 or 1788, when he was succeeded by—

FERNANDO DE LA CONCHA, who held the position until 1794, and again for a short time in 1800.

FERNANDO CHACON was appointed in 1794 and continued in office for eleven years, until 1805, except an interval in 1800 and 1801.

These breaks in official tenure, and the appearance of so many *ad interim* officials, is in a great measure accounted for by visits of the Governors to the City of Mexico, which at that period required a large amount of time.

During all of this century, New Mexico was the extreme outpost of Mexican authority and colonization, receiving all its supplies of articles not produced at home, by the long routes from the south, through Durango and Chihuahua. The time was very shortly to come when by the opening of communication with the American States to the eastward, it was to become of itself a great point of trade and distribution for the northern portions of Mexico.

In 1796 a census was taken by the Franciscan Fathers, which showed a population of 14,167 whites and 9,453 Indians—only the civilized Pueblos being enumerated. This is exclusive of the City of Santa Fé, which for some reason is omitted in the computation. In 1798 a similar census showed a slight increase, there being 15,031 whites and 9,732 Indians. These reports are signed by Father Francisco de Hezio, Custo. In 1799 Governor Chacon made an official report of the last census, in accordance with a royal decree, making the population, including Santa Fé and its garrison—white, 18,826; Pueblo, 9,732; or counting the jurisdiction of El Paso—white, 23,769; Indian, 10,369. This showed the population of Santa Fé to be at that time 3,795.

CHAPTER XVI.

FROM 1800 TO 1846.

A.—THE GOVERNORS.

IN Chapter XV., on the Eighteenth Century, the line of Governors ended with Fernando Chacon, who remained in office till 1805. This list then continues as follows,—

JOAQUIN DEL REAL ALENCASTER.—He was in office from 1805 to 1808.

JOSÉ MANRIQUE.—He was a Lieutenant-Colonel in the army, and was Governor or Governor *ad interim* from 1808 to 1814; and again for a short time in 1819. In 1811 General Nemecio Salcedo, General of the Department, with head-quarters at Chihuahua, made certain orders respecting lands in New Mexico, which have led to his name being placed in some lists of Governors; but he never seems to have had that or any other civil title, and the powers he exercised he probably assumed by virtue of his military authority.

ALBERTO MAYNEZ was the next executive, with the title of Civil and Military Governor. He served in 1814 and 1815, and again in 1817.

PEDRO MARIA DE ALLANDE succeeded to the title in 1816, and again in 1818, after the second period of Maynez's authority.

FACUNDO MELGARES.—He was the last of the Spanish Governors, the revolution of 1821 being successful in establishing Mexican independence. By the law of May 6, 1822, his term as Governor expired on the succeeding 5th of July. It was Governor Melgares who, as Lieutenant, commanded the brilliant expedition into the Indian

Territory in 1806; and subsequently had charge of the escort of Pike, to Chihuahua, in 1807. During the year 1821, from certain documents it appears that—

ALEJO GARCIA CONDE, Inspector-General, acted as Governor for a time, with the title of "Superior Political Chief of the four Internal Provinces." This was probably in the revolutionary days, before the arrangements under the Mexican *regime* became settled.

FRANCISCO XAVIER CHAVEZ was the first regular executive under Mexican authority. The title was now changed from Governor to "Political Chief." Governor Chavez succeeded Melgares on July 5, 1822, and was also Acting Civil Governor from June 17 to July 21, 1823.

ANTONIO VISCARA quickly succeeded Chavez in 1822, holding office but a short time; but was again in power for a brief period, in 1828.

BARTOLOMÉ BACA was in authority in 1824, and until September 13, 1825, when he was succeeded by—

ANTONIO NARBONA, who held the office until May 20, 1827. He was a Canadian.

MANUEL ARMIJO then obtained the position, holding it at this time but about a year, when—

JOSÉ ANTONIO CHAVEZ succeeded, and held the office for three years, a long period in those days of rapid changes and short administrations.

SANTIAGO ABREU became Political Chief in 1831, and continued until some time in 1832. He and his two brothers, Ramon and Marcelino, all came from Mexico shortly before, and all were killed in the revolution of 1837. Governor Abreu was Chief Justice down to the time of that revolution.

FRANCISCO SARRACINO.—Political Chief, 1833 to May 14, 1835, when—

MARIANO CHAVEZ became Acting Jefe Politico for three months, until the arrival from Mexico of—

ALBINO PEREZ, who served as Political Chief until the new Mexican constitution went into effect and New

Mexico was changed from a Territory into a Department, and its executive from a Political Chief to a Governor. The new arrangement went into operation in May 1837, Perez being appointed the first Governor, and holding the position until he was cruelly murdered in the revolution of that year. During the insurrection, and while Gonzales was claiming to be governor, the legitimate authority was held by—

Pedro Muñoz, a Colonel in the army, as Acting-Governor, until the executive power was assumed by—

Manuel Armijo, first as Commanding General, and after the execution of Gonzales in January 1838, as Governor. He was soon after regularly appointed to the latter office, and held it until January 1845, when he was suspended by the Inspector General. For a brief time in 1841—

Antonio Sandoval appears as Acting-Governor; and during the suspension of Armijo—

Mariano Martinez de Lejanza was Acting-Governor from some time in 1844 to September 18, 1845, and—

José Chavez from the latter date to December, when Armijo was elected to the executive office, and again assumed its duties.

Manuel Armijo was the last Mexican Governor, holding the position until the American occupation.

Juan Bautista Vigil y Alarid appears as Acting-Governor for a short time after Armijo's retreat, and as such delivered the capital to General Kearney, August 18, 1846.

B.—PRINCIPAL EVENTS.

In 1805 a census was taken, the report of which signed by Governor Alencaster, under date of Nov. 20, 1805, shows a population (exclusive of El Paso and its surroundings not now included in the territory), of Spaniards: Male, 10,390; female, 10,236; total, 20,626. Pueblo Indians: Male, 4,094; female, 4,078; total, 8,172. Total population, 28,798, exclusive of wild tribes.

1800 TO 1846.

The population of the Pueblo towns was as follows: Taos 508, Picuris 250, San Juan 194, Santa Clara 186, San Yldefonso 175, Nambé 143, Pojuaque 100, Tesuque 131, Pecos 104, Cochití 656, Santo Domingo 333, San Felipe 289, Sandia 314, Jemez 264, Zia 254, Santa Ana 450, Isleta 419, Acoma 731, Laguna 940, Zuñi 1,470, Abiquiu 134, Belem (so spelled) 107. From this it will be seen that though the aggregate number has not greatly varied in three-quarters of a century, yet considerable changes have taken place in particular pueblos.

In the year 1806, during the same administration, much excitement was caused by the belief that an invasion from the United States was contemplated. Rumors of Burr's conspiracy had been received, at the same time that information came of the fitting out of government expeditions to explore the territory newly acquired by the Americans by the purchase of Louisiana. In consequence of this, Lieutenant Facundo Melgares was sent with 600 men to descend Red River and make treaties with the Indian tribes to the eastward, a duty which he performed most admirably. Early in the next year, the expedition of Lieutenant Pike, which had been sent to explore the south-western United States territory, was found encamped by mistake on Mexican soil, and was brought in to Santa Fé. As this constitutes the first historical connection between the United States and New Mexico, a separate chapter has been devoted to the subject. (See Chap. XVII).

In 1810 came the first revolutionary attempt in Mexico, under Hidalgo, commencing at Dolores on September 16th, and ending with the execution of the great leader at Chihuahua, in the ensuing year. But New Mexico was so isolated by its geographical position that the stirring events to the south scarcely caused a ripple of excitement in the territory. In 1814 a conspiracy against the authority of the Governor, Alberte

Maynez, was arranged by Dionicio Valdez and Antonio Armijo; but it was discovered before the plans were fully matured, or any active steps taken, and the projectors were sentenced to ten years' imprisonment at the well known "Trias Hacienda," at Encinillas, north of Chihuahua.

All through this period, down to the final overthrow of the Navajoes long after the American occupation, there existed an almost constant condition of warfare with that powerful tribe. They made frequent incursions into the settlements—much as the Comanches did in the preceding century; and in turn armed expeditions were made into their country, with a view to their punishment and the destruction of their villages and property. The military reputation of Melgares was won in such expeditions, before he was sent to negotiate with the Pawnees in the east. They served as a school of military experience. Governor Vigil took part in no less than four of these campaigns, in 1823, 1833, 1836, and 1838. The hostility of these Indians was intensified by instances of bad faith on the part of the whites. A notable case of this kind occurred in 1820, when a party of Navajo Indians came into the village of Jemez for the purpose of concluding a peace. They were received in a friendly manner, but after a short time the authorities of the town determined to put them to death; so the people were secretly arranged in position so as to surround them while they were unarmed, and cruelly killed them with clubs. Complaint of this outrage was made to the government, and the leaders were arrested; but the cases dragged along until 1824, when they were all set at liberty. Ten years after, the principal perpetrators of this cruelty fell by the hands of other members of this same tribe, it seeming as if Providence would not allow the crime to pass without retribution. Gregg speaks of a similar outrage, which occurred at Cochití.

About the year 1830 the Navajoes were kept in very

good order for a time by the energy of Colonel Vizcarra, but after his departure no one arose capable of inspiring them with fear. The ordinary custom was for peace to be made in the spring, which permitted the sowing of grain to be done without danger; but the fall was very likely to see a renewal of hostilities. An expedition organized in 1835, in which most of the leading men of the territory enlisted as volunteers, was surprised by an ambush in a narrow defile, and forced to retreat with some loss. The Apaches also made periodical raids into certain parts of the territory, and by attacks on frontier settlements prevented to a great extent the spread of population. They were more troublesome, however, in Chihuahua than in New Mexico.

On the 28th day of September, 1821, Mexico declared its independence of the mother country, and shortly afterwards succeeded in making it a reality. This necessarily caused an entire change in the relations of New Mexico, which became a part of the new country—an empire under Iturbide, and a republic after his fall. One principle of the new government of Mexico was popular education; and accordingly, in 1822, we find the first steps taken in the Territory towards the establishment of public schools.

In 1824, Durango, Chihuahua, and New Mexico were united in constituting a State of the Mexican Union; but this arrangement did not last for any great length of time.

In 1828 the Mexican Congress passed a law expelling all native-born Spaniards (called Cachupines) from the republic. This of course affected a number in New Mexico, including several Franciscan Friars, who were all forced to leave, with the exception of two, named Albino and Castro, who were permitted to remain on account of their advanced age—*and* the payment of $500 each! It was not believed that any large proportion of this sum reached the official treasury.

In 1833 the Bishop of Durango made a visitation throughout New Mexico, and was received with great enthusiasm. Special preparations were made at all points for his reception; the roads and bridges on the route were repaired and decorated, and the houses decked with flags, colored cloths, and flowers, in profusion. He made quite a protracted stay in Santa Fé, and visited a number of towns in the territory. A year before, Padre Ortiz (Juan Felipe) had been appointed as Vicar-general of New Mexico.

In 1835 the first newspaper enterprise was attempted —Padre Martinez, of Taos, issuing a paper, of the size of foolscap, entitled "El Crepúsculo" (meaning "The Dawn"), weekly for about a month, when its particular mission being accomplished, and the number of its subscribers (about fifty) not justifying a continuance, it was abandoned. This was the only attempt at a newspaper while the territory was under Mexican control.

In 1837 occurred the change in the general system of government throughout the republic, which metamorphosed New Mexico from a Territory into a Department, and by its augmented taxation and other unpopular features led to an insurrection of large importance, and at the time, of very doubtful result. This was the first revolution, of any real moment, in a century and a half; for which reason it has appeared best to treat it briefly in a separate chapter. (See Chap. XIX.)

Through many years, since the first passage across the plains in the early part of the century, the traffic with the United States had been steadily increasing, until it had grown to very large proportions, and the goods thus brought to Santa Fé were distributed over a large part of northern Mexico. The importance of this business and the general interest attached to the history of the "Santa Fé Trail," has caused that subject also to have a separate chapter devoted to it. (See Chap. XVIII.) This intercourse between the valleys of the Mississippi and the Rio Grande, naturally brought into New Mexico merchants and traders from the East, and they, together with trappers and hunters who gradually accumulated a competence and settled down near the scenes of their active life, constituted a population now generally known as the "Pioneers." Their history should be separately written, and when their adventures and exploits are faithfully recorded, will be as interesting as the most fascinating romance. Many of the first of them to settle on the western border of the plains were of the parentage known as "St. Louis French;" and hence come the French names which exist throughout the north of the Territory, whose existence would otherwise be a mystery.

First among those thus to establish a business in New Mexico was Mr. Roubidoux, who settled at Taos in 1822. Charles Beaubien came to the same town in 1827, and a year later married the sister of Don Pedro Valdez. He was one of the grantees of the enormous "Beaubien and Miranda Grant," to which his son-in-law gave the name of the "Maxwell Grant." His daughters married respectively Lucien B. Maxwell, Jesus G. Abreu, Joseph Clouthier, and Frederick Müller. Colonel Ceran St. Vrain, perhaps the most celebrated of south-western pioneers, lived for many years at Taos, and subsequently at Mora, where he owned a large mill, and where his grave now is. The Bents built "Bents' Fort" in 1829, and in 1832 Bent and St. Vrain commenced business at Taos. There Charles Bent married, and lived until his appointment as Governor, and violent death in 1847. Kit Carson first came from Missouri to Santa Fé in 1826; afterwards going to Taos, where he studied Spanish with Kinkead, and through all the travels and vicissitudes of his after life, retained that as his home. Maxwell, on his "Home Ranch" on the Cimarron, lived like a feudal chief, dispensing a lavish hospitality, and literally "lord of all he surveyed." He employed 500 men, had 1,000 horses, 10,000 cattle, and 40,000 sheep; and after the hardships of early frontier life, enjoyed leisure and profusion in his later days. The oldest living "American" in Santa Fé for many years was James Conklin, who came in 1825, and died in June, 1883. Samuel B. Watrous, now the father of the town of that name, arrived in 1835, and for a considerable time lived at the Placers. James Bonney, whose hospitality both Emory and Abert record, was the original settler at La Junta, in 1842, his house being the first one seen in 1846 for a distance of 775 miles in coming from the east. Peter Joseph, a native of the Azores, came to Taos in 1844, and established himself in business.

In the year 1841 great excitement was produced by reports of the coming of an invading army from Texas, for the purpose of conquering the territory. George W. Kendall, the editor of the New Orleans "Picayune," who accompanied this expedition simply as a traveller, has left a very graphic account of its history in his "Santa Fé Expedition," published in 1844. According to his statement, it had no intention of making war; it was believed in Texas, which claimed all the country east of the Rio Grande as part of her territory, that the majority of the New Mexican people were dissatisfied with the government of Mexico, and would gladly unite with the Texans, if not overawed by military power. The intention of the expedition, then, was to ascertain with regard to this feeling, and if the people so desired, to raise the "Lone Star" flag, and protect them against Mexican coercion; but if there was no such popular feeling, then simply to endeavor to open a mercantile trade. The Mexican authorities, however, naturally regarded it as a direct invasion of their territory; and terrible stories were circulated as to the ferocity of the Texans, who, it was said, would burn, slay, and destroy wherever they went.

The expedition set out from Austin on the 18th of June, 1841, under command of General McLeod; and consisted of 270 mounted volunteers, divided into six companies, of which one was of artillery and provided with a brass six-pounder; and about fifty others, including commissioners, merchants, tourists, and servants. Their march was a very dangerous and arduous one, as it passed through a country entirely untravelled; and of the rivers, deserts, ravines, and other obstacles to be encountered, those in the expedition knew nothing. When a long distance out on the plains, Lieutenant Hull and four men were killed by the Caygua Indians; and soon, on account of the difficulty in finding water, it was determined to divide the party, Captain Sutton, with eighty-seven soldiers and twelve civilians, being sent in advance on the best horses to find the nearest settlements and send word back to the remainder. They took rations for five days, but owing to their lack of knowledge of the country, and the time lost in trying to cross a very deep and perpendicular cañon, it was thirteen before they met any human beings, when they fell in with a party of Mexicans returning from trading with the Indians, at a point in the vicinity of the present Fort Bascom. Near the Gallinas they found a sheep ranch, and for the first time in many days had enough food to eat. From here two of the party, Captain Lewis and Mr. Van Ness, who spoke Spanish, were sent ahead to confer with the authorities, and two merchants with Mr. Kendall accompanied them. At Anton Chico they found the people in a terrible condition of fear and excitement, owing to the stories that had been circulated of Texan ferocity and cruelty; and were informed that the whole country was in arms, and that they would no doubt be taken prisoners the next day and be shot.

The following morning they proceeded through La Cuesta to San Miguel, and on the way were met by

Damacio Salazar, with 100 roughly dressed but well mounted soldiers. In answer to his questions they told him that they were messengers from a large party behind, and desired to see the Governor. This seemed satisfactory, but at the first stop, having surrounded the party with his men, Salazar said that he must demand their arms, at the same time expressing regret at the necessity of carrying out his orders. These were given up, and soon after Salazar said that his instructions were to take all papers and similar articles, and the party had to submit to being searched. Thus far the Mexican officer had expressed so much regret at having to incommode the travellers that they had not doubted his sincerity, but they were shocked a little later to see twelve men drawn up before them with the evident intent of shooting them then and there; and this would have been quickly accomplished but for the intervention of Don Gregorio Vigil, who stopped the bloody deed. The prisoners—for such they now were—were then marched through La Cuesta and Puertocito to San Miguel, where they were confined in a room; the women all along the route showing a kindness and sympathy in marked contrast with the unnecessary cruelty of their captors. The next day on the road to Santa Fé, they met Governor Armijo, who directed them to be retaken to San Miguel. Here, from their little window, they saw two of their late companions shot for having attempted to escape after being taken; and they soon after heard that through the treachery of one of their party, named Lewis, who had been used by Armijo to deceive the Texans, and on his assurance that they would be well treated and allowed to trade, but that the universal custom was for Santa Fé traders to give up their arms on entering the settlements and receive them when their business was done, the entire party had delivered up all their arms; and thereupon had been surrounded and treated as prisoners.

On the 17th of October the whole Texan expedition were marched out of San Miguel, on the way to the City of Mexico, under a strong guard commanded by Salazar. The story of their sufferings and privations, of the numberless cruelties and persecutions inflicted by Salazar, who seems to have been a disgrace to the Mexican name; of the great contrast in their treatment when they were transferred at El Paso to the care of General J. M. Elias Gonzales, who put Salazar under arrest; of the kindness and hospitality of this General "Elias" and Padre Ortiz, and of their long imprisonment in Mexico—is graphically told by Mr. Kendall, but cannot have further space here. The sequel to this history, in the attacks made during the next year on Mexican traders, will be found in the chapter on the Santa Fé Trail.

In 1844 Governor Martinez issued a proclamation which is interesting as containing the last arrangement of civil divisions under the Mexican rule, and also as giving the estimated populations. It states that the Department of New Mexico is divided into three districts, to be called the Central, the North, and the South-east. The whole is divided into seven counties. The districts are as follows.—

Central District.—Counties of Santa Fé, Santa Ana, and San Miguel del Bado, with populations of 12,500, 10,500, and 18,800.

North District.—Counties of Rio Arriba and Taos, with populations of 15,000 and 14,200.

South-east District.—Counties of Valencia and Bernalillo. Populations 20,000 and 8,204.

This gives the total population of the territory as 99,204. The proclamation is dated June 17, 1844.

Governor Martinez was a special friend of education. He sent a number of the most promising young men in the territory to Durango and the City of Mexico to receive military educations; and established additional government schools in Santa Fé.

The news of the breaking out of hostilities between the United States and Mexico in May, 1846, naturally created a great excitement at Santa Fé; the more so as all of New Mexico east of the Rio Grande was included in the territory in dispute, the ownership of which was the occasion of the war. Almost immediately thereafter news arrived that an expedition was being fitted out in Missouri for the invasion of New Mexico, so that it was certain that the territory would become the theatre of actual warfare; and this raised the excitement still higher.

General Armijo was Governor, but for various reasons was unpopular with a large proportion of the influential citizens; and they distrusted his ability and that of his army to repel an invasion. An important private meeting of leading New Mexicans was therefore held to determine what steps should be taken in the emergency; and it was decided that the best course would be to organize a volunteer army composed in part of those who had experience in Indian wars, and were of most approved bravery. As commander they naturally turned to Don Manuel Chavez, of Santa Fé, who had acquired a high reputation as an Indian-fighter; and the other officers designated were Miguel E. Pino, Nicolas Pino, and Tomas C. de Baca, the latter from Peüa Blanca. A petition embodying this programme was presented to the Governor; and Manuel Chavez assured him that if this plan were adopted, he could surely defeat the Americans, as they would be far from their base of supplies and unacquainted with the country. Armijo appeared well pleased with the proposition, but put off a decision until the last moment, and then answered that he was confident of success with his dragoons. The result is known, and finds a place in the chapter on the "American Occupation;" but these facts are here mentioned because they were the foundation of subsequent erroneous charges against some of those who were the leaders in the movement.

C.—MINES AND MINING.

At the time of the journey of Lieutenant Pike, in 1807, as appears in the chapter on his expedition, but one mine was being worked in the territory; to use his words, " There are no mines known in the Province except one of copper, situated in a mountain on the west side of the Rio del Norte, in latitude 34°. It is worked, and produces 20,000 mule-loads of copper annually. It contains gold, but not quite sufficient to pay for its extraction." The locality named above would be directly west of Socorro, in the Magdalenas; but it is very possible that the latitude given is wrong, and that the description refers to the Santa Rita mine, near Silver City. This was discovered in 1800 by Lieutenant Colonel Carrisco, through the aid of an Indian. In 1804 he sold it to Don Francisco Manuel Elguea, a wealthy merchant of Chihuahua, who at once commenced extensive developments, and found the metal of such fine quality that the whole product was contracted to the royal mint for coinage; and was transported to the City of Mexico by pack-mules and wagons— 100 mules, carrying 300 pounds each, being constantly employed.

The next discovery of importance was that in the district now called the " Old Placers." In 1828 a citizen of Sonora, who was herding some cattle in that vicinity, in following some animals that had strayed into the mountains, saw a stone which resembled those in the gold regions of his native State. A further examination revealed particles of gold, and the news of the discovery occasioned much excitement. Many men flocked to the spot, and washing was carried on for a number of years, with what, under the circumstances, was good success. The appliances were of the rudest description, and the lack of water a great drawback. The winter season was the favorite time for operations, on account of the facilities afforded for obtaining water from snow.

This was thrown into a sink and melted with hot stones. The washing was done in a round wooden bowl called "batea," about eighteen inches in diameter, which was filled with earth and then immersed in the pool, and constantly stirred until nothing was left but the heavy black sand and grains of gold. From 1832 to 1835 the annual product was from $60,000 to $80,000; but then diminished somewhat, the poorest years not producing more than $30,000 or $40,000.

Soon after the discovery of the Placers, a vein of gold ore was found on the property of Ortiz in the same vicinity; and in order to work it he formed a partnership with Lopez, a Spaniard, with some experience in mining. By the skill of the latter a considerable sum was realized, whereupon a feeling of jealousy arose, and the old decree which ordered the expulsion of all natives of Spain from Mexico, though long considered obsolete, was revived by the officials, who desired to obtain possession themselves, and Lopez was immediately ordered to the frontier, the vigilant officers assuring him that it was against their consciences "longer to connive at his residence so near the Capital, in contravention of the laws." A new company, including several officials, with Ortiz, then proceeded with the wealth-producing work; but from lack of knowledge did not obtain a grain of gold. Subsequently an order was made prohibiting any but natives from working at the mines; and thus foreign capital and energy were prevented from taking any part in the necessary development. The greater part of the work was done by poor men working on their own account, and satisfied if they could realize scanty wages. Each miner was allowed ten paces in all directions from his pit, as his "claim," and no newcomer could interfere with the right thus acquired, unless the "*labor*" was abandoned for a specified time, when the ground again become open to location. The gold was mainly in dust, but occasionally large nuggets were found, the most valuable being worth $3,400, although it was sold by its finder for $1,400.

In 1839 the "New Placers" were discovered a short distance to the south-west, and the miners speedily deserted their old "diggings" for the greater charms of the new; and the little village of Tuerto rose into large importance as a business point. In 1845 this town contained twenty-two stores, transacting more business in the aggregate than the establishments of Santa Fé. At that time the annual "output" of both districts had reached $250,000, and as many as 2,000 men congregated there to work in the winter. Machinery was introduced, but the lack of a sufficient supply of water prevented very extensive operations. At the time of the American occupation, Samuel B. Watrous, for whom the town of Watrous has since been named, and Richard Dallum, the first U. S. Marshal, were residents of the "Placers." The "Ramirez" mine is described as being at that time the most important in operation. Among other Placers which were discovered and worked before 1846, were a number in the north, in the vicinity of Taos, and as far distant as Sangre de Cristo; and Gregg speaks (1844) of some in the mountains, near Abiquiu. At that time no silver mines were in operation, though discoveries had been made near Manzano; but the ore was considered too refractory to be worked by the appliances at hand. Two years later, however, Lieutenant Abert tells of visiting Don Pedro Baca, at Manzano, and receiving some fine specimens of ore from mines of which his host had charge. Some discoveries had also been made of silver near Socorro. This may be said to be the substance of the mining development as it existed when our history closes, showing how almost entirely that branch of industry had been abandoned since the Pueblo revolution, and giving but little earnest of the enormous proportions which it was to assume in the future.

L—SANTA FÉ IN 1846.

The following description of Santa Fé, as it appeared in 1846, is taken from the works of Cooke, Abert, Edwards, and Meline, and is of interest as showing the condition at that time of the Capital city: The city, though spread over a large extent, was thinly inhabited, and with the exception of the buildings around the plaza, consisted of scattered houses surrounded by corn-fields. On one side of the plaza (which is about 350 feet square) stood the Palace, a long adobe building, one story high, with a portico formed by extending the roof some distance over the street, supported by the smooth trunks of trees. This portico extended in front of all the buildings fronting the plaza. The Palace was the only building having glazed windows. At one end of it was the government printing-office, and at the other the guard-house and prison. Fearful stories were connected with the prison; and Edwards says that he found, on examining the walls of the small rooms, locks of human hair stuffed into holes, with rude crosses drawn over them.

Fronting the Palace, on the south side of the plaza, stood the remains of the Capilla de los Soldados, or military chapel, the real name of which was The Church of Our Lady of Light. It was said to have been the richest church in the Territory, but had not then been in use for a number of years, and the roof had fallen in, allowing the elements to complete the work of destruction. On each side of the altar was the remains of fine carving, and a weather-beaten picture above gave evidence of having been a beautiful painting. Over the door was a large oblong slab of freestone, elaborately carved, representing "Our Lady of Light" rescuing a human being from the jaws of Satan. A large tablet, beautifully executed in relief, stood behind the altar, representing various saints, with an inscription stating that it was erected by Governor Francisco Antonio Maria del Valle, and his wife, in 1761.

The other sides of the square were occupied by the shops used by those engaged in the trade of the Santa Fé Trail. There were no trees in the center of the plaza, which was simply an open square, dusty in the spring, and muddy in the rainy season; but on each side was an acequia, with a row of young cottonwoods. The houses were lighted by small grated windows, generally about a foot square; but the dazzling whiteness of the walls made them sufficiently light. The church services were held in the *Parroquia*, or parochial church (now the cathedral), which had two towers or steeples, in which hung three or four bells. The music was furnished by a violin and a triangle. "The wall back of the altar was covered with innumerable mirrors, paintings, and bright-colored tapestry."

During the month of November, 1846, a dramatic society was organized among the soldiers; and Governor Bent having kindly given the use of the ball-room in the Palace, it was soon transformed into a theatre. The "season" opened with Pizarro and Bombastes Furioso about the middle of the month, and continued until many of the troops were ordered South in December. On the night after Christmas, the Governor gave a grand ball in the Palace, to which the leading people of both nationalities were invited, and which was considered one of the finest entertainments that Santa Fé had ever seen.

CHAPTER XVII.

THE EXPEDITION OF LIEUTENANT PIKE—1806.

VERY shortly after the acquisition of the vast territory then embraced under the one name of Louisiana from the French by the United States, the Government of the latter undertook the exploration of such portions of this immense domain as were then unknown, save to the aborigines. Captains Merriwether Lewis, and C. Clark were selected by the President to explore the then unvisited sources of the Missouri, and Lieutenant Zebulon Montgomery Pike, of the sixth infantry, to follow the Mississippi to its source; both expeditions having to traverse unbroken wildernesses and encounter untold hardships and privations. The expedition of Lieutenant Pike occupied nearly nine months, extending from August 9, 1805, when he sailed from St. Louis, to the last day of April, 1806, when he returned.

Soon after his arrival he was requested by General Wilkinson to take command of another expedition then being fitted out at St. Louis, the primary object of which was to conduct a number of Osage Indian captives, and also a deputation of that tribe recently returned from Washington, up the Missouri and Osage Rivers to the Indian town of Grand Osage. The instructions then provided that Lieutenant Pike should endeavor to bring about a permanent peace between the Kansas and Osage nations; and afterwards to "establish a good understanding with the Yanctons, Tetaus, or Camanches," and finally "to ascertain the direction, extent, and navigation of the Arkansaw and Red Rivers." As to the possibility of meeting inhabitants of New Mexico, the instructions of the General were as follows:

"As your interview with the Camanches will probably lead you to the head branches of the Arkansaw and Red Rivers, you may find yourself approximated to the settlements of New Mexico, and there it will be necessary you should move with great circumspection to keep clear of any hunting or reconnoitering parties from that province and to prevent alarm or offense; because the affairs of Spain and the United States appear to be on the point of amicable adjustment, and moreover it is the desire of the President to cultivate the friendship and harmonious intercourse of all the nations of the earth, and particularly our near neighbors, the Spaniards."

This expedition started from the landing at Belle Fontaine on July 15, 1806—the party consisting of two lieutenants, one surgeon, one sergeant, two corporals, sixteen privates, and one interpreter. It had in charge fifty-one Indians, the most of whom were Osages who had been redeemed from captivity among the Pottawatomies, and were now to be returned to their own country. The surgeon was Dr. Robinson, who was a volunteer, giving his services as compensation for transportation and accommodation. Without dwelling on this expedition until it neared the Spanish boundary, it may be said that from August 20th to September 1st, Lieutenant Pike remained at Grand Osage, holding councils with the chiefs of the Osage nation, and that on September 29th he held a grand council with the Pawnees at their principal village, not less than 400 warriors being present.

At this point he saw the first evidences of the Spanish expedition which had recently visited there from New Mexico. This expedition, which was the most important that ever penetrated to the eastward into the Indian country, at least in modern times, consisted of 100 dragoons of the regular army drawn from Chihuahua, and 500 mounted militia of New Mexico, all equipped with ammunition for six months, and each man leading two horses and a mule, making the whole number of animals 2,075. The whole force was under the command of Don Facundo Melgares, a lieutenant in the Spanish army, a man of large wealth and liberal education, who had gained much distinction in previous expeditions against the Apaches and other hostile Indians. They descended the Red River 233 leagues, held councils there with the Chief of the Tetaus, and afterwards struck off north-east to the Arkansas River, and thence to the Pawnee nation, where they held a grand council, presented Spanish flags and medals, and also a commission to Characterish, the head chief, from the Governor of New Mexico (dated Santa Fé, June 15, 1806), and finally returned to Santa Fé in October. When the distance travelled and the country and tribes passed through are considered, this expedition rivals those of Lewis and Clark, and Pike, for its extent, difficulty, and importance.

After leaving the Pawnee capital, Lieutenant Pike proceeded westerly between the Arkansas and the Kansas rivers, (always called in his narrative " Arkansaw " and " Kans "), seeing many prairie-dogs, which he calls *Wishtonwishes* from the sound of their cry, and of which he tells us almost the exact story afterwards repeated by Horace Greeley with a slight variation, of their living in the same hole with a rattlesnake, a horned frog, and a land tortoise. On the 28th of October, in accordance with instructions, he detached Lieutenant Wilkinson with five soldiers to make the trip down the Arkansas River in canoes, for the purpose of exploring its whole course to the Mississippi. On the 15th of November he came in sight of the Rocky Mountains, and soon after encountered almost constant snows, suffering great hardships—as the company had only summer cotton clothes—and on the 3d of December reached and calculated the altitude of the great mountain which bears his name to those who otherwise might never have heard of this intrepid explorer—"Pike's Peak." He mentions it as known to all the savage nations for hundreds of miles around, and spoken of with admiration by the Spaniards, being the bounds of their travels to the northward. Pike's measurement made it 10,581 feet above the level of the prairie, which he estimated at 8,000 feet, thus making the total elevation 18,581, whereas the latest estimates make it only 14,147; and he says that in all the wanderings of the party for over two months, from November 14th to January 27th, it was never out of their sight.

The hardships endured during this period are almost beyond description; the feet of the men became frosted so that they could only proceed with the utmost pain, and finally several had to be left in sheltered localities, and supplied with food from time to time by the remainder. The party subsisted entirely on the product of the chase, and sometimes for as long as three full days were without a mouthful to eat. In December the expedition determined to leave the valley of the Arkansas and proceed southerly, to strike the head-waters of the Red River, which they expected to find at that point. Soon after they met a stream which they followed eastward slowly, on account of their wretched physical condition, and the necessity of stopping daily to hunt; but imagine their feelings, almost of despair, when on January 5th they found that they had thus been led back to the Arkansas, and were at the camp which they had occupied nearly a month before! Again they started southerly, in search of the Red River, determining to cross the mountains before them on foot; each of the party, including the commander himself and Dr. Robinson, carrying forty-five pounds of baggage, besides provisions and arms, making an aggregate of seventy pounds burden. At length, on the 30th of January, they arrived in the evening on the banks of a stream of some magnitude, which they believed to be the long-looked-for Red River. Here they concluded to build a kind of stockade, where four or five might defend themselves while the others went back to carry assistance to the poor fellows who had necessarily been left at various points, on account of inability to travel; the intention being, when all should be assembled, to proceed in canoes or on rafts down the Red River to Natchitoches, then the most westerly U. S. post in southern Louisiana. At this point Dr. Robinson, who had business in New Mexico, left the party in order to proceed to Santa Fé, which they calculated was then nearer than it would be from any other point.

While most of the men were absent, in search of those left behind, and the remainder were at work building the fort, Pike himself usually employed himself in hunting; and on February 15th, while thus occupied with a single soldier, he discovered two horsemen near the summit of a hill, but half a mile distant. After much parleying they were induced to come to the camp, and proved to be a Spanish dragoon and a civilized Indian, both well armed. They reported that Robinson had arrived in Santa Fé, and been received with great kindness by the Governor. They seemed surprised at the appearance of the fort, but Pike informed them of his intention of going down the river to Natchitoches as soon as his party was prepared; and at the same time said that if the Governor of New Mexico would send an officer with an interpreter, it would be a pleasure to satisfy any doubts he might have as to the intentions of this American party in being so near his borders. The two visitors stated that they could reach Santa Fé in two days (which was not true), but never intimated that Pike was wrong in supposing himself on the banks of the Red River. The building of the fort continued, and gradually the frozen men who had been left behind were brought in—with the exception of two still unable to walk. Of them Pike says, "they sent me some of the bones taken out of their feet, and conjured me by all that was sacred not to leave them to perish far from the civilized world."

On the 26th of February the report of the guard's gun announced the appearance of strangers, and soon after two Frenchmen arrived. These informed Pike that Governor Alencaster, of New Mexico, had heard that the Ute Indians were about to attack the little expedition, and therefore had sent an officer with fifty dragoons to protect them. Scarcely had this notification been received, when the Spanish party came in sight, consisting not only of the fifty dragoons but also fifty mounted militia of the province. Pike sent the Frenchman to arrange a meeting between himself and the commander of the troops, and then sallied forth to hold the interview on the prairie near the fort. The officers in command of the Spanish expedition were Don Ygnacio Saltelo and Don Bartolomé Fernandez, both lieutenants. After some conversation, Pike invited them to enter his fortification and they breakfasted together, after which the Spanish officers said that the Governor, having learned that Pike's party had lost its route, had sent them to offer all necessary assistance to reach the Red River, the nearest navigable point of which was eight days' journey from Santa Fé. "What," said Pike, interrupting him, " is not this the Red River?" Imagine his amazement at the answer "No, sir! it is the Rio del Norte." These words showed that he had unwittingly passed the frontiers of the United States, and actually erected a fort on Spanish soil, within the borders of New Mexico. His first act, on receiving this astonishing information, was to order his men to take down the American flag, which had been hoisted over the works. The Spanish commander then said that the Governor was anxious to see them at Santa Fé as soon as possible, and had provided 100 horses and mules to take the party and their baggage to the capital. Pike at first refused to go until the detachment which he had sent under a sergeant to bring in the two men still absent had returned; but it was finally arranged that he should proceed with one of the lieutenants and half the Spanish force, leaving two men to meet the sergeant's party on their return, to inform them of the changed aspect of affairs. Pike in telling of this event expresses the reluctance with which he abandoned the fort built with so much labor, and which was admirably situated for defense; but finding that he had really, though unintentionally, trespassed on Spanish territory, and being confident that the officers sent had orders to bring him and his men to Santa Fé by force, if necessary, he thought it best to show an entire willingness to make an explanation to the Governor, rather than appear to go under constraint.

Much discussion has taken place as to the exact locality of Pike's Fort; but by a careful reading of his narrative it can be determined almost to a certainty. He first saw the Rio Grande from the top of a high hill, two days after his party struck a small river running west, which they hailed as a tributary to the Red River, and followed through what would now be called a cañon, along the foot of the White Mountains (Sierra Blanca). A glance at a modern map will show that the small river was the Sangre de Cristo; and the point from which the Rio Grande was first seen, near the site of Fort Garland. After reaching the Rio Grande they descended eighteen miles, where they found a large western branch emptying into the main stream. This must have been the present Conejos River. Five miles up this river, on the north bank, and with the water itself forming the defense on one side, was where he built his fort; which was so ingeniously constructed that it could only be entered by creeping through a hole, after passing a draw-bridge over the ditch. The description which

Lieutenant Pike gives of the surrounding country is just such a burst of enthusiasm as we might expect from the first writer who ever attempted to tell the loveliness of the San Luis Park. "From a high hill south of our camp," he says, "we had a view of all the prairie and rivers to the north of us; it was at the same time one of the most sublime and beautiful inland prospects ever presented to the eyes of man. The prairie, lying nearly north and south, was probably sixty miles by forty-five. The main river, bursting out of the western mountain and meeting from the north-east a large branch which divides the chain of mountains, proceeds down the prairie, making many large and beautiful islands—one of which I judge contains 100,000 acres of land, all meadow-ground, covered with innumerable herds of deer. In short, this view combined the sublime and beautiful. The great and lofty mountains, covered with eternal snows, seemed to surround the luxuriant vale, crowned with perennial flowers like a terrestrial paradise shut out from the view of man."

The description of the journey to Santa Fé shows the above to be the correct location of the fort. The first town of importance which they saw, was after a march of a little more than 100 miles, being the village of Warm Spring, or "L' Eau Chaud," as Pike calls it, or, as now known, Ojo Caliente. Here he found the first real Mexican houses which he had seen, and describes at some length the flat roofs, water-spouts, narrow doors, and small windows—some with mica lights. The springs he describes as two in number, about ten yards apart, each affording water enough for a mill, and the temperature of the water as more than thirty-three degrees above blood-heat. The next day they marched down Ojo Caliente River to its junction with the Chama (which he calls Conejos), observing on the way the well-known ruins of ancient pueblo towns, as well as several little inhabited villages, all of which had round towers to defend the inhabitants from Indian incursions. Here they first experienced the characteristic hospitality of the Mexican people; who invited them into their houses, dressed the feet of the lads who had been frozen—and in short, to use the language of Pike, "brought to my recollection the hospitality of the ancient patriarchs, and caused me to sigh with regret at the corruption of that noble principle by the polish of modern ages."

The same day they continued down the Chama to the Rio Grande and across to "the village of St. John's" (Pueblo of San Juan), which he says was the residence of the President Priest of the province, who had resided in it forty years. The house-tops were crowded when the party entered, just as they would be on a similar occasion to-day; and all the officers and men were hospitably treated. The next morning they marched after breakfast, and in about six miles came to a village of 2,000 souls, and in seven miles further to a small town of 500 inhabitants. These places are not named by the narrator, but must be Santa Cruz and San Yldefonso. Seventeen miles further on they came to a Pueblo town (the Pueblos are always distinguished by Pike as "civilized Indians") containing 400 people. While the estimate of population is a good deal exaggerated, this is evidently Tesuque. Here they changed horses and prepared for their entry into the capitol and appearance before the Governor. The condition of Pike's party as to clothing was so lamentable as to be almost ludicrous. When they left their horses on the Arkansas, and commenced carrying everything on their backs, all articles were abandoned that were not essential to safety. Ammunition, tools, leather, etc., claimed the first places; the ornamental was a minor consideration. So on arriving at Santa Fé the commander was dressed in blue trousers, moccasins (mockinsons) blanket, coat, and a cap made of scarlet cloth lined with fur skin; and the men, in leggings, breech-cloths, and leather coats—and not a hat in the whole company. In such garb they did not make a very imposing appearance.

They had left the fort on the Conejos, February 26th, and arrived at Santa Fé on the evening of Tuesday, March 3rd. Pike describes the length of the city on the creek as about a mile, and that it was about three streets in width. "Its appearance from a distance struck my mind with the same effect as a fleet of the flat-boats which are seen in the spring and fall seasons descending the Ohio. On the north side of the town is the square of soldiers' houses. The public square is in the center of the town, on the north side of which is situated the palace or government house, with the quarters for the guards, etc. The other side of the square is occupied by the clergy and public offices. In general the houses have a shed before the front, some of which have a flooring of brick; the consequence is that the streets are very narrow, say in general 25 feet. The supposed population is 4,500." In another description of Santa Fé, which Captain Pike included in the appendix to his report, he gives a fuller description of the place and its surroundings, as follows: " In the center is the public square, one side of which forms the flank of the soldiers' square, which is closed and in some degree defended by round towers in the angles which flank the four curtains; another side of the square is formed by the palace of the Governor, his guard-houses, etc. The third side is occupied by the priests and their suite, and the fourth by the chapetones who reside in the city."

On entering the city, Lieutenant Pike was conducted to the palace, where he says, "we were ushered in through various rooms, the floors of which were covered with skins of buffalo, bear, or some other animal. We waited in a chamber for some time until his Excellency appeared, wnen we arose, and the following conversation took place in French,—

Gov. Do you speak French?

Pike. Yes, sir.

Gov. You come to reconnoitre our country, do you?

Pike. I marched to reconnoitre our own.

Gov. In what character are you?

Pike. In my proper character, an officer of the United States Army.

Gov. How many men have you?

Pike. Fifteen.

Gov. When did you leave St. Louis?

Pike. 15th of July.

Gov. I think you marched in June.

Pike. No, sir.

Gov. Well, return with Mr. Bartholomew to his house, and come here again at seven o'clock, and bring your papers.

"At the hour appointed we returned, when the Governor demanded my papers. I told him I understood my trunk was taken possession of by his guard. He expressed his surprise, and immediately ordered it in; and also sent for one Solomon Colly, formerly a sergeant in our army, and one of the unfortunate company of Nolan. We were seated, when he ordered Colly to demand my name, to which I replied; he then demanded in what province I was born. I answered in English, and then addressed his Excellency in French, and told him that I did not think it necessary to enter into such a catechising; that if he would be at the pains of reading my commission from the United States, and my orders from my General, it would be all that I presumed would be necessary to convince his Excellency that I came with no hostile intentions towards the Spanish government; on the contrary, that I had express instructions to guard against giving them offense or alarm, and that his Excellency would be convinced that myself and party were rather to be considered objects on which the so much celebrated generosity of the Spanish nation might be exercised, than proper subjects to occasion the opposite sentiments." He then requested to see my commission and orders, which I read to him in French; on which he got up and gave me his hand for the first time, and said he was happy to be acquainted with me as a man of honor and a gentleman, that I could retire this evening and take my trunk with me; that on the morrow he would make further arrangements.

The next day, after examining the contents of Pike's trunk, the Governor informed him that he must go with his men to Chihuahua, in the then province of Biscay, to appear before the Commandant-General. The following conversation then ensued, which Pike has preserved in full in his journal,—

Pike. If we go to Chihuahua, we must be considered as prisoners of war.

Gov. By no means.

Pike. You have already disarmed my men without my knowledge; are their arms to be returned, or not?

Gov. They can receive them at any moment.

Pike. But, sir, I cannot consent to be led 300 or 400 leagues out of my route without its being by force of arms.

Gov. I know you do not go voluntarily, but I will give you a certificate from under my hand of my having obliged you to march.

Pike. I will address you a letter on the subject.

Gov. You will dine with me to-day, and march afterwards to a village about six miles distant, escorted by Captain Antony D'Almansa, with a detachment of dragoons, who will accompany you to where the remainder of your escort is now waiting for you, under the command of the officer who commanded the expedition to the Pawnees."

After the dinner—which Captain Pike characterizes

as "rather splendid," having a variety of dishes, and wines of the southern provinces—the Governor drove Pike, D'Almansa, and a Mr. Bartholomew, who had proved a special friend to the Americans, three miles on the road to the south, the coach being attended by a guard of cavalry; and on parting said to his prisoner-guest: "Remember Alencaster in peace or war."

Accompanied by his friend Bartholomew and the guard, Pike continued on through a blinding sand, and passed the night at the priest's house, at what apparently was the present village of La Bajada; as he says that they "came to a precipice which we descended, meeting with great difficulty from the obscurity of the night." Shortly after noon of the next day they arrived at the Pueblo of Santo Domingo, which they describe as "a large village—the population being about 1,000 natives, governed by its own chief." The insignia of the Governor appears to have been nearly the same then as at present, as it is stated that he was distinguished by "a cane with a silver head and black tassel." Pike visited the old church, and speaks enthusiastically of its rich paintings and the image of the Saint, "as large as life—elegantly ornamented with gold and silver."

On Friday, March 6th, they arrived at San Felipe, where they crossed the Rio Grande on a bridge of eight arches, which seems to have attracted Pike's attention specially, as he gives a full description of its construction. Here they stopped at the house of the padre, Father Rubi, whose hospitality and extended information made the stay a pleasant one. At Albuquerque they were similarly entertained by Father Ambrosio Guerra, and Pike seems to have been particularly impressed with the beauty of some of the orphan girls, whom the good padre had adopted, and was bringing up in his household; and enthusiastically writes, after describing the dinner, "and to crown all, we were waited on by half a dozen of those beautiful girls, who, like

Hebe at the feast of the gods, converted our wine to nectar, and with their ambrosial breath shed incense on our cups."

A short distance further south Pike was rejoiced to meet Dr. Robinson, who had left the party, it will be recollected, while they still believed they were on the Red River, to find his way to Santa Fé. He had received much the same treatment as Lieuten't Pike's command, and was being conveyed to Chihuahua by Don Facundo Melgares, who was now also to assume command of the guard that was conducting Pike. This Melgares was the same who had commanded the Spanish Pawnee expedition, and was described by Robinson to Pike in the highest terms as a gentleman and soldier of gallantry and honor, praise in which Pike himself heartily joined after a brief acquaintance.

After passing towns which the Lieutenant calls Tousac, St. Fernandez, Sabinez, and Xaxales, the expedition reached Cebolleta, spelled by Pike "Sibilleta," which he calls the neatest and most symmetrical village he had seen, being built in a regular square, with an unbroken wall on the outside, all the doors and windows facing the square. At this point, at that time, the semi-annual caravan for the south was formed, leaving in the month of February for El Paso, and returning in March; and making a similar expedition in the fall. The spring caravan which Pike saw consisted of about 300 men, escorted by an officer and 35 or 40 troops, and was conducting 15,000 sheep, which had been collected from various parts of New Mexico, and were to be sold or exchanged for merchandise.

On the 21st of March the whole party arrived at El Paso, and Pike, with the officers, stayed at the house of Don Francisco Garcia, a wealthy merchant and planter, possessing 20,000 sheep and 1,000 cows.

On April 2d they reached Chihuahua, and Pike immediately had an audience with the General Commanding, Don Nemecio Salcedo, who took his papers for examination, and also requested him to write a brief sketch of his travels and adventures on this expedition, which he shortly after did.

After being detained for some time, which however was spent quite pleasantly, owing to the hospitality of many of the leading citizens, Pike and Robinson were sent by a route nearly directly eastward, toward Natchitoches, which was the nearest United States post. On June 7th they arrived at San Antonio, where they were very hospitably treated by Governor Cordero, of Coahuila and Texas, and Governor Herrera, of the Kingdom of New Leon, who treated them, in the language of Pike, "like their children."

Captain Pike speaks in the most exalted terms of both of these gentlemen, and relates the following anecdote as evidence of the extreme popularity of the latter: "When his last term as Governor expired, he repaired immediately to Mexico attended by three hundred of the most respectable people of his government, who carried with them the sighs, tears, and prayers of thousands that he might be continued in that government. The Viceroy thought proper to accord to their wishes *pro tempore*, and the King has since confirmed his nomination. When I saw him, he had been about one year absent, during which time the citizens of rank in Mont Elrey had not suffered a marriage or baptism to take place in any of their families, until their common father could be there to give joy to the occasion by his presence."

At length, on the 1st of July, 1807—but three weeks short of a year from the time of his departure from St. Louis—after crossing the whole of what is now the State of Texas, late in the afternoon, but so eager to arrive that they left their jaded horses and pressed forward on foot, Pike entered the town of Natchitoches with Dr. Robinson. "Language," says he, "cannot express the gaiety of my heart when I once more beheld the standard of my country waved aloft. 'All hail,' cried I, 'the ever sacred name of *country*, in which is embraced that of kindred, friends, and every other tie which is dear to the soul of man!'"

It will be interesting to make a few extracts from the description which Captain Pike gave of New Mexico in the "Observations" which form part of the appendix to the history of his expedition; as showing the condition of the country at that period, in several respects in which time has wrought changes, and in other instances illustrating the characteristics which are still distinguishing marks of the Territory and its people,—

MINES, ETC.—" There are no mines known in the province, except one of copper, situated in a mountain on the west side of Rio del Norte, in latitude 34° north. It is worked, and produces twenty thousand mule-loads of copper annually. It also furnishes that article for the manufactories of nearly all the internal provinces. It contains gold, but not quite sufficient to pay for its extraction; consequently it has not been pursued."

The above extract sounds strangely at this day, when gold and silver are considered the chief resources of the Territory; and it is also singular as showing how little knowledge or recollection there could have been in the community of the operations of the early conquerors, which had ceased a century and a quarter before. It is not easy to fix the identity of the copper mine referred to, but latitude 34° is just below Socorro, and so the mine may have been in the Magdalena Range; although it is possible that the latitude given is incorrect, and that the mine referred to was the "Santa Rita," then being actively worked. This extract may be read in connection with one soon to be given on trade and commerce, in which "wrought copper vessels" appear among the exports, and "gold and silver" among the imports.

MINERALS.—" There is, near Santa Fé, in some of the mountains, a stratum of talc, which is so large and flexible as to render it capable of being subdivided into thin flakes, of which the greater proportion of the houses in Santa Fé, and all the villages to the north, have their window-lights made."

These mica mines, especially at Petaca and in the vicinity of Mora (where one of the villages is called Talco), are well known at present. As late as the time of the American occupation, in 1846, we are told that no house in Santa Fé, except the Palace, had windows of glass.

TRADE AND COMMERCE.—"New Mexico carries on a trade direct with Mexico through Biscay (Chihuahua), also with Sonora and Sinaloa; it sends out about 30,000 sheep annually, tobacco, dressed deer and cabrie skins, some fur, buffalo-robes, salt, and wrought copper vessels of a superior quality. It receives in return from Biscay and Mexico, dry-goods, confectionery, arms, iron, steel, ammunition, and some choice European wines and liquors; and from Sonora and Sinaloa gold, silver, and cheese. The following articles sell as stated (in this province), which will show the cheapness of provisions and the extreme dearness of imported goods :—

Flour sells per hundred at..	$ 2 00
Salt per mule-load...	5 00
Sheep each...	1 00
Beeves each..	5 00
Wine del Passo per barrel...	15 00
Horses each..	11 00
Mules each..	30 00
Superfine cloths per yard..	25 00
Fine cloths per yard..	20 00
Linen per yard..	4 00

and all other dry-goods in proportion.

"The journey from Santa Fé to Mexico and returning to Santa Fé takes five months. They manufacture rough leather, segars, a vast variety and quantity of potters' ware, cotton, some coarse woolen cloths, and blankets of a superior quality. All these manufactures are carried on by the civilized Indians, as the Spaniards think it more honorable to be agriculturists than mechanics. The Indians likewise far exceed their conquerors in their genius for, and execution of, all mechanical operations. New Mexico has the exclusive right of cultivating tobacco."

From this it will be seen that the manufacture of pottery, the evidences of which are found in great quantities in the ruins of the oldest pueblos, and which is still carried on to such an extent by the Pueblo Indians, was never intermitted by that industrious people. The blankets were probably the forerunners of the present celebrated productions of the Navajoes, which tribe is mentioned by Pike under the name of "Nanahaws." Then, as now, the Apaches were the most troublesome of the natives, as the "Observations" say, "The Apaches are a nation of Indians who extend from the Black Mountains in New Mexico to the frontiers of Cogquilla (Coahuila), keeping the frontiers of these provinces in a continual state of alarm, and making it necessary to employ nearly 2,000 dragoons to escort the caravans, protect the villages, and revenge the attacks they are continually making."

GOVERNMENT AND LAWS.—"The government of New Mexico may be termed military, in the pure sense of the word; for although they have their alcaldes, or inferior officers, their judgments are subject to a reversion by the military commandants of districts. The whole male population are subject to military duty, without pay or emolument, and are obliged to find their own horses, arms, and provisions. The only thing furnished by the government is ammunition, and it is extraordinary with what subordination they act when they are turned out to do military duty; a strong proof of which was exhibited in the expedition of Melgares to the Pawnees. His command consisted of 100 dragoons of the regular service and 500 drafts from the province. He had continued down the Red River until their provisions began to be short; they then demanded of the lieutenant where he was bound and the intention of the expedition. To this he haughtily replied, 'wherever his horse led him.' A few mornings after, he was presented with a petition, signed by 200 men of the militia, to return home. He halted immediately, and caused his dragoons to erect a gallows; then beat to arms; the troops fell in, he separated the petitioners from the others, then took the man who had presented the petition, tied him up, and gave him fifty lashes, and threatened to put to death on the gallows erected any man who should dare to grumble. This effectually silenced them and quelled the rising spirit of sedition, but it was remarked that it was the first instance of a Spaniard receiving corporal punishment ever known in the province

In the following paragraph Captain Pike pays a warm tribute to the bravery of the New Mexicans, and makes a richly merited recognition of that generosity and hospitality for which they are everywhere noted, and which the lapse of three-quarters of a century has not lessened, but which form as noticeable a characteristic to-day as when the Captain wrote these words in 1807.

MANNERS, ETC.—"There is nothing peculiarly characteristic in this province that will not be embraced in my general observations on New Spain, except that being frontier and cut off, as it were, from the more inhabited parts of the kingdom, together with their continual wars with some of the savage nations who surround them, render them the bravest and most hardy subjects in New Spain; being generally armed, they know the use of them. Their want of gold and silver renders them laborious, in order that the productions of their labor may be the means of establishing the equilibrium between them and the other provinces where those metals abound. Their isolated and remote situation also causes them to exhibit in a superior degree the heaven like qualities of hospitality and kindness, in which they appear to endeavor to fulfill the injunction of the scripture, which enjoins us to feed the hungry, clothe the naked, and give comfort to the oppressed in spirit; and I shall always take pleasure in expressing my gratitude for their noble reception of myself and the men under my command."

CHAPTER XVIII.

THE SANTA FÉ TRAIL.

THOUGH Mexico was settled early in the sixteenth century, and the Spaniards soon after penetrated over 1,500 miles to the north and occupied the valley of the Rio Grande as far as Taos and the Chama in northern New Mexico, and another colonization from England and France had populated the eastern shores of what is now the United States and Canada early in the seventeenth century, and had extended westward to the Mississippi Valley, and was constantly pushing on further into the wilderness and advancing the pioneer line of its civilization toward the setting sun; yet strangely enough, it was left for the nineteenth century, in which we live, to see any communication whatever between these two populations, situated on the same continent, yet separated by mountains and rivers and by the great expanse of what was then believed to be desert plain.

The French and Spaniards had successively been the rulers of the vast territory extending westward from the Mississippi to the limits of Mexico and the shores of the Pacific, and then all included under the name of Louisiana; yet the people of neither of those nationalities had displayed the enterprise or spirit of adventure requisite for an attempt to cross the intervening space beween themselves and New Mexico, and brave the hostility of the tribes which roamed over the plains between.

It was not until after the acquisition of Louisiana by the United States that such a journey was accomplished, or even attempted. In 1803 President Jefferson completed the negotiation for the purchase of Louisiana from the Emperor Napoleon, and the sovereignty of that vast domain was transferred from the French to the Americans. The chief city of the Mississippi Valley, in the newly acquired territory, was St. Louis; the principal settlement on the easterly side of the river, within the old boundaries of the United States, was Kaskaskia. Each of these places claims the credit of sending the first adventurers across the plains to meet the tide of Spanish colonization coming from the south, at Santa Fé; and it is difficult to say which has the prior right. In both cases, however, the accomplishment was rather the result of accident than intention.

In 1804 Mr. Morrison, an enterprising merchant of Kaskaskia, sent a man called Baptiste La Lande, whose name shows his French parentage, but who was born in Louisiana, to the head-waters of the Missouri and Platte, and furnished him with goods with which to trade with the Indians. Although the relative geographical position of places in that remote section was not well understood, still the astute Kaskaskia merchant directed this La Lande, if it should be possible, to press on to Santa Fé. La Lande was evidently a man of energy, though we cannot admire some of his other qualities; and succeeded in reaching the Rocky Mountains, and finally in sending in some Indians to the Spanish borders, who gave a report of the arrival of this stranger from the far and almost unknown East. A party of Mexicans on horseback ventured into the mountains to meet him, and conveyed him and his goods into some of the northern settlements near Taos, from where he travelled on to Santa Fé, selling his merchandise as he went. Pleased with the country, in which he obtained far higher prices than he had dreamed of elsewhere, and where the hospitable people offered him land and other inducements if he would stay; and captivated by some of the bright-eyed brunettes of the city, he concluded to return no more, not even to account to Mr. Morrison for his goods;

and so, with the proceeds thus simply obtained, he settled down in the capital of the province.

Two years before La Lande left the banks of the Mississippi, James Pursley, an enterprising Kentuckian, who was by turns a hunter, trapper, and trader, and a fair type of the pioneers of those early days, left St Louis on a hunting expedition to the head-waters of the Osage River, in what is now south-western Missouri, with two companions; and from thence with their peltries they started across the country to the White River, with the idea of descending that stream and the Mississippi to New Orleans. But they had scarcely set out when the Kansas Indians stole their horses. They started in pursuit and recognized the horses at the Indian village, but could not regain them. Shortly after, Pursley saw his own horse carrying a burly Indian outside of the town, going to a little stream for water. He pursued stealthily and killed the horse at the river bank; whereupon the Indian rushed back to his wigwam, brought out his gun and attempted to shoot the pioneer. But the weapon missed fire, and Pursley, turning, chased the assailant into the center of the village, where the latter, apparently panic-stricken at the temerity of his pursuer, took refuge in the midst of the women and children, while the other Indians were so struck with admiration that they restored the remaining horses.

Concluding to return to St. Louis, Pursley and his companions were already sailing down the Missouri in a canoe, when they met a French trader bound to the Mandan country; and Pursley, always ready for adventure, left his companions and the prospect of home, and turned up the river in the employ of the Frenchman. The next spring he was sent with some goods in company with several bands of Paducahs and Kyaways on a hunting and trading tour through part of what is now Nebraska; but the party was driven by hostile Sioux into the mountains of Colorado, and travelled over the head-waters of the Platte and the Arkansas—a vast company of 2,000 souls, with 10,000 beasts of various kinds—until they reached the northern border of New Mexico. Wishing to ascertain whether the Spaniards would receive them in a friendly way and enter into trade, the Indians sent Pursley, with a small escort, to Santa Fé as a kind of ambassador. The Governor (Alencaster) acceded to the request, and shortly afterward the whole band followed its advance-guard, and after some time spent in trading, set out on its return to the North.

But Pursley, tired of life among the savages, and glad enough again to be in the midst of Europeans and their civilization, which he had feared he would never more enjoy, concluded to remain in Santa Fé. He arrived there in June, 1805—over three years after his departure from St. Louis—and settled down to the pursuit of his trade as a carpenter; at which, we are told, "he made a great deal of money, except when working for the officers, who paid him little or nothing." Here Pike found him in 1807, and had the celebrated conversation which has given to Pursley the fame not only of being the second (if not the first) who crossed the unknown country which separated the United States from Mexico, but of being the first discoverer of the gold of Colorado— more than half a century before the discovery which brought so many thousands to Pike's Peak and the cañons and mountains of the centennial State. "He assured me," says Pike, "that he had found gold on the head of La Platte, and had carried some of the virgin mineral in his shot-pouch for months; but that being in doubt whether he should ever again behold the civilized world, and losing in his mind all the ideal value which mankind have stamped on that metal, he threw the sample away; that he had imprudently mentioned it to the Spaniards, who had frequently solicited him to go and show a detachment of cavalry the place, but that conceiving it to be in United States territory, he had refused."

How different would have been the history of this great section of the continent, had this patriotic pioneer pursued a different course; and the mineral wealth of Colorado been poured south into Mexico in the beginning of the century, instead of waiting for fifty years for the Anglo-Saxon immigration from the east to rediscover and profit by it!

These two adventurous traders may be called the Fathers of the Santa Fé Trail, although the route which they travelled was far from direct, and their final arrival in New Mexico more the result of chance than of any calculation. The latter at any rate had no intention whatever of visiting the Spanish dominion; and the little that was known of the relative position of the different parts of the continent is strongly illustrated by the fact that Lieutenant Pike, who was the next one to arrive at Santa Fé, and who had every advantage which instruments and the best maps of the period could give, and was actively engaged in an official exploring expedition at the time, yet supposed himself on the waters of the Red River when he was really on the Rio Grande, and had not only crossed the boundary and trespassed on Spanish domain, but had actually built a fort and raised the United States flag on that foreign soil. His visit to Santa Fé in 1807 was rather involuntary than otherwise, yet from it flowed important results; for the descriptions which he published of his travels on his return created much interest and some excitement throughout the West, and many of the adventurous sons of the border yearned to follow the path which led to the city whose very isolation gave it an air of romance.

The first expedition, however, of which we have any record, was undertaken in 1812 by a company of about a dozen enterprising men of St. Louis, who fitted out a party under command of Mr. McKnight, which followed nearly the route described by Captain Pike. They arrived after various hardships, in safety, at Santa Fé, but only to encounter unexpected troubles. Unfortunately, their appearance at the capital was exactly at the wrong time. The attempted revolution under Hidalgo had just been put down, and every American adventurer was looked upon with suspicion as a probable agent of some newly projected revolt. McKnight and his party found themselves arrested as spies, their merchandise, which had been transported with so much labor across the plains, seized and confiscated; and they were themselves soon sent to follow Pike to Chihuahua, in the prison of which city they languished in rigorous confinement until the success of the republican movement under Iturbide brought their release.

Almost simultaneously with their restoration to liberty, another adventurous spirit, an Ohio merchant named Glenn, arrived in Santa Fé with a little caravan, having come by what appears still to have been the only known route—into the mountains of the present Colorado, and thence down the Rio Grande. From this time the trips across the plains became more frequent. The profits made on American goods successfully transported were immense, because the only other route by which they could be received was by the sea to Vera Cruz, across the country to the City of Mexico, thence over the long and difficult road to El Paso, and finally by the semi-annual caravans up the Rio Grande, and crossing the Jornada, to Santa Fé. As an illustration of the enormous prices which such a long, expensive, and perilous trip occasioned, we are told that common calicoes and even plain domestic cottons sold as high as $2.00 or $3.00 per yard, on the plaza of the Capital. It is not strange that the reports of such profits should have stimulated enterprise, and caused the adventurous merchant to esteem the Santa Fé market as better than a gold-field.

In the same year, 1812, Captain Becknell, a Missourian, who had made an expedition from Franklin to the Rocky Mountains, to trade with the Indians, concluded to seek the new Mecca of merchants to the south; and found at Santa Fé a far better market than among the Comanches. Returning that winter with the fruits of his enterprise, and glowing accounts of the country he had visited, he raised a company of thirty friends, and with them and an assortment of goods which cost about $5,000, and was the largest venture of the kind yet made, started across the plains. Knowing from experience that the trail by the mountains of Colorado was a very circuitous one, they determined to try a more direct route, and so branched off from the Arkansas River at the point called "the Caches," intending to march directly southwest to Santa Fé. But this daring enterprise came near costing them all their lives, for the unknown country into which they thus started as pioneers was utterly devoid of water. Their scanty supply was soon exhausted, and the horrors of thirst took possession of them. They killed their dogs and cut off the ears of their mules in order to endeavor to find a moment's relief by drinking the warm blood of the animals. Probably all would have perished, had not a buffalo, coming from a river whose nearness they had not suspected, appeared among them; and the water in his stomach afforded relief which enabled them to reach the river itself. Even then they did not find the route since so well known as the "Santa Fé Trail," for they passed to the north of the Raton range, and first reached the Spanish settlements at Taos

Early in May, Colonel Cooper, a neighbor of Captain Becknell, had left Missouri, about fifteen being in the party, and by pursuing the better known route up the Arkansas, had successfully made the journey. Down to this time, and indeed until 1824, all of the expeditions were on mule-back, and of course the amount of goods that could be transported was comparatively inconsiderable; but in the latter year a new departure was made by the employment of vehicles. The caravan which then started consisted of twenty-five wagons of different kinds, the largest part being what were then called "Dearborn carriages," besides a number of the pack-mules which had usually been employed; and their success in making the trip, which presented fewer difficulties than had been anticipated, gave a great impetus to the Santa Fé trade. The original cost of the goods brought by this caravan was $25,000 to $30,000.

Thus far the occasional passing of a few adventurers had apparently not been noticed by the Indians, or rather, the first traversers of the plains traded almost as much for skins and furs with the Indians as with Spaniards, and took pains to keep on good terms with them. But as the traffic increased, among the men employed were many of the reckless and unprincipled, who seemed to regard neither the keeping of faith with an Indian, nor even the taking of his life, as of any importance. To use the language of Joseph Gregg, who spoke from long personal experience, "Many seemed to forget the wholesome precept, that they should not be savages themselves because they dealt with savages. Instead of cultivating friendly feelings with those who remained peaceful and honest, there was an occasional one always disposed to kill, even in cold blood, every Indian that fell into their power."

As the amount carried to the East by traders increased, troubles with bands of Indian thieves and marauders became alarmingly frequent and grew more and more serious. The first difficulty of this kind was experienced by a small party returning from a trading trip in 1826. They were encamped on the Cimarron, and very foolishly had but four guns among the twelve persons who comprised it. A small party of Arrapahoes approached in a friendly way, but seeing the weakness of the trading party, went away for a short time and returned thirty strong. Their chief then told the Americans that his men needed horses, as they had none; and the traders, hoping to satisfy them, gave them one apiece. Then the Indians' demand increased to two horses for each of their number, and the traders, knowing resistance to be useless, again acquiesced; whereupon the Indians, mounting their newly acquired steeds, and each swinging a lasso in his hand, took possession of the whole drove of animals belonging to the caravan, numbering about 500. This however only affected property; soon lives were found to be unsafe. The first victims were two young men named McNees and Monroe, who had strayed a little way from their camp, and were wantonly shot almost within sight of their tents. While the party to which they belonged was engaged in burying them as best they could on the lone prairie, near the banks of the Cimarron, a small party of Indians, no doubt entire strangers to the murder, came near; and the Americans, full of indignation at the death of their comrades, and stopping to ask no questions, shot down all of them save one, who escaped to bear tidings of the slaughter to his tribe. They in turn pursued the caravan of the traders, bent on avenging the death of their brethren; and overtaking them at the Arkansas River, carried off nearly 1,000 head of horses and mules, though the owners themselves succeeded in escaping. Turning back towards their village, their vengeance far from satisfied until blood had been paid for blood, the Indians soon encountered another little returning prairie caravan, which they attacked, killing one man and running off all the horses. The profits of the trade at that time may be guessed from the fact that the men thus left to travel towards home afoot had each to carry with him over eighty pounds of silver coin, which was his share of the gains of the trip.

The news of these assaults caused the Government next year to furnish an armed escort, consisting of four companies of troops under Major Riley, which was to protect the caravan as far as Chouteau's Island, in the Arkansas, and the various traders consolidated their trains into one long caravan. It was supposed that the road past that point was comparatively free from danger, but the fallacy of this was shown on the first possible occasion; for the caravan had proceeded but two hours' march on its way, after parting with the troops, when the advance guard was attacked by Kiawas, and one man so unfortunate as not to escape was killed and scalped. Major Riley was at once sent for, and arrived with all speed, but the Indians had retired at the first sign of the presence of soldiers. The escort remained in camp on the Arkansas until the returning caravan in the fall required their services. But for some unexplained reason the Government failed to furnish a similar military protection the next year, and it was only repeated on special occasions thereafter, as in 1834, when Captain Wharton's dragoons were detailed for the service, and in 1843, when a formidable army under Captain Cooke escorted two large caravans past the principal points of danger.

As early as 1825 the Government had taken the first steps in favor of encouraging the traffickers of the plains by appointing a commission, consisting of Messrs. Reeves, Sibley, and Matthews, to lay out a road from the border of Missouri to the confines of Santa Fé. While this work was never completed, yet it was commenced with some spirit by the commissioners, who held a council with the Osages in a beautiful strip of woods called Council Grove, long an important point on the Santa Fé Trail, and now the seat of justice of Morris County, Kansas. Here a treaty was made whereby the

Indians agreed to permit all traders to pass and repass, without interference, and in case of necessity, to lend their assistance to trading caravans. The line of the proposed road was determined as far as the Arkansas, and designated by mounds of earth; but it never seems to have been used by the travellers, who persistently refused to be carried off from the old trail, which had been the route of their predecessors, and which had the sanction of experience if not of scientific engineering.

The first route followed, as we have seen, was by a line almost directly westward to the mountains of Colorado, and thence south to Taos. Afterwards, when the trade assumed importance, a road along the Arkansas, and thence south-west to the Raton Pass, following substantially the present line of the Atchison, Topeka & Santa Fé Railroad, was sometimes used; but the route which was the ordinary and favorite one for a long series of years was that along the Arkansas, thence across to the Cimarron, and so entering New Mexico, proceeding in an almost direct line to the Wagon Mound—which made a conspicuous landmark—and thence to Las Vegas, San Miguel, and Santa Fé. A few trips were made by a more southerly route, starting from Van Buren, in Arkansas, instead of Independence; and Mr. Gregg pronounced this the most excellent natural line of travel. But it never became popular, or was more than an experiment.

In 1839 an attempt was made to establish a route from Chihuahua and El Paso to the East, without going to Santa Fé at all. This was undertaken chiefly by Mexican merchants, but Dr. Connolly took a leading part in the enterprise also. The expedition set out from Chihuahua, April 3, 1839, amid general acclamations, as the people saw in it the commencement of a great wholesale trade for their city. Seven wagons, with about $250,000 in bullion, constituted the caravan; and for lack of knowledge of the country, lost considerable time, both in going and returning, having much trouble in crossing some of the intervening rivers, and did not reach Chihuahua, on their return (when they brought sixty or seventy wagons laden with merchandise), until August 27, 1840. A change, meanwhile, had taken place in the Mexican officials, which greatly affected the duties to be paid, so that the enterprise was a financial failure, and was never repeated.

Down to 1824 only pack-animals were employed; in 1824 and 1825 pack-animals and wagons; and commencing in 1826, nothing but wagons. Oxen were first used in 1830. The following statistics, taken from Gregg's "Commerce of the Prairies," show the gradual increase in the business from its commencement in 1822 until 1843, when the trade was temporarily closed:—

Years.	Cost of Merchandise.	No. Wagons.	Men.
1822	$ 15,000		70
1823	12,000		50
1824	35,000	26	100
1825	65,000	37	130
1826	90,000	60	100
1827	85,000	55	90
1828	150,000	100	200
1829	60,000	30	50
1830	120,000	70	140
1831	250,000	130	320
1832	140,000	70	150
1833	180,000	105	185
1834	150,000	80	160
1835	140,000	75	140
1836	130,000	70	135
1837	150,000	80	160
1838	90,000	50	100
1839	250,000	130	250
1840	50,000	30	60
1841	150,000	60	100
1842	160,000	70	120
1843	450,000	230	350

In the beginning of the traffic across the plains, those engaged in it were nearly all Americans or French, from the western States; but gradually New Mexicans of wealth began to take part in the business, until in

1843, Gregg says, "the greater part of the traders were New Mexicans, and they bid fair to secure a monopoly."

While the time occupied in making the passage, of course, varied considerably according to circumstances, yet an average trip to Santa Fé, with loaded wagons, usually occupied about seventy days, and the return trip about forty days. The eastward loads then comparatively light, usually from 1,000 to 2,000 pounds, and the approaching winter compelled haste. On one occasion a young man of Canadian descent, named F. X. Aubrey, rode, on a wager, from Santa Fé to Independence in five days and ten hours; his own mare Nellie carrying him 150 miles of the distance.

Gregg, in his "Commerce of the Prairies," gives a graphic account of the way in which the movements of the caravan were managed and governed. The first business was to elect a "Captain of the Caravan," who directed the order of travel and designated the camping-grounds. While he had no legal authority, yet all by common consent obeyed his directions. The proprietors then furnished a full list of the wagons and men, and the caravan was then apportioned into about four divisions, each with a lieutenant in command, as they generally marched in four lines abreast. The guards were then arranged, the number of watchmen generally being eight, each man standing guard a quarter of each alternate night. From this duty no one, no matter what his circumstances, was exempt; except in case of very apparent sickness.

The place of rendezvous for the caravan was usually Council Grove, the wagons leaving Independence at somewhat different times; and at the time of starting, which was generally after an early breakfast, the cry of "catch-up" was sounded from the captain's wagon and re-echoed throughout the camp, until the answering shouts of "all's set" from the teamsters in turn, announced that the wagons were ready for the journey.

It was the custom when about 200 miles from Santa Fé to send a party of couriers, composed generally of proprietors or agents, and known on the plain as "runners," ahead to that city, with a view to procuring provisions, securing good store-houses, and if possible arriving at an understanding with the custom-house officials. At the crossing of Red River, some part of the caravan frequently left the main body to proceed westerly to Taos; and a little further on they were met by the custom-house guard, who came to escort the caravan into Santa Fé to prevent smuggling. In the early days the village of San Miguel was the first reached, but subsequently Las Vegas was settled, and still later some American families built in the valley of the Mora, near the present town of Watrous.

When the caravan finally arrived in sight of Santa Fé, great excitement prevailed both among those connected with the wagons, and in the city. To use the language of Mr. Bigelow: "It was truly a scene for the artist's pencil to revel in; even the animals seemed to participate in the humor of their riders, who grew more and more merry and obstreperous as they descended toward the city. I doubt whether the first sight of the walls of Jerusalem was beheld by the Crusaders with much more tumultuous and soul-enrapturing joy."

The arrival produced a great deal of bustle among the natives. "*Los Americanos!*" "*Los Carros!*" "*La entrada de la Caravana!*" were to be heard in every direction; and crowds of women and boys flocked around to see the new-comers. The wagoners were by no means free from excitement on this occasion. Each one must tie a brand-new cracker to the lash of his whip, for on driving through the streets and the *plaza publica*, every one strives to outvie his comrades in the dexterity with which he flourishes this favorite badge of his authority."

"Our wagons were soon discharged in the warerooms

of the custom-house; and a few days' leisure being now at our disposal, we had time to take that recreation which a fatiguing journey of ten weeks had rendered so necessary. The wagoners and many of the traders, particularly the novices, flocked to the numerous fandangoes, which are regularly kept up after the arrival of a caravan. But the merchants generally were anxiously and actively engaged in their affairs, striving who should first get his goods out of the custom-house, and obtain a chance at the 'hard chink' of the numerous country dealers who annually resort to the Capital on these occasions."

"The *derechos de arancel* (tariff imposts) of Mexico are extremely oppressive, averaging about 100% upon the United States' cost of an ordinary Santa Fé assortment. Those on cotton textures are particularly so. According to the *arancel* of 1837 (and it was still heavier before) all plain-wove cottons, whether white or printed, pay twelve and a half cents duty per *vara*, besides the *derecho de consumo* (consumption duty), which brings it up to at least fifteen. For a few years, Governor Armijo, of Santa Fé, established a tariff of his own, entirely arbitrary,—exacting $500 for each wagon-load, whether large or small, of fine or coarse goods! Of course this was very advantageous to such traders as had large wagons, and costly assortments, while it was no less onerous to those with smaller vehicles of coarse heavy goods. As might have been anticipated, the traders soon took to carrying their merchandise only in the largest wagons, drawn by ten or twelve mules, and omitting the coarser and more weighty articles of trade. This caused the Governor to return to the *ad valorem* system, though still without regard to the *arancel general* of the nation.*"* It was calculated that the amount collected each year at this time amounted to between $50,000 and $60,000.

The return trip usually commenced four or five

weeks after the arrival at Santa Fé; generally about the 1st of September. Usually the caravan consisted of only thirty or forty wagons, a large portion of those taken out being disposed of in the country. The return cargo, which was the proceeds of the venture, was silver bullion from Chihuahua—and in later years, gold-dust from the placers south of Santa Fé—buffalo-rugs, furs, coarse Mexican blankets and wool, the latter, however, hardly paying a fair freight, but being used to fill wagons which would otherwise have been empty.

Stories of tragedies on the plains, during the early days, could be multiplied almost indefinitely. Generally they resulted from the carelessness or overconfidence of the traders. The death of Captain Smith, in 1831, illustrates this. He had for years been a pioneer in the Indian country and the Rocky Mountains, and had the firmest belief in his knowledge of border affairs. In the spring of that year he concluded to enter the Santa Fé trade, and started off in a caravan numbering eighty-four men, under the general command of Captain Sublette. Strangely enough, no one among the eighty-four had ever been over the Santa Fé Trail; and shortly after crossing the Arkansas the party became lost in the labyrinth of buffalo-tracks which crossed the plains in every direction. After days of wandering the water was exhausted and none could be found. Parties went out in various directions in search of a stream or spring, and among them Smith started alone, in what he thought a promising direction. After long travelling he at length reached the goal of his hopes; a small stream was before him, or rather the now dry bed of what had been a stream. Well versed in the nature of the western waters, he dug with his hands a hole in the center of the channel, and soon was rejoiced to see it become a little pool. But as he stooped and was in the very act of assuaging his long-continued and burning thirst, he fell a victim to the deadly arrows of the Comanche.

After the year 1831, however, Indian attacks on the regular route ceased; but soon after, new difficulties arose. The treatment of the Texan "Santa Fé Expedition," in 1841, which is narrated elsewhere, aroused great indignation in the "Lone Star" Republic, and rumors were rife in 1842 that a band of Texans was preparing for an organized attack on any Mexicans whom they could find on the Santa Fé Trail. Early in the next year one Colonel Warfield, said to have held a Texan commission, formed a company, with which he attacked the town of Mora—then the most advanced settlement in that direction—killing five men and driving off a lot of horses. He was pursued, however, by a party of Mexicans, who succeeded not only in retaking their own horses, but in capturing those of the Texans, so that Warfield's company had to go on foot to Bents' Fort. About the same time a Texan named John McDaniel, claiming to hold a captain's commission, raised a party of men on the border of Missouri, and started to join Warfield. On the way he met Don Antonio José Chavez, of New Mexico, travelling towards Independence with a small party, consisting of five servants, with two wagons and fifty-five mules, and $10,000 or $12,000 in specie and bullion. Although within the United States territory, the marauders did not hesitate to attack Chavez, and rifle his baggage, from which each member of McDaniel's party obtained about $500 as his share of the booty; and immediately after, seven of them left for the settlements, satisfied with this exploit. The remaining eight for some reason determined to murder Chavez, and soon after carried their cruel design into execution—carrying their victim a few rods from the camp and shooting him in cold blood. A considerable amount of gold was found on his person and in his trunk, and was divided among the murderers, who thereupon fled towards Missouri.

This outrage was the more abominable because

Chavez belonged to a very influential family, who were not at all friendly to Armijo and his action in regard to the Texans, Don Mariano Chavez, the elder brother of the murdered man, and his wife, having done all that kind hearts could dictate to alleviate the sufferings of the Texan prisoners, on their march down the Rio Grande.

Before the perpetration of this murder a company of United States dragoons had started to intercept and capture McDaniel's party, but were not in time; but as soon as the outlaws reached the borders of civilization, ten of them were arrested and sent to St. Louis for trial, five others escaping. Those of the prisoners who were found guilty of participation in the murder of Chavez, including Captain McDaniel, were executed according to law, and the others were convicted of robbery and sentenced accordingly.

About May 1st, of the same year, a company of 175 men was organized in northern Texas, under Colonel Snively, for operations against Mexicans engaged in the Santa Fé trade, and were soon after joined by Colonel Warfield and a few followers. They soon after encountered a Mexican caravan, containing about 100 men, attacked it, and killed eighteen besides five who subsequently died, and captured nearly all of the remainder. This was in Mexican or Texan territory, and has been justified by some as a fair act of warfare, the two countries being then engaged in the struggle which succeeded the Texan declaration of independence; but by others it has been held to be beyond the proper limits of belligerency. Snively, who had meanwhile moved to a point on territory claimed by the United States, was soon after met by Captain Cook, in command of 200 American dragoons, acting as escort to the annual caravan from Independence; and the Texans were speedily disarmed by the United States troops.

The occurrence of such events, however, determined

President Santa Ana to close the north of the Mexican Republic against any further commerce; which for a time ended the business of the Santa Fé Trail. The decree is dated at Tacubaya, August 7, 1843, and was to take effect in forty-five days. The next spring, however, the custom-houses were re-opened and the trade renewed. In 1846 the number of wagons in the caravan was 414, and the value of the merchandise transported was estimated at $1,752,250. After the American occupation the business of the Santa Fé Trail still further increased; new and large commercial establishments being founded at the capital city, from which a great part of northern Mexico as well as New Mexico and Arizona were supplied.

CHAPTER XIX.

THE INSURRECTION OF 1837.

FOR the commencement of the causes which led to this outbreak, we must go back two years, to the time when Albino Perez, a Colonel of the Mexican army, was appointed Political Chief by President Santa Ana, in 1835. For some time before, the people of the territory had been governed by native New Mexicans, or by those who had become identified with their interests. Bacas and Chavez, and Armijos, had been among their recent rulers, and the last Spanish Governor, Melgares, was one of whose brilliant record they were all proud; but Governor Perez was an entire stranger, sent from Mexico; and even if he had been absolutely perfect, his appointment would have occasioned discontent. The feeling was increased during the next year by events connected with the trial of the disbursing officers of the territory, who were charged with peculation—two of the three judges of the Supreme Court, Nafero and Santiago Abreu, being among those accused as accomplices; and the highest pitch of excitement was reached when in May, 1837, the new Mexican constitution went into effect, which changed the Territory into a Department, centralized power in many respects, and imposed taxes to which the people had never before been subject. The opponents of the government exaggerated the bad features of the new system so as to render them still more obnoxious, until the people, especially in the north, were ready to break into revolt at the first signal. An occasion soon presented itself in the arrest and imprisonment of a local judicial officer on what the people considered a false charge; a large assemblage hurriedly gathered, released him by force, and raised the standard of revolution. This was on the 1st of August, 1837. Santa Cruz became the head-quarters of the movement, and within two days a large number of men dissatisfied with the government had collected there, embracing many Mexicans from the northern counties, especially from the vicinity of Chimayó, and the majority of the Pueblo Indians from the adjacent villages, except San Juan. On August 3d they issued the following "Plan," which was published and circulated:—

"Viva! God and the Nation! and the faith of Jesus Christ! For the principal points which we defend are the following:

"1st. To be with God and the Nation, and the faith of Jesus Christ.

"2d. To defend our country until we spill every drop of our blood in order to obtain the victory we have in view.

"3d. Not to admit the departmental 'plan.'

"4th. Not to admit any tax.

"5th. Not to admit the disorder desired by those who are attempting to procure it. God and the Nation!

"Encampment, Santa Cruz de la Cañada, August 3d, 1837."

As soon as Governor Perez received news of this revolt, he assembled what troops he had at command, and called on the militia to report for duty; but to this call received a very lukewarm response. The Indians of San Juan and Santo Domingo, however, remained apparently true, and accompanied by the warriors from those pueblos and his own soldiers, he marched to put down the rebels. These he met on the second day, near San Yldefonso, but upon approaching them, nearly all of the Governor's army deserted and fraternized with their opponents; leaving so few faithful to his standard that Perez was forced to move with all speed toward Santa Fé. Lieutenant Miguel Sena, Sergeant Sais, and Loreto

Romero, who were among those who remained loyal, were killed by the revolutionists near the Puertocito, between Santa Cruz and Pojuaque. Finding that there was no security at the palace, the Governor left the city at 10 o'clock at night to escape to the south, but the roads were all blocked by squads of revolutionists, and his party was soon forced to retreat and again retire towards the capital. Travelling on foot, the better to conceal his identity, Governor Perez reached the house of Salvador Martinez, about a league south-west of Santa Fé and near Agua Fria, and took refuge there, but was soon found by Indians from Santo Domingo, who were following his track, and almost instantly killed. Before his pulse had ceased to beat, they cut off his head—compelling Santiago Prada, one of his own soldiers, to perform the deed—and carried it to the head-quarters of the insurgents, which were now near the Church of our Lady of the Rosary (Rosario Church), in the western outskirts of Santa Fé. On the same day Jesus Maria Alarid, Secretary of State, and Santiago Abreu, formerly Governor, were taken together near the Mesita of Santo Domingo, and killed; the latter with special cruelty. Ramon Abreu and Marcelino Abreu, brother of the Ex-Governor, and Lieutenant Madrigal and another, were overtaken on the same road, at a place called "Las Palacias," between Cieneguilla and Agua Fria, and killed. Colonel Aponti was wounded at the same time, and taken prisoner.

All this was on the 9th of August; and the next day the insurgents entered the city without opposition, under command of General "Chopon," of Taos, and the Montoya brothers took possession of the palace, and offered up thanks in the parish church for their victory. José Gonzalez, a Pueblo Indian, of Taos, was elected Governor, and duly installed in office in the palace; and the revolutionary army, having now accomplished its object, immediately disbanded—its members returning to their homes.

There can be no doubt that the movement had the secret support and approval of many of the leading men of the northern counties, including Santa Fé itself; but in the end they seem to have been entirely out-generaled by Governor Armijo, who soon after organized a counter-revolution in the lower country, and prepared to march to Santa Fé with a considerable force. Meanwhile, a General Assembly, composed of the alcaldes and other influential citizens in the northern half of the territory, met at Santa Fé in the palace, and ratified the acts of the revolutionists.

When Gonzales heard, however, that Armijo was marching up from Albuquerque, he withdrew from the capital to Santa Cruz, which was the center of the revolutionary feeling. Armijo thereupon entered Santa Fé, assumed charge of the government, and proclaimed himself Commandant-General of the Province. He immediately sent dispatches to the central government at Mexico, stating that he had overthrown the rebellion; and as a result was appointed Governor of New Mexico—a position which he held for the greater part of nine years. At the same time the national authorities dispatched troops from Zacatecas and Chihuahua to assist in the final suppression of the insurrection. With these and his own soldiers, Armijo made a rapid march to Santa Cruz, in January, and succeeded in defeating the entire rebel army, and capturing all the leaders. Immediate punishment followed, no mercy being shown. The two brothers Montoya, General "Chopon," and Alcalde Esquibel were shot near the old powder-house, or "Garita," on the little hill in the northern part of Santa Fé; Juan Antonio Vigil was executed near Cuyamungué; and Gonzales was killed by the immediate command of Armijo himself. The story is that Gonzalez, on being captured at Cañada, was brought before Armijo, who was then in the outskirts of the town, and on seeing the General, Gonzalez came forward with hand extended, saying "How do you do, Compañero?" as was proper between two of equal rank as governors. Armijo replied, "How do you do, Compañero? Confess yourself, Compañero." Then turning to his soldiers, added, "Now shoot my compañero!"—which command was immediately executed. This effectually ended the revolution of 1837.

CHAPTER XX.

THE AMERICAN OCCUPATION.

It is not necessary in this place to trace the causes which led to the war between the United States and Mexico, or to follow its history further than relates specially to the operations and results in New Mexico. Suffice it to say that the origin of the hostilities was found in the dispute as to the ownership of the territory between the Rio Grande and the Nueces River. When Texas declared its independence in 1836, it claimed all the region from the Sabine on the east to the Rio Grande on the west, and when the annexation to the United States took place ten years later, it transferred that claim of course to the American Union. The latter therefore claimed the whole country east of the Rio Grande from its source to its mouth, including half of New Mexico, with Taos, Santa Fé, Albuquerque, San Miguel, etc., as well as the long strip of country to the south extending to the Gulf of Mexico.

This claim was stoutly resisted by Mexico, which insisted that the Territory of Texas had never extended farther west than the Nueces River, and determined to oppose any attempt of the United States to carry its authority beyond that line. General Taylor having been ordered into the disputed district, was met by the Mexican forces, under General Santa Ana, and the battles of Palo Alto and Resaca de la Palma on successive days in May, 1846, opened the bloody drama of war, and startled the American people, who had been at peace so long that more than a generation had heard no sounds of armed hostilities, except as echoed from the lands across the ocean.

A formal declaration of war by the American Congress followed almost immediately, on the 10th of May; and so the war was formally and legally, as well as actually, begun. The first plan of operations looked to an invasion of Mexican territory at various points near the boundary line, General Taylor crossing the Rio Grande near its mouth, with Monterey as his first objective point, General Wool organizing a force at San Antonio to proceed westerly towards Chihuahua, and Colonel Stephen W. Kearney being ordered to march from Fort Leavenworth along the general line of the Santa Fé Trail, for the conquest of New Mexico and the region beyond, with what was denominated the Army of the West." Our interest, of course, is exclusively with the latter.

Colonel Kearney was the commandant of the First Dragoons, U. S. A., and troops from that regiment constituted the nucleus of the army which was to start on the long and perilous trip across the plains. Volunteers were called for from Missouri, and a regiment of cavalry was speedily organized, and on June 18th elected, as its Colonel, Alexander W. Doniphan, an eminent lawyer who had enlisted as a private. Missouri also furnished a battalion of light artillery, commanded by Major Clark, consisting of two companies, under Captains Weightman and Fischer, two companies of infantry, commanded by Captains Angney and Murphy, and the LaClede Rangers from St. Louis, under Captain Hudson. It was also proposed to form a Mormon battalion from the Latter Day Saints who had recently been driven from their settlements at Nauvoo and had set out on their journey towards a new home in the wilderness of the far West, and Captain Allen was dispatched to Council Bluffs to meet the Mormon caravan and endeavor to obtain volunteers for the purpose.

The companies which composed the regiment of dragoons, like most of our army in times of peace, were widely scattered; two companies stationed on the Upper Mississippi, under Captain P. St. George Cooke and Captain E. V. Sumner, were firstly ordered to New Orleans to join the more southerly expeditions, but at St. Louis found new orders to proceed with Colonel Kearney across the plains.

Kearney himself commenced his march from Fort Leavenworth in the latter part of June, 1846. The two companies just mentioned proceeded up the Missouri River in boats, and set out on July 6th. The troops, all told, consisted of six companies of the First Dragoons —who were all the regulars in the command—and the volunteers before mentioned, who, while possessing the high spirit, bravery, and love of adventure characteristic of the western soldier, yet had had little time for drilling or even the acquirement of discipline. Altogether, the "Army of the West," with its high sounding title, and which was expected to march across 1,000 miles of desert and conquer a whole province, consisted of 1,658 men and sixteen pieces of ordnance. The whole did not come together until the plains had been traversed and they had reached Bents' Fort, the most important and best known of frontier trading posts, and then the great point of rendezvous for the hunters and trappers of the mountain regions. This fort was situated on the north bank of the Arkansas, about 650 miles west of Fort Leavenworth, in latitude 38°02′ and longitude 103°03′. It was 180 feet long and 135 feet wide, and the walls, which were of adobe, were fifteen feet high and four feet thick. Altogether, it was certainly the strongest post established by private enterprise in the country. Here the army found the most of the great caravan of traders' wagons which had started over the trail that year, the whole consisting of 414 loaded wagons.

From Bents' Fort Lieutenant DeCourcey was dispatched with twenty men to the Taos Valley to ascertain the disposition of the people and report to the General at the most practicable point on the road. It may be added here that he rejoined the main body on the 11th of August, at the Poñil, bringing 14 Mexican prisoners, who reported that the Pueblos, Utes, and other Indians, to the number of 5,000, had joined the Mexican forces, and that the United States Army would be opposed at every point between San Miguel and Santa Fé.

After spending three days in greatly needed rest, the army resumed its march on August 2d, and Captain Cooke was sent in advance, as a kind of ambassador, to proceed under a flag of truce to Santa Fé and carry the proclamation of the General declaring the annexation to the United States of all the territory east of the Rio Grande as part of the old Republic of Texas. Cooke was accompanied by twelve picked men of his own company as an escort, and also by Mr Jas. Magoffin, of Kentucky, and Señor Gonzales, of Chihuahua, two merchants extensively engaged in the trade of the Santa Fé Trail, and then bound for the New Mexican capital. They crossed the Purgatoire near where Trinidad now is, and passed through the Raton Mountains, following almost exactly the stage route of a later day, and not far from the present line of the Atchison, Topeka & Santa Fé Railroad, finding the first habitations on the banks of the Mora River, the proprietor being Mr. James Bonney, who had settled there four years before.

On August 9th they came in sight of Las Vegas, which Cooke describes, as so many others have done both before and since, as resembling "an extensive brick-yard and kilns." It was then a comparatively new town, Don Miguel Romero, the father of the distinguished family of that name, having been its virtual founder a little before the year 1840. Here the envoy met the Alcalde (Juan de Dios Maes), and enjoyed his hospitality, while the latter sent a swift express by the short trail across the mountains to carry the information of the foreign arrival to Governor Armijo at Santa Fé. The next day Cooke's party passed through Tecolote and San Miguel, in both of which places crowds of inhabitants turned out to see the strangers, and on the morning of August 12th arrived at Santa Fé. They found the city crowded with soldiers and citizens, who had come in to form a volunteer army to resist the American approach, and had some difficulty in forcing their way through the throng to the front of the Palace. Here they halted and were met by Captain Ortiz (Mayor de Plaza), who carried news of their arrival to the Governor. That official they found in the large hall of the Palace (which we are told then had a carpeted earth floor), seated at a table and surrounded by military and civil officers. Cooke described him as a "large fine looking man," dressed in a blue frock coat, with a rolling collar and general's shoulder-straps, blue striped trousers, with gold lace, and a red sash.

Cooke informed the Governor that he had been sent by the General commanding the American army, with a letter, which he would present when it should be agreeable to his Excellency. The Governor directed that the envoy and his escort should be properly cared for, and set a later hour for an official reception of his communication. At the time appointed Cooke presented his documents, and later in the evening the Governor returned his call, and said that he would send a Commissioner to meet General Kearney, the person selected for that office being Dr. Connolly. The Governor also stated that he would march himself very shortly with 6,000 men to meet the invaders.

Meanwhile the army under Kearney had been proceeding by rapid marches, in which the infantry sometimes outwalked the cavalry, over the same route from Bents' Fort towards Santa Fé, and had reached Santa Clara Springs on the 13th, the Mora River on the 14th, and on the 15th entered Las Vegas. Just before reaching this town Major Swords arrived from Fort Leavenworth with the mail, which contained Colonel Kearney's commission as Brigadier-General U. S. A., the announcement of which caused great rejoicing and congratulation among the troops. Las Vegas was the first Mexican town reached by the expedition, and was then a place of small importance; San Miguel being the county seat and center of business and population in that section.

General Kearney halted his army and called the people together in the plaza, standing, with his staff and other officers, and the Alcalde of the town, on the flat roof of a building situated on the north side of the plaza, near the middle of the block (owned in 1883 by Mr. Kihlberg). He explained to the people the objects of the invasion, and assured them that neither they nor their property should be molested so long as they were quiet and peaceable. The Alcalde, Juan de Dios Maes, then took the oath of allegiance to the United States, being the first Mexican who had thus voluntarily assumed the obligations of American citizenship; and he was immediately confirmed in his office by the commanding General.

Continuing on their march, Kearney and his troops next reached the little village of Tecolote; and here proceedings quite similar to those at Las Vegas were enacted. The General addressed the Alcalde and the leading citizens, informing them of the annexation and its advantages, and requiring an oath of allegiance from the former, whom he then confirmed in his office. Here they met Colonel Cooke and Dr. Connolly, but no change of programme seems to have been caused by any communication from the latter. The ceremony at Tecolote only occupied the time required for watering the horses, and at night the army bivouacked by the sparkling and refreshing waters of the Bernal Spring.

The next day they arrived at San Miguel, then the

cabecera of the county, and much the most important town east of the mountains. It was quite a changed scene from that of a few years before, when the Texans of Kendall's expedition, foot-sore and weary, and as prisoners, marched through the same streets; and singularly enough, that night the American pickets captured a son of General Salazar, who had taken the first Texans in 1841. General Kearney and his staff, with the Alcalde, the padre, and some other officers, ascended to the roof of a house overlooking the plaza, and delivered an address to the crowds that had congregated from the surrounding country, similar to those at Las Vegas and Tecolote; but at first the Alcalde positively refused to take the oath of allegiance, and was only induced to comply after much persuasion. Soon after leaving the town, two prisoners were captured, and by order of the General, conducted through the camp and shown the number and quality of the cannon, and then set at liberty. To the exaggerated accounts of the Americans' strength given by these men to the Mexican volunteers, and the consternation thus caused, have been ascribed largely the demoralization and subsequent melting away of the Mexican army.

On the night of August 17th the army encamped near the deserted Pueblo of Pecos, where the church and some other buildings were then standing in far better condition than their present ruinous appearance would indicate, and but a short distance from the narrow defile at Apache Cañon, or Cañoncito, where Governor Armijo's army was posted in an almost impregnable position, sustained by a good supply of artillery, and strongly defended by a breastwork of huge trees. It was intended to take a circuitous route which passed around this narrow defile, and so avoid, if possible, a conflict under the terrible disadvantages which that position presented; but during the night news came that the Mexican army had abandoned its position, and retired toward Santa Fé. While considerable in numbers, it was heterogeneous in material, the regular troops were few, and the great bulk of the force was made up of undisciplined countrymen, armed with such weapons as they could best obtain, and General Armijo seems to have had little confidence in their ability to stand a charge of cavalry, and indeed to some extent in their enthusiasm and earnestness in his cause. Greatly exaggerated accounts of the strength of the invading army had been spread, the size of the coming host increasing with each repetition, until a feeling of fear and despondency was quite general, and the hasty levies from the country had become demoralized. So the American army, which had expected to take a circuitous and difficult mountain track in order to pass around the strategic point occupied by Armijo, found themselves able to march directly on by the high road, only incommoded by the trees and other obstructions which had been thrown across the track to act as a kind of breastwork; and marched rapidly all day, in order, if possible, to accomplish the whole distance to the Capital City (twenty-eight miles) before night-fall.

The head of the column arrived in sight of the city soon after three o'clock, but waited until about six for the rear and the artillery to come up, as it was desired to enter the city in good military form. General Kearney and several officers proceeded to the Palace, where he was received by Juan Bautista Vigil, the Lieutenant-Governor, and the government of the city formally transferred. A little before sunset the troops marched into the plaza, raised and saluted the "stars and stripes," and then retired, without food or fuel, to make a camp on top of one of the surrounding hills south-east of the town. The baggage had not arrived, but before dark the enterprising drivers of burros laden with wood had supplied material for fires, and the soldiers, hungry and thirsty, soon filled the saloons and hotels until literally driven to the encampment by the guard. General Kearney slept on the floor in the Palace. Colonel Cooke, with fifty men, was put in charge of the city.

Meanwhile General Armijo had proceeded toward Albuquerque, disbanding the militia and taking with him only the regular troops, but having to abandon his artillery, which was soon after found and brought into the city. This consisted of nine pieces in all, and among them, an old Spanish cannon with the inscription, " Barcelona, 1778," and one fine Texan piece bearing the name of President Lamar, and which had been taken from the Texan " Santa Fé Expedition."

Thus was accomplished, without the shedding of a drop of blood, an entire change in the government of the Territory; and without having to strike a blow, what has been called the " Conquest of New Mexico" was effected. Few such campaigns have been known in history. A little army, hardly larger than a full regiment, had marched 900 miles from its base of supplies, largely through a desert region, with its communications liable at any time to be cut off, and without sufficient provisions, or money to procure them, for the long period required. The heat was excessive during much of the march, and the suffering therefrom, when water could not be obtained, was intense. In crossing what was then called the " Great American Desert," through what is now western Kansas and southern Colorado, they suffered greatly for want of water. In the language of the historian of Doniphan's expedition, "In the course of a day's march we could scarcely find a pool of water to quench the thirst, a patch of grass to prevent our animals from perishing, or an oasis to relieve the weary mind. Dreary, sultry, desolate, boundless solitude reigned as far as the eye could reach, and seemed to bound the distant horizon. We suffered much with the heat and thirst, and the driven sand, which filled our eyes, and nostrils, and mouths almost to suffocation.

Many of our animals perished on the desert." The volunteer troops were badly furnished as to wagons and teams, often reduced to half rations, and the provisions frequently so far behind as not to arrive before midnight.

At Bents' Fort, in consequence of the scarcity of provisions, the daily allowance was reduced to half a pound of flour, and three-eighths of a pound of pork—thus cutting off the rations of coffee, sugar, salt, rice, etc., which had previously been furnished. After entering New Mexico the army subsisted, until its arrival at Santa Fé, on about one-third of the regular rations. Even with this reduction, there were on hand only sufficient rations to last the number of days required to reach Santa Fé by the most rapid and uninterrupted marching; no allowance had been made for delays or detentions; and although making forced marches, the army arrived at the Capital entirely destitute of provisions. And even here there was but little improvement for a time, for the expedition had not been properly supplied with money, and the people having been declared citizens of the United States, and therefore entitled to full protection of their property, no supplies could be had from them except by cash payment. Had the country been treated as conquered territory, supplies of course could have been seized and used; but carrying out the opposite theory, no property could be taken or disturbed except as purchased from the owners; and so the army found itself in a very extraordinary and embarrassing position—compelled on the one hand to be on its guard against a people who might at any moment rise in hostility, and on the other, not having any of the advantages as to supplies which would have resulted from a condition of open war.

The first business of the General, after attending to the pressing wants of the soldiers, was to secure the fruits of victory, and guard against any uprising of the people or the coming of a Mexican army from the south;

and so the erection of Fort Marcy (named for Hon. Wm. L. Marcy, of New York, then the Secretary of War) was immediately commenced. This was situated on the hill north-east of the city, which commanded the entire town, and on the very spot where, centuries before, the Pueblo chiefs had established their head-quarters in the rebellion of 1680. The fort was planned by Lieutenant Gilmer, of the topographical corps, and L. A. McLean, a civil engineer in a Missouri company, and was built by the volunteers, a certain number of whom were detailed each day for the purpose. This was a source of great complaint, as the men felt that they had volunteered to fight, but not to act as laborers; and even the small extra compensation (eighteen cents a day) allowed, failed to reconcile them to what many considered a hardship and imposition. The fort, however, was finally completed, its form being an irregular tridecagon, and its walls being massively built of adobes. In size it was sufficient to accommodate 1,000 soldiers, and it was armed with fourteen cannon.

This fortress was the more necessary because the "Army of the West" was not to be an army of occupation; but was intended to push on to greater conquests on the Pacific coast.

General Kearney, with characteristic vigor, proceeded to set in order a provisional government. In this he showed tact and discretion as well as energy. The instructions which he had received were conceived in the proper spirit, the fundamental idea being that the people of the Territory were not to consider themselves as conquered, but simply as brought under the good influences of the free liberal, and stable institutions of the United States. The confidential instructions from the Secretary of War, dated June 3, 1846, contained these extracts: "Should you conquer and take possession of New Mexico and Upper California, you will establish temporary civil governments therein, abolishing all arbitrary restrictions that may exist so far as it may be done with safety. In performing this duty, it would be wise and prudent to continue in their employment all such of the existing officers as are known to be friendly to the United States, and will take the oath of allegiance to them. You may assure the people of those provinces that it is the wish and design of the United States to provide for them a free government, with the least possible delay, similar to that which exists in our Territories. Then they will be called upon to exercise the rights of freemen, in electing their own representatives to the Territorial Legislature. In your conduct you will act in such a manner as best to conciliate the inhabitants, and render them friendly to the United States."

On the morning of the 19th General Kearney assembled the people in the plaza and addressed them as follows, his words being translated by the interpreter Roubidoux: " New Mexicans! we have come amongst you to take possession of New Mexico, which we do in the name of the Government of the United States. We have come with peaceable intentions and kind feelings towards you all. We come as friends to better your condition, and make you a part of the Republic of the United States. We mean not to murder you, or rob you of your property. Your families shall be free from molestation; your women secure from violence. My soldiers will take nothing from you but what they pay you for. In taking possession of New Mexico, we do not mean to take away your religion from you. Religion and government have no connection in our country. There, all religions are equal; one has no preference over the other; the Catholic and Protestant are esteemed alike. Every man has a right to serve God according to his heart. When a man dies he must render to his God an account of his acts here on earth, whether they be good or bad. In our Government all men are equal. We esteem the most peaceable man the best man. I advise you to attend to your domestic pursuits—cultivate industry, be peaceable and obedient to the laws. Do not resort to violent means to correct abuses. I do hereby proclaim that, being in possession of Santa Fé, I am, therefore, virtually in possession of all New Mexico. Armijo is no longer your Governor. His power is departed. But he will return and be as one of you. When he shall return you are not to molest him. You are no longer Mexican subjects; you are now become American citizens, subject only to the laws of the United States. A change of government has taken place in New Mexico, and you no longer owe allegiance to the Mexican Government. I do hereby proclaim my intention to establish in this Department a civil government, on a republican basis, similar to those of our own States. It is my intention, also, to continue in office those by whom you have been governed, except the Governor, and such other persons as I shall appoint to office by virtue of the authority vested in me. I am your Governor—henceforth look to me for protection."

The General next proceeded to inquire if they were willing to take the oath of allegiance to the United States Government, to which having given their consent, he then administered to the Governor *ad interim*, the Secretary of State, the Prefects, the Alcaldes, and other officers of state, the following oath: "Do you swear in good faith that under all circumstances you will bear allegiance to the laws and Government of the United States, and that through good and evil you will demean yourselves as obedient citizens of the same, in the name of the Father, and of the Son, and of the Holy Spirit, Amen." This address of the General's was received with many manifestations of satisfaction and applause by the people; and General Kearney then proceeded to administer a similar oath to several delegations of Pueblo Indians who came in to offer their submission.

His next act was to cause a flag-staff, 100 feet in height, to be erected in the center of the plaza; and the American flag to be flung to the breeze from its top. A grazing camp was then established on the Galisteo River, twenty-seven miles southerly from the capital, to which the horses of the army, wearied from their long and arduous journey, were sent to recuperate in the midst of plentiful grass and water. Three days after the taking of the oath of allegiance, General Kearney issued the following proclamation, in which for the first time the intention was expressed to take possession of territory west of the Rio Grande, and consequently beyond the limits claimed by Texas,—

PROCLAMATION!

"As by the act of the Republic of Mexico, a state of war exists between that government and the United States, and as the undersigned, at the head of his troops, on the 18th instant took possession of Santa Fé, the capital of the Department of New Mexico, he now announces his intention to hold the Department, with its original boundaries (on both sides of the Del Norte), as a part of the United States, and under the name of the Territory of New Mexico. The undersigned has come to New Mexico with a strong military force, and an equally strong one is following close in his rear. He has more troops than necessary to put down any opposition that can possibly be brought against him, and therefore it would be folly and madness for any dissatisfied or discontented persons to think of resisting him. The undersigned has instructions from his Government to respect the religious institutions of New Mexico, to protect the property of the Church, to cause the worship of those belonging to it to be undisturbed, and their religious rights in the amplest manner preserved to them. Also to protect the persons and property of all quiet and peaceable inhabitants within its boundaries, against their enemies, the Utes, Navajoes, and others. And while he assures all that it will be his pleasure as well as his duty to comply with those instructions, he calls upon them to exert themselves in preserving order, in promoting concord, and in maintaining the authority and efficiency of the laws; to require of those who have left their homes and taken up arms against the troops of the United States to return forthwith to them, or else they will be considered as enemies and traitors, subjecting their persons to punishment and their property to seizure and confiscation for the benefit of the public treasury. It is the wish and intention of the United States to provide for New Mexico a free government, with the least possible delay, similar to those in the United States, and the people of New Mexico will then be called on to exercise the rights of free men in electing their own representatives to the Territorial Legislature; but until this can be done, the laws hitherto in existence will be continued until changed or modified by competent authority; and those persons holding office will continue in the same for the present, provided they will consider themselves good citizens and willing to take the oath of allegiance to the United States. The undersigned hereby absolves all persons residing within the boundary of New Mexico from further allegiance to the Republic of Mexico, and hereby claims them as citizens of the United States. Those who remain quiet and peaceable will be considered as good citizens and receive protection. Those who are found in arms, or instigating others against the United States, will be considered as traitors, and treated accordingly. Don Manuel Armijo, the late Governor of this Department, has fled from it. The undersigned has taken possession of it without firing a gun or shedding a drop of blood—in which he most truly rejoices; and for the present will be considered as Governor of this Territory.

"Given at Santa Fé, the Capital of the Territory of New Mexico, this 22d day of August, 1846, and in the seventy-first year of the Independence of the United States. By the Governor,

"S. W. KEARNEY,
"Brigadier-General."

While everything at the capital was quiet, and the best of feeling appeared to exist among the people of Santa Fé towards the American authorities, rumors arrived of the concentration of quite a large Mexican force near Albuquerque, with a view to renew hostilities, and General Kearney determined to march in that direction in person, in order to prevent the execution of any such plan; and by personal acquaintance, to gain the confidence of the people of the Territory at large. He started on September 2d, taking with him a battery of eight pieces, with 100 artillery-men, a battalion of 100 dragoons under Captain Burgwin, and 500 mounted volunteers. Including his staff, the force consisted of 725 men, besides fifty or sixty Mexicans, who accompanied the expedition as a kind of honorary escort. When near Santo Domingo they were met by the "Gobernador" of the pueblo, carrying his official cane, and accompanied by the other officers of the pueblo; and after the usual salutations, the "Gobernador" said: "We shall meet some Indians presently, mounted and dressed for war, but they are young men of my town—friends come to receive you—and I wish to caution your men not to fire upon them." And this was soon verified by the appearance of a band of Pueblos, most grotesquely dressed, and painted to represent different animals, their heads surmounted by buffalo-horns, etc., who dashed by at full speed, enveloped in a cloud of dust, and firing volleys under the bodies of the horses of the Americans as they passed. After arriving in the town the General addressed the people in a speech which had to be doubly translated;—into Spanish, and from that language into the Pueblo tongue.

From here the little army proceeded to San Felipe, Algodones (then the largest town of the valley), and Bernalillo, and arrived at Albuquerque on the morning of the 25th, receiving a salute of twenty guns from the top of the parish church, which was the first assurance they had that the city was not occupied by a hostile force. The next day a deputation came up from the town of Peralta to offer their submission to the new Government, and to say that the people of the Rio Abajo

(Lower River) desired to be considered as friends. The army continued its march, however, stopping a short time at Peralta, then the residence of many of the Chavez family, who were friends to the Americans, and going as far as Tomé, where the officers attended an imposing religious ceremony; and then returned to Santa Fé, having accomplished all that was most essential by demonstrating to every inhabitant of the country that the Americans had come as friends and not as enemies, and recognized every New Mexican as now an American citizen.

One of the most important and yet difficult and delicate tasks which had to be performed was with regard to the civil law to be observed and enforced under the new *regime*. This of course required immediate action, and General Kearney committed the work of preparing a Code to Colonel Doniphan and Willard P. Hall, of the Missouri volunteers. Just as this work was being completed, and while he was actually engaged in a room in the Palace in transcribing part of the laws, Mr. Hall received the intelligence of his election as a Member of Congress from the district in Missouri in which he resided. As preliminary to the work the General directed a translation to be made of all the laws and decrees found in the official archives at Santa Fé—a work which was rapidly accomplished by Captain David Waldo.

This Code, much of which has remained as the law of the Territory for nearly forty years, contained a Bill of Rights quite similar to those in many of the States, proclaiming the broadest principles of liberty, and was made up largely from Missouri statutes and existing Mexican laws. It was to be promulgated in both Spanish and English, and the labor of translation was confided to Captain Waldo, whose varied accomplishments and scholarship were frequently of much value in similar matters. Considerable difficulty was experienced in printing the work, the only press in the Territory being a small one which had been used by the former government in printing proclamations, public notices, manifestos, etc. The type was worn, and ink and other materials difficult to obtain; but finally the work was accomplished. The type being Spanish, and consequently containing no "W," we are told that whenever that letter occurred in the book, the compositors had to substitute two " V's." This "Kearney Code" was promulgated on September 22d, and took effect immediately.

General Kearney promptly established a provisional government by the appointment of a Governor, Judges, etc. The following was the official notice which was circulated throughout the Territory, in both English and Spanish,—

NOTICE.

"Being duly authorized by the President of the United States of America, I hereby make the following appointments for the government of New Mexico, a Territory of the United States. The officers thus appointed will be obeyed and respected accordingly: Charles Bent to be Governor; Donaciano Vigil to be Secretary of the Territory; Richard Dallam to be Marshal; Francis P. Blair to be U. S. District Attorney; Charles Blumner to be Treasurer; Eugene Leitensdorfer to be Auditor of Public Accounts; Joab Houghton, Antonio José Otero, Charles Beaubien, to be Judges of the Superior Court.

"Given at Santa Fé, the Capital of the Territory of New Mexico, this 22d day of September, 1846, and in the seventy-first year of the Independence of the United States. S. W. KEARNEY,
Brigadier General, U. S. A."

Charles Bent was an old resident of the Territory, and with his brother, the owner of Bents' Fort. He was an able and popular man, and married to a native-born New Mexican lady of Taos.

Donaciano Vigil was a native New Mexican, born September 6, 1802, who had held a number of public positions, both civil and military, and enjoyed the confidence and respect of the whole people. He had been active in expeditions against the Navajoes in 1823, 1833, 1836, and 1838; for over four years military secretary of the Governor; twice a member of the Departmental Assembly, etc.; and so had an official experience of great value.

Francis P. Blair, Jr., was the well-known member of the Blair family who afterwards represented the St. Louis District in the United States Congress, being the first Republican representative ever elected in a slave State.

Richard Dallam was an American, residing at the Placers and engaged in mining operations there.

Eugene Leitensdorfer was a Santa Fé merchant, who had married the daughter, Soledad, of Governor Santiago Abreu.

Joab Houghton was a well-known lawyer, who afterwards held the office of Associate Justice, under the regular Territorial government, for a number of years, from 1865 to 1869.

Antonio José Otero was the representative of one of the most important Spanish families in New Mexico, a man of high character and reputation, and influential connections.

Charles Beaubien had been a resident of Taos since about 1827, and had married a sister of Don Pedro Valdez, in 1828. He was widely known and respected.

On the 26th of September the column for California, under command of General Kearney, set off on the long journey to conquer an empire on the Pacific, choosing as the least of two unknown evils the southern route along the Gila, and really making what General Cooke aptly calls, "a leap in the dark of a thousand miles of wild plain and mountain." General Kearney, on leaving the Territory, which he had practically annexed, and to which he had given a new government and code of laws, turned over the command to Colonel Doniphan.

Two days afterward, on September 28, General Sterling

Price arrived at Santa Fé, in a feeble state of health, and accompanied only by his staff. The troops under his command, consisting of 1,200 mounted volunteers from Missouri, and a Mormon battalion of 500 infantry organized at Council Bluffs, reached the city a few days later, having completed the march across the plains in fifty-three days. The capital was now literally alive with artillery, baggage-wagons, commissary teams, beef-cattle, and a promiscuous throng of American soldiers, traders, visitors, straglers, trappers, amateurs, mountaineers, Mexicans, Pueblo Indians, women and children, numbering perhaps not less than 14,000 souls. The aggregate effective force of the American army in New Mexico at this time was about 3,500 men.

Colonel Doniphan had been ordered to march to Chihuahua, where it was supposed General Wool had arrived from San Antonio, and great preparations were made for the campaign; but just as he was about starting, the attacks made by bands of Navajoes on Polvedero and other towns made necessary some efficient action against that tribe, and so the Colonel was directed, by a special order sent by General Kearney from La Joya while *en route* for California, to make a campaign against them, before proceeding on his more adventurous southern trip. Thus a part of the army which had started out in hostility to Mexicans found its first active duty in the protection of the Mexican people themselves against their inveterate enemies.

With characteristic promptitude Doniphan performed the task. Leaving Colonel Price at Santa Fé, he set out on October 26th, dividing his forces into two parts. With one he proceeded to Albuquerque, and thence up the Rio Puerco to the head-waters of its western branch; while Major Gilpin, in command of 200 men, marched up the valley of the Chama from Abiquiu, crossed the "Great Continental Divide," and proceeded down the San Juan to the valley of the Little

Colorado. Nothing more romantic or daring is recorded in the pages of history than Captain Reid's expedition, with an escort of only thirty men, to the center of the Indian population; and Gilpin's march across the Cordilleras. The whole country of the Navajoes was visited, and the tribe brought together at Ojo del Oso, where a treaty was successfully concluded, and the regiment returned to the Rio Grande, reaching Socorro on December 12th, having accomplished its whole work most efficiently in little more than six weeks.

The novel position which the American army thus assumed, as the champions and protectors of the people who had so lately been their enemies, is well illustrated by a part of the proceedings at the "long talk," which preceded the making of this treaty with the Navajoes. After the first statement by Colonel Doniphan, a young Navajo Chief, Sarcilla Largo, a very bright man, responded that he was gratified to learn the views of the Americans. "He admired their spirit and enterprise, but detested the Mexicans." The next day Colonel Doniphan explained to the council " that the United States had taken military possession of New Mexico; that her laws were now extended over that Territory; that the New Mexicans would be protected against violence and invasion; and that their rights would be amply preserved to them: that the United States was also anxious to enter into a treaty of peace and lasting friendship with her red children, the Navajoes; that the same protection would be given them against encroachments, and the usurpation of their rights, as had been guaranteed to the New Mexicans; that the United States claimed all the country by the right of conquest, and both they and the New Mexicans were now equally become her children." Then the same young Chief, with great acuteness boldly replied: "Americans! you have a strange cause of war against the Navajoes. We have waged war against the New Mexicans for many years. We have plundered their villages and killed many of their people, and made many prisoners. We had just cause for all this. *You* have lately commenced a war against the same people. You are powerful. You have great guns and many brave soldiers. You have therefore conquered them, the very thing we have been attempting to do for so many years. You now turn upon us for attempting to do what you have done yourselves. We cannot see why you have cause to quarrel with us for fighting the New Mexicans on the west, while you do the same thing on the east. Look how matters stand. This is *our war*. We have more right to complain of you for interfering in our war than you have to quarrel with us for continuing a war we had begun long before you got here. If you will act justly, you will allow us to settle our own differences."

Colonel Doniphan then explained that the New Mexicans had surrendered; that they desired no more fighting; that it was a custom with the Americans, when a people gave up, to treat them as friends thenceforward; that we now had full possession of New Mexico and had attached it to our Government; that the whole country and every thing in it had become ours by conquest; and that when they *now* stole property from the New Mexicans they were stealing from us, and when they killed them they were killing our people, for they had now become ours; that this could not be suffered any longer. Finally after some consideration the Chief responded: "If New Mexico be really in your possession, and if it be the intention of your Government to hold it, we will cease our depredations, and refrain from future wars upon that people; for we have no cause of quarrel with you, and do not desire to have any war with so powerful a nation. Let there be peace between us." This was the end of the speaking, and so the treaty was signed.

This expedition to the westward, with all its dangers and hardships, was a fitting prelude to that extraordinary march and conquest which have rendered the name of Doniphan immortal, and which have been not inappropriately compared by as high authority as William Cullen Bryant to Xenophon's celebrated "Retreat of the Ten Thousand."

On October 12th the Mormon battalion, which was to be formed at Council Bluffs of refugees from Nauvoo, arrived at Santa Fé; and its commander having died, it was put in charge of Lieutenant Colonel Cooke, and a week later started south and west to follow the route taken by General Kearney to California.

Doniphan's march to Chihuahua commenced on December 14th, leaving Colonel Price, of the Second Missouri Mounted Volunteers, in command of the few remaining troops in New Mexico.

CHAPTER XXI.

THE REVOLT OF 1847.

SCARCELY had a day passed after the departure of General Doniphan, before information came that preparations were being made for a general revolt against the American authority. While the people generally had apparently submitted to the new order of things with a good grace, yet there was naturally much discontent beneath the quiet external appearance, especially among the wealthy and those who had been local leaders, and who thought that the attainment of their ambition or the pursuit of their pleasures might be interfered with by the new *regime*. Besides, we are to remember in judging of the acts of those days, that the people were Mexicans, and their territory a part of the Republic of Mexico, which had been invaded by an American army and was being held by force of arms; and that so long as the war continued it was simply an act of patriotism, from their point of view, to drive from their soil these invaders of their country, or to destroy them from the face of the earth. What afterwards, when they had accepted American citizenship, would have been treason and rebellion, at that time, while war was raging between the two countries, was for them, as Mexican citizens held under foreign military control, a natural manifestation of love of country. This view of the matter was officially taken by the President of the United States himself, who pardoned several of those engaged in the revolt, after they had been convicted of treason and sentenced to be hung, on the ground that as actual war was existing between the two governments, a Mexican citizen could not commit treason against the

United States; and this should be carefully borne in mind, in reading and judging of the events connected with the American occupation and the revolt of 1847; and it is also to be noted that those who were most patriotic Mexicans, while they were Mexicans, have been among the most valuable and loyal American citizens in civil affairs, in Indian wars, and the war of the Rebellion, since the treaty of peace transferred their allegiance.

The leaders in the attempt to recapture the country from the Americans were Don Diego Archuleta, of Los Luceros, who had been a delegate to the Mexican Congress from New Mexico, and Don Tomas Ortiz, of Santa Fé, who had been second in command to Armijo; both men of extensive connections and large influence. They were supported in the enterprise by many leading citizens of the Territory, including— according to the histories of Hughes and W. W. H. Davis, and as was generally believed at the time—Tomas C. de Baca, of Peña Blanca, Manuel Chavez, Miguel E. Pino, Nicolas Pino, and Pablo Dominguez; and Hughes also mentions Santiago Armijo, Domingo Baca, and Juan Lopez. It subsequently appeared, however, that several of these parties were not concerned in this attempt. Among those specially active in the affair were some of the Mexican priesthood, the most prominent being Padre José Manuel Gallegos and Padre Juan Felipe Ortiz. These two took an important part in arranging the preliminaries of the revolt. Padre Ortiz went to the north as far as La Joya at the time of the festival of Nuestra Señora de Guadalupe (December 12th) to perform the religious services appropriate to the occasion, and from there visited the Rio Arriba and Taos regions to excite the people to action. Padre Gallegos simultaneously came up from Albuquerque to perfect arrangements with the leaders around Santa Fé. The first general meeting was held on December 12th, and it was then decided that the revolution should take place one week from that date— a general rising being made all over the country. The programme was to kill or drive out of the Territory all Americans, and also all Mexicans who had taken office under the American Government since the occupation.

Everything was arranged with the utmost secrecy, and organized so that each leader should have his appointed part in the work to perform. It was agreed that on the night of the appointed day (December 19th) those engaged in the conspiracy in Santa Fé were to gather in the parochial church and remain concealed. Meanwhile, friends from the surrounding country, under the lead of Don Diego Archuleta, who was to be the General-in-Chief, were to be brought into the city and distributed in various houses where they would be unobserved. At midnight the church bell was to sound, and then the men within the church were to sally forth and all were to rendezvous immediately in the plaza, seize the cannon there and aim them so as to command the leading points, while detachments under special orders were to attack the Palace and the quarters of the American Commandant (Colonel Price), and make them prisoners. The people throughout the whole north of the Territory had been secretly notified, and were only awaiting news of the rising at Santa Fé to join in the revolt and make it a sure success. In fact, everything seemed favorable, and but for a postponement, agreed to at a final preparatory meeting, the object might have been accomplished. Some timid spirits then argued that more time was needed for preparation, and so the date of the rising was changed to Christmas eve, which it was thought was the most propitious occasion, as discipline would then be relaxed, the soldiers would be engaged in festivities at various *bailes* and saloons in the town, and so—dispersed and unarmed—could be easily killed or captured.

The postponement, however, was fatal to action at

that time, for in the interim information of the conspiracy reached the American authorities, as is said by some, through a mulatto woman, who was the wife of one of those engaged in the project and who had friends among the Americans whom she wished to serve; and according to another account, from Agustin Duran. Very possibly the news came from more than one source, as is apt to be the case with secrets too long kept. At all events, the Governor took vigorous measures to repress the outbreak, and promptly arrested and imprisoned a number of the supposed leaders; among whom were Manuel Chavez and the Pino brothers. An investigation ensued, from which it appeared that these three were not concerned in this conspiracy at all, the suspicions against them having been excited by the prominent part they took in endeavoring to raise a volunteer army to meet the Americans in the field before the coming of General Kearney, as narrated in Chapter XVI. They were acquitted and released, and soon after showed their loyalty to the new order of things by enlisting (Manuel Chavez and Nicolas Pino, Miguel E. Pino being sick) in the volunteer company under Colonel St. Vrain, which marched to put down the Taos insurrection. Ortiz and Archuleta, who were to have been, respectively, Governor and Commanding General under the revolutionary government, escaped to the south, notwithstanding the efforts of Lieutenant Walker to make an arrest, and succeeded in reaching the City of Mexico, where they remained until the end of the war.

This opportune discovery prevented the projected revolt for the time, but did not allay the determination of the people to free themselves from foreign control as soon as a fitting opportunity presented itself. On the contrary, preparations for a future rising were secretly undertaken on a scale more extended than before. This time certain of the Pueblo Indians, and especially those of Taos, were enlisted in the cause, and added much to the strength and prospects of the enterprise. The time for the revolt was well chosen, as was the place of the first outbreak.

Governor Bent, supposing all danger past, left the capital on January 14th to visit his home and family at Taos, and arrived there after a two days' trip. He was accompanied by five persons, including the sheriff, prefect of the county, and the circuit attorney. On the night of the 19th a large body of men, partly Mexicans and partly Pueblo Indians, attacked his residence, and succeeded that night not only in killing the Governor, but also the sheriff of the county, Stephen Lee; J. W. Leal, the circuit attorney; Cornelio Vigil, the prefect; Narciso Beaubien, a son of Judge Beaubien; and Pablo Jaramillo. The prefect represented the class of natives of the Territory who had accepted office under the United States authorities, and his death showed a determination to destroy all those who had taken similar positions. Jaramillo was a brother-in-law of Governor Bent, and no doubt was killed for that reason.

The animosity of the people had evidently been aroused to the highest pitch against all connected with the invaders, as we told that the most cruel feautures were connected with the murders of some of these officials, as well as with others that took place almost simultaneously in the vicinity; S. Turley, the owner of the distillery, and six other Americans at work at the Arroyo Hondo, twelve miles above Taos, and two others still farther north on the Rio Colorado, being among the victims, the former after a resistance of two days.

At Mora, at the same time, an attack was made on a party of Americans who had just arrived there from Las Vegas, and all of them were killed. The principal one in this party was Mr. L. Waldo, a brother of Captain Waldo of the Missouri volunteers, and father of Henry L. Waldo, afterward Chief Justice of New

Mexico. He had been merchandising for some years in the Territory, was well known and much respected. He had a wagon in which he travelled, and on this occasion the other seven Americans who fell victims had accompanied him in the wagon from Las Vegas. The bodies of all those thus killed at Mora, with the exception of one that could not be found, were subsequently brought into Las Vegas and interred there.

The startling news of the assassination of the Governor was swiftly carried to Santa Fé, and reached Colonel Price the next day. Simultaneously, letters were discovered calling on the people of the Rio Abajo to secure Albuquerque and march northward to aid the other insurgents; and news speedily followed that a united Mexican and Pueblo force of large magnitude was marching down the Rio Grande valley towards the capital, flushed with the success of the revolt at Taos. Very few troops were in Santa Fé, ; in fact, the number remaining in the whole Territory was very small, and these were scattered at Albuquerque, Las Vegas, and other distant points. At the first named town were Major Edmondson and Captain Burgwin ; the former in command of the town, and the latter with a company of the First Dragoons.

Colonel Price lost no time in taking such measures as his limited resources permitted. Edmondson was directed to come immediately to Santa Fé to take command of the capital; and Burgwin to follow Price as fast as possible towards the scene of hostilities. The Colonel himself collected the few troops at Santa Fé, which were all on foot, but fortunately included the little battalion which under Captain Angney had made such extraordinary marches on the journey across the plains as to almost outwalk the cavalry. With these was a volunteer company formed of nearly all of the American inhabitants of the city, under command of Colonel St. Vrain, who happened to be in Santa Fé, together with Judge Beaubien, at the time of the rising at Taos. With this little force, amounting in all to 310 men, Colonel Price started to march towards Taos, or at all events to meet the army which was coming towards the capital from the north and which grew as it marched by constant accessions from the surrounding country. The city of Santa Fé was left in charge of a garrison under Lieutenant-Colonel Willock. While the force was small and the volunteers without experience in regular warfare, yet all were nerved almost to desperation by the belief, since the Taos murders, that the only alternative was victory or annihilation.

The expedition set out on January 23d, and the next day the Mexican army, under command of General Montoya as Commander-in-Chief, aided by Generals Tafoya and Chavez, was found occupying the heights commanding the road near La Cañada (Santa Cruz), with detachments in some strong adobe houses near the river banks. The advance had been seen shortly before at the rocky pass, on the road from Pojuaque; and near there and before reaching the river, the San Juan Pueblo Indians, who had joined the revolutionists reluctantly and under a kind of compulsion, surrendered and were disarmed by removing the locks from their guns. On arriving at the Cañada, Price ordered his howitzers to the front and opened fire; and after a sharp cannonade, directed an assault on the nearest houses by Angney's battalion. Meanwhile an attempt by a Mexican detachment to cut off the American baggage-wagons which had not yet come up was frustrated by the activity of St. Vrain's volunteers. A charge all along the line was then ordered and handsomely executed; the houses, which being of adobe, had been practically so many ready-made forts, were successively carried, and St. Vrain started in advance to gain the Mexican rear. Seeing this manœuver, and fearing its effects, the Mexicans retreated, leaving thirty-six dead on the field.

Among those killed was General Tafoya, who bravely remained on the field after the remainder had abandoned it, and was shot.

Colonel Price pressed on up the river as fast as possible, passing San Juan, and at Los Luceros, on the 28th, his little army was rejoiced at the arrival of re-inforcements, consisting of a mounted company of cavalry, Captain Burgwin's company, which had been pushed up by forced marches on foot from Albuquerque, and a six-pounder brought by Lieutenant Wilson. Thus enlarged, the American force consisted of 480 men, and continued its advance up the valley to La Joya, which was as far as the river road at that time extended. Meanwhile the Mexicans had established themselves in a narrow pass near Embudo, where the forest was dense, and the road impracticable for wagons or cannon, the troops occupying the sides of the mountain on both sides of the cañon. Burgwin was sent with three companies to dislodge them and open a passage—no easy task. But St. Vrain's company took the west slope, and another the right, while Burgwin himself marched through the gorge between. The sharp-shooting of these troops did such terrible execution that the pass was soon cleared, though not without the display of great heroism, and some loss; and the Americans entered Embudo without further opposition. The difficulties of this campaign were greatly increased by the severity of the weather, the mountains being thickly covered with snow, and the cold so intense that a number of men were frost-bitten and disabled. The next day Burgwin reached Las Trampas, where Price arrived with the remainder of the American army on the last day of January, and all together they marched into Chamisal.

Notwithstanding the cold and snow they pressed on over the mountain, and on the 3d of February reached the town of Fernando de Taos, only to find that the

Mexican and Pueblo force had fortified itself in the celebrated Pueblo of Taos, about three miles distant. That force had diminished considerably during the retreat from La Cañada, many of the Mexicans returning to their homes, and its greater part now consisting of Pueblo Indians. The American troops were worn out with fatigue and exposure, and in most urgent need of rest; but their intrepid commander, desiring to give his opponents no more time to strengthen their works, and full of zeal and energy, if not of prudence, determined to commence an immediate attack.

The two great buildings at this Pueblo, certainly the most interesting and extraordinary inhabited structures in America, are well known from descriptions and engravings. They are five stories high and irregularly pyramidal in shape, each story being smaller than the one below, in order to allow ingress to the outer rooms of each tier from the roofs. Before the advent of artillery these buildings were practically impregnable, as when the exterior ladders were drawn up, there were no means of ingress, the side walls being solid without openings, and of immense thickness. Between these great buildings, each of which can accommodate a multitude of men, runs the clear water of the Taos Creek; and to the west of the northerly building stood the old church, with walls of adobe from three to seven and a half feet in thickness. Outside of all, and having its north-west corner just beyond the church, ran an adobe wall, built for protection against hostile Indians, and which now answered for an outer earth-work. The church was turned into a fortification, and was the point where the insurgents concentrated their strength; and against this Colonel Price directed his principal attack. The six-pounder and the howitzer were brought into position without delay, under the command of Lieutenant Dyer, then a young graduate of West Point, and since then Chief of Ordnance of the U. S. Army, and opened a fire on the thick adobe walls. But cannon balls made little impression on the massive banks of earth, in which they imbedded themselves without doing damage; and after a fire of two hours, the battery was withdrawn, and the troops allowed to return to the town of Taos for their much-needed rest.

Early the next morning, the troops, now refreshed and ready for the combat, advanced again to the Pueblo, but found those within equally prepared. The story of the attack and capture of this place is so interesting, both on account of the meeting here of old and new systems of warfare—of modern artillery with an aboriginal stronghold—and because the precise localities can be distinguished by the modern tourist from the description, that it seems best to insert the official report as presented by Colonel Price. Nothing could show more plainly how superior strong earth-works are to many more ambitious structures of defense, or more forcibly display the courage and heroism of those who took part in the battle, or the signal bravery of the accomplished Captain Burgwin which led to his untimely death. Colonel Price writes,—

"Posting the dragoons under Captain Burgwin about two hundred and sixty yards from the western flank of the church, I ordered the mounted men under Captains St. Vrain and Slack to a position on the opposite side of the town, whence they could discover and intercept any fugitives who might attempt to escape towards the mountains, or in the direction of San Fernando. The residue of the troops took ground about three hundred yards from the north wall. Here, too, Lieutenant Dyer established himself with the six-pounder and two howitzers, while Lieutenant Hassendaubel, of Major Clark's battalion, light artillery, remained with Captain Burgwin, in command of two howitzers. By this arrangement a cross-fire was obtained, sweeping the front and eastern flank of the church. All these arrangements being made, the batteries opened upon the town at nine o'clock A. M. At eleven o'clock, finding it impossible to breach the walls of the church with the six-pounder and howitzers, I determined to storm the building. At a signal, Captain Burgwin, at the head of his own company and that of Captain McMillin, charged the western flank of the church, while Captain Angney, infantry battalion, and Captain Barber and Lieutenant Boon, Second Missouri Mounted Volunteers, charged the northern wall. As soon as the troops above mentioned had established themselves under the western wall of the church, axes were used in the attempt to breach it, and a temporary ladder having been made, the roof was fired. About this time, Captain Burgwin, at the head of a small party, left the cover afforded by the flank of the church, and penetrating into the corral in front of that building, endeavored to force the door. In this exposed situation, Captain Burgwin received a severe wound, which deprived me of his valuable services, and of which he died on the 7th instant. Lieutenants McIlvaine, First U S. Dragoons, and Royall and Lackland, Second Regiment Volunteers, accompanied Captain Burgwin into the corral, but the attempt on the church door proved fruitless, and they were compelled to retire behind the wall. In the meantime, small holes had been cut in the western wall, and shells were thrown in by hand, doing good execution. The six-pounder was now brought around by Lieutenant Wilson, who, at the distance of two hundred yards, poured a heavy fire of grape into the town. The enemy, during all of this time, kept up a destructive fire upon our troops. About half-past three o'clock, the six-pounder was run up within sixty yards of the church, and after ten rounds, one of the holes which had been cut with the axes was widened into a practicable breach. The storming party, among whom were Lieutenant Dyer, of the ordnance, and Lieutenants Wilson and Taylor, First Dragoons, entered and took possession of the church without opposition. The interior was filled with dense smoke, but for which circumstance our storming party would have suffered great loss. A few of the enemy were seen in the gallery, where an open door admitted the air, but they retired without firing a gun. The troops left to support the battery on the north side were now ordered to charge on that side.

"The enemy then abandoned the western part of the town. Many took refuge in the large houses on the east, while others endeavored to escape toward the mountains. These latter were pursued by the mounted men under Captains Slack and St. Vrain, who killed fifty-one of them, only two or three men escaping. It was now night, and our troops were quietly quartered in the houses which the enemy had abandoned. On the next morning the enemy sued for peace, and thinking the severe loss they had sustained would prove a salutary lesson, I granted their supplication, on the condition that they should deliver up to me Tomas, one of their principal men, who had instigated and been actively engaged in the murder of Governor Bent and others. The number of the enemy at the battle of Pueblo de Taos was between six and seven hundred, and and of these one hundred and fifty were killed, wounded not known. Our own loss was seven killed and forty-five wounded; many of the wounded have since died."

The capture of the Taos Pueblo practically ended the main attempt to expel the Americans from the Territory. Governor Montoya, who was a very influential man in the conspiracy and styled himself the "Santa Ana of the north," was tried by court-martial, convicted, and executed on Febuary 7th, in presence of the army. Fourteen others were tried for participating in the murder of Governor Bent and the others who were killed on the 19th of January, and were convicted and executed. Thus, fifteen in all were hung, being an equal number to those murdered at Taos, the Arroyo Hondo and Rio Colorado. Of these, eight were Mexicans and seven were Pueblo Indians. Several more were sentenced to be hung for "treason," but the President very properly pardoned them, on the ground that treason against the United States was not a crime of which a Mexican citizen could be found guilty, while his country was actually at war with the United States.

In other parts of New Mexico attempts were made to revolt simultaneously with the rising at Taos, or very soon after, all being part of the one general plan; it having been intended to have a universal destruction of all the Americans, including Mexicans holding office under the American Government, in the entire Territory.

The projected rising at Las Vegas was prevented by the faithfulness of the Alcalde to his oath, and the proximity of the troops under Captain Hendley. The day after the killing of Mr. Waldo and his seven companions at Mora, a swift messenger came in from that town to Juan de Dios Maes, the Alcalde, at Las Vegas, bringing a letter which told of the revolt of the people in the north, the killing of Governor Bent and others at Taos, and of the eight Americans at Mora, and called on the Mexicans of Las Vegas and its vicinity to join their northern brethren in the work; to rise immediately and kill all the Americans among them. The Alcalde showed the letter to Levi J. Keithley, a neighbor on the plaza, and the latter advised that they should consult Antonio Sais, a citizen of excellent judgment. Sais advised the Alcalde to keep faith with the United States at all hazards, and to call a meeting of the citizens without delay to take such action as they deemed necessary. This was accordingly done—the call being made by beating a drum around the plaza. When the crowd had assembled, the Alcalde read to them the letter which he had received, and then addressed them as to their duty. "You all saw me take the oath of allegiance to the

United States," he said, "on the house-top across the plaza. I consider that you all took that oath through me, as your Alcalde, and are bound as much as myself. As for me, I assure you I am determined to live and die by that oath." This position taken by the local authority had great weight, and the people agreed to follow his advice. Just then Captain Hendley, who was in command of a detachment of soldiers at a grazing-camp near Apache Spring, came into town, and was informed of what had occurred. He said he had no orders to move his company, but that if any attempt was made by insurgents from Mora, or elsewhere, to make trouble, he could be depended on to protect the peaceable citizens. He then left town, but had scarcely started when threats were heard which alarmed the Americans, and they sent a swift messenger (a Frenchman) to urge him to bring up his company. The Captain replied that he could not move without orders, but that if any were afraid, they could come to his camp and be protected. "No!" said the excited Frenchman, with an oath, "I am an American citizen, and demand protection *here*! D——n the orders!" Finally Hendley consented to come—and arrived early the next morning with his company, and occupied the town. Here a number of volunteers joined him, so that his total force was increased to about 250 men.

Full particulars of the killing of Mr. Waldo and his seven companions at Mora had now been received, creating great indignation, and on the 22d of January Captain Hendley started on an expedition against that town with eighty men, with the intention of avenging their deaths. He arrived in front of Mora on the 24th, but found the town occupied by over 150 armed Mexicans. He ordered an assault, and had succeeded in taking possession of a number of houses, and penetrated to the old fort, or block house, built for protection against Indians, in which his antagonists had entrenched themselves, when he fell, a victim of his own bravery; and his command withdrew. A few days subsequently, February 1st, the town was again attacked by Captain Morin, and was captured and much of it demolished.

About the same time Captain Robinson's camp was surprised and 200 horses and mules captured, one man killed and several wounded. Captain Edmondson started from Las Vegas in pursuit of the band that had made the attack, came up with them in the narrow cañon near the junction of the Canadian and Mora, "the hills literally covered with Indians and Mexicans," and after a sharp skirmish succeeded in dispersing them.

A few more isolated outbreaks occurred, generally at points remote from the Capital, as at Las Valles, in San Miguel County, and at Captain Morin's camp, at the Cienega, eighteen miles below Taos, where Lieutenant Larkin and four men were killed. But they were promptly met, and seem to have arisen more from bands of freebooters in search of plunder than from any concerted and patriotic attempt as Mexicans to drive the invaders from their country. Later in the year large re-inforcements came to the American army; and the people began to learn that they had really more freedom and more protection under the American flag than under that of Mexico. Many of the stories that had been circulated to influence their minds against the new-comers, time proved to be untrue; and so they became reconciled to the change in government.

By the treaty of Guadalupe Hidalgo, all inhabitants of New Mexico, except those who chose formally to retain the character of Mexican citizens, became citizens of the United States, with the same rights and privileges as all other citizens. Thus New Mexico became, beyond dispute, a part of the "Great Republic," and her people legally, actually, and unalterably united, with the millions of their brother freemen under the stars and stripes, in sustaining the honor of the American nation, enhancing its glory, and fulfilling its great mission.

www.ingramcontent.com/pod-product-compliance
Lightning Source LLC
Chambersburg PA
CBHW030126240426
43672CB00005B/43